PORTUGUESE
HOME COOKING

PORTUGUESE
HOME COOKING

Ana Patuleia Ortins

Photography by Hiltrud Schulz

Interlink Books

I dedicate *Portuguese Home Cooking* to my father, Rufino Patuleia, whose love and passion for our wonderful Portuguese food is his enduring legacy to me and to my children. Here's to you, Pai!

Meu Pai é um amigo,	*My Father is a friend,*
Que eu nunca esquecerei.	*Whom I never will forget.*
Por que amor igual ao dele	*For love equal to his*
Nunca mais encontrarei.	*Never more will I have met.*

This verse is one of the many quaint Portuguese sayings painted on the artful blue-and-white pottery of Alcobaça, a town north of Lisbon.

First published in 2021 by
Interlink Books
An imprint of Interlink Publishing Group, Inc.
46 Crosby Street, Northampton, Massachusetts 01060
www.interlinkbooks.com

Library of Congress Cataloging-in-Publication Data available
ISBN 978-1-62371-880-0

Publisher: Michel Moushabeck
Editor: Leyla Moushabeck
Design: Harrison Williams
Recipe testing and styling: Hiltrud Schulz
Proofreading: Jennifer Staltare

Printed and bound in Korea
10 9 8 7 6 5 4 3 2 1

CONTENTS

PREFACE

This book preserves and shares the everyday food of my heritage, introducing it to those who are interested in exploring this soul-comforting, understated peasant food of the Portuguese. It seems not long ago, *Portuguese Home Cooking* was not even a passing thought, but events in life often make us change direction, if only temporarily. Some years ago, it occurred to me that treasured family recipes of my heritage would be lost to our children if I failed to record them. As a first-generation Portuguese-American, I knew these recipes needed to be captured on paper, preserved not only for my children but for future generations of descendants of Portuguese immigrants—before the recipes adapt and change.

What was to be a simple notebook of family recipes soon expanded to include common, yet popular, everyday homestyle dishes of our extended family and Portuguese friends. Before I knew it, my thoughts of writing this book were echoed aloud by my brother Rufino Jr. and encouraged by others. Today, Portuguese food is still relatively unknown outside Portugal. Many confuse it with Spanish fare, and still more toss it into books and articles as an aside to Spanish cooking. I feel that it is time for Portuguese food to stand on its own and be more closely examined for itself. With an overview of the diverse influences of the cuisine, this book is a guide to the heartwarming recipes of authentic Portuguese food.

For questions or comments, contact the author at: ana@portuguesecooking.com.

INTRODUCTION

My family's origins are in the Alto Alentejo province, just south of Ponte Sor, in a small town originally called Aldeia das Laranjeiras, Grove of Oranges. However, name changes were neither unusual nor difficult to accomplish, according to my grandfather, who liked to tell the story of how Aldeia das Laranjeiras became known as Galveias. There were two neighbors, so the story goes, one of whom owned hens, the other, a rooster. When the owner of the hens complained that the rooster was bothering his hens, the owner of the rooster was said to have replied, "Can I help it if my rooster (*gallo*) sees (*veia*)?"

Like so many others, my grandfather Jose Nunes Patuleia came to the United States by way of Ellis Island, seeking a better life for his family. He left Galveias in the winter of 1920 and settled in Peabody, Massachusetts, where he was joined by my grandmother, father, and aunt in 1937. Wherever they settled, Portuguese immigrants transplanted their love of family, food, wine, friendship, hospitality, and their strong religious beliefs, from which they drew their courage and perseverance. I remember that any visitor to our home was always invited to share our meal or, at the very least, to have something to drink. It was not unusual for my father to offer a guest his last beer or glass of wine. "Come in, come in," was a standard greeting in our home. No matter how meager our dinner might be, unexpected guests were always invited to sit down and join us. Friends never left our home empty-handed, either, especially in the summertime. They would take with them a bag heavy with sun-ripened tomatoes and other vegetables from the garden. Pai (Dad) was even known to climb our pear tree to pick the ripened fruit for our guests. Sharing what we have been blessed with, however meager, is who we are.

As a child, I often stood by my father's side in the kitchen as he prepared dinner. "Watch how I do this, so you learn," he would say in his imperfect English. For past generations it was expected training: watch and learn. I was a willing student, my zest for learning was surpassed only by my father's pleasure in teaching me all he knew—something he enjoyed almost as much as he enjoyed soccer! Along with Pai's teaching, I absorbed his passion for cooking and eating wonderful food, for sharing it with others, and for savoring the taste of their satisfaction as keenly as the food offered. This book is my way of sharing his passion and handing on my culinary heritage.

Traditional Portuguese dishes blend the flavors and techniques of many cultures, dating back centuries. Phoenicians, Turks, Moors, and Arabs are just a few of the peoples who left their mark on what is now Portuguese cuisine. From the Arab countries around the Mediterranean came wheat, rice, citrus fruits, almonds, sugar, saffron, and salt. In Portuguese cooking, braising is done the Arabic way: meat is cooked in a liquid *before* it is seared; in the Western, the meat is seared first. Almond trees, introduced into the Algarve region of southern Portugal by the Moors, bloom so profusely during the winter that the effect is what my father called "Portuguese snow." Phoenicians brought wine and olives, and the Turks taught us the uses of sugar. Although other ingredients essential to Portuguese cuisine are common to Mediterranean countries— olive oil, onions, bay leaves, garlic, cilantro, paprika, chili peppers, and red sweet peppers—the ways these ingredients are used are what makes Portuguese fare unique.

Its location on the edge of the Atlantic Ocean played a large part in Portugal's decision to take to the sea. Access to the sea led to the discovery of new lands and exciting new ingredients, creating unprecedented trade opportunities. From the east, the Orient and Indies brought Portuguese cooks tea and a variety of spices including cloves, cinnamon, curry, and nutmeg. Voyages west to the Americas filled ships with tropical fruit, corn, tomatoes, green peppers, and potatoes, giving bright new colors and flavors to traditional dishes. Coffee is believed to have come originally from Ethiopia and eventually spread by Portuguese sailors to Brazil. These influences during the Age of Discovery fed the evolution of a cuisine.

Today, native legumes and leafy greens are still used abundantly in soups and stews. Kale, fresh fennel, and baby turnip tops—a few of the greens that lend distinct flavor to soups—are lightly sautéed and seasoned, or mixed with rice to create tasty side dishes. Red and white kidney beans, chickpeas, pinto, and fava beans not only provide body to sustaining soups, but make interesting accompaniments to main courses. Some dishes combine meat and shellfish. Easy-to-prepare seafood dishes, luscious egg- and sugar-rich desserts, and the way certain spices and herbs are used to flavor foods, give the cuisine its character. And last but not least, infusions of wine and garlic give meat a comforting taste that is unmistakably Portuguese.

Even though the country is small, there are some regional culinary differences. Most obviously, the food of the mainland and that of the Portuguese Azores—lying almost halfway between Portugal and the United States—are quite different. The cheeses in the Azores are made mostly with cow milk, while the mainland uses sheep and goat milk. There is greater use of beef and butter in the islands as well. The recipe for Tripe (*Dobrada*, page 134), is more likely in the Azores to be spicier and to contain kidney beans; its continental cousin uses lima beans, has a thicker texture, and is milder in spice. The overall flavor of Azorean-style cooking is spicier than mainland fare. On the mainland, seafood use is heaviest along the coast, especially in the southern region of the Algarve. To the northwest, surrounding Lisbon, there is a fair mix of regional dishes. In the north, around the city of Oporto, bean stews like *dobrada* and *feijoada* stand out. If you go to Beira Alta, boiled dinners are very common, as is more frequent use of lamb.

The cuisine I learned at home is that of the Alentejo area, known for its delicious pork, as well as for its wheat, regal olive groves, and picturesque cork trees. A signature of this region is Sweet Red Pepper Paste, *massa de pimentão* (recipe on page 219), which flavors sausages, and the popular **Carne de Porco à Alentejana** (page 128), a noteworthy dish of fried, marinated pork meat with clams, which is said to have originated during the era of the Inquisition. *Cóentros* (cilantro) is used especially in the Alentejo. The primary oil in soups is olive oil, but other dishes from this region use lard or pork fat. Other culinary offerings from the Alentejo include *açordas* (bread soups) and sweet egg desserts.

Portuguese cooking has always been resourceful and creative, the recipes easy to make from scratch. As in the old country, here in America traditional culinary methods were handed down from mother to daughter or shared among family and friends through watching, helping, and tasting. Naturally, this method of passing on recipes means that each dish has many variations. Daughters might not have paid close attention, or perhaps they followed their own tastes. Recipes were rarely written down; instructions were universally imprecise; measurements always inexact. Just how much is a handful? Measured by whose hand? Additionally, when immigrants first settled in a new land, some traditional methods and recipes were changed out of necessity because certain ingredients were simply not available.

Most Portuguese recipes are, as we say, "*com gusto*"—to your liking. No matter what ingredients are specified for a dish, individual quantities are assumed to be according to one's personal preference. This encourages culinary creativity. The recipes included here have been collected over the years from relatives and friends and are presented as they would be prepared in a Portuguese home. To standardize these heirlooms, ingredients have been measured and recipes tested carefully. With the increased availability of traditional ingredients, the dishes can be prepared authentically. Still variations and substitutions have been noted for times when traditional ingredients cannot be found. I encourage you to first cook the recipes as presented, then change the quantities of ingredients *com gusto*.

In the pages that follow, I describe the basic methods of cooking, traditional marinades, and spices most often found in Portuguese cooking, as well as breads and desserts. The instructions are detailed and easy to follow. An informational chapter about Portuguese wine includes a description of the traditional method of making wine at home. These recipes—from different regions of mainland Portugal, the Azores, and the United States—are an introduction to authentic, homestyle Portuguese food at its best—heartwarming, flavorful, delicious! After all, no matter what area, region, or island we as a people came from, "*somos todos Portugueses*," we are all Portuguese.

My father's immigration, 1936

My grandparents enjoy a picnic with friends, 1940s

The author (center) in the Holy Ghost Procession, Peabody, Massachusetts, 1957

Grandmother Theresa & Aunt Ana's arrival in the USA, 1937

INGREDIENTS, METHODS & EQUIPMENT

INGREDIENTS

When Portuguese immigrants came to the United States, bringing their culinary traditions with them, some had never previously traveled outside their home regions in Portugal. Here, they met Portuguese from other regions. Regional versions of dishes were compared, shared, and carried on. Seafood dishes were adjusted to use fish available in American markets. Fortunately, many immigrants brought the seeds of familiar varieties of tomatoes, kale, wild fennel, herbs, and spices, which enabled them to continue cooking traditionally.

Onions, garlic, tomatoes, paprika, bay leaves, red pepper paste, cumin, chili peppers, parsley, cilantro, olive oil, vinegar, and wine are the common flavors that, when combined with meats, fish, and vegetables, distinguish this cuisine from any other. Components in a well-known dish may vary slightly from region to region, town to town, or cook to cook, but certain ingredients are inherent to Portuguese cooking—such as *linguiça, chourico*, and red pepper paste. While I encourage substitutions when necessary, I have attempted to remain true to authentic Portuguese homestyle fare, but the essential ingredients are simple and readily available to almost everyone.

As with any cuisine, the quality of ingredients is reflected in the flavor of the dish, so use the freshest ingredients possible. The following ingredients (in alphabetical order) are the most fundamental to the Portuguese kitchen.

BREAD

Traditionally baked in wood-fired ovens, bread is a constant element in any Portuguese meal. Since as early as the Middle Ages, bread provided basic sustenance. From the Romans came wheat, which was made into a bread that the Portuguese liked very much. Ever since the first feast in honor of the Holy Ghost, bread—considered to represent the body of Christ—is still the major ingredient, with meat, in the celebratory Soup of the Holy Ghost (page 62). Today, Portuguese breads are characterized by crisp crusts, delicate flavors, and textures varying from dense and chewy to cotton-like. Most Portuguese bakeries carry the following breads, but many bakeries now sell crusty artisan breads that make good substitutes.

Cornbread (*pão de milho* or *broa*)

Years ago, traditional cornbread was made of ground corn, water, and salt. This resulted in a very hard crusted bread with a slightly moist interior. Today's bread is made with a combination of wheat flour and cornmeal—some prefer white cornmeal to yellow. The crisp crust is softer than that of the old cornbread, but the texture is still slightly moist, open-grained, and dense. Cornbread, eaten both in the Azores and in continental Portugal, is produced in many Portuguese-American bakeries, some of which have switched from cornmeal to corn flour to save time in production. Find the recipe on page 232.

Crusty Rolls (*papo-secos*)

These rolls (page 238), made with wheat flour, are frequently served with grilled sausage; *presunto*, a salt-cured ham; sautéed medallions of marinated meat; fresh sardines; or cheese. The name *papo-seco* denotes the crusty puffed-up shape of these tasty rolls.

Flatbread (*pão estendido*)

This baked bread (page 235) and the fried version, *pão de sertã* (page 233), hail back to the time before breads were leavened. Both combine wheat and corn flours.

Homestyle Bread (*pão caseiro*)

This popular homemade bread has a crispy crust, a cotton-like texture, and an earthy flavor. Made with a *fermente* (sponge) and wheat flour, it contains no fats Find the recipe on page 236.

CHEESE

The different regions of Portugal have homemade cheeses with their own distinct flavors. Variations in climate, soil, native pasture grasses, all influence a region's cheese. Made primarily from sheep and goat milk, the cheeses range in flavor from mild to intensely sharp. Textures range from soft and creamy to semi-hard. The very mature cheeses are often grated. Typically eaten with fruit or bread, before or after a meal, these cheeses are intrinsic to the Portuguese diet.

Many cheeses are named after the towns of their origin. A few popular Portuguese cheeses can be found in Portuguese grocery stores in the United States.

Blue Island Cheese (*queijo da Ilha Azul*)
The island of Faial (the "blue island"), in the Azores, produces this cheese. Light yellow in color, it has a semi-soft texture and a mild, smooth flavor.

Cheese from the Mountain Ridge (*queijo da serra*)
Wrapped in linen, this cheese comes from the high mountain plateaus of mainland Portugal. Intensely flavored, with a creamy texture, *queijo da serra* requires a spoon for eating. As it ages, the texture becomes harder. It is sold in whole wheels only, starting at about 2½ pounds. The hefty price tag relegates it to holidays and special occasions. In spite of this, it is Portugal's most popular sheep-milk cheese.

Cheese of St. Michael (*queijo da São Miguel*)
This specialty cheese from the island of St. Michael in the Azores is made from cow milk. It has a semi-soft texture and a mild flavor.

Cheese of St. George (*queijo da São Jorge*)
Sliced or grated, this popular semi-hard cheese made from cow milk comes from the island of São Jorge. This cheese delivers a spicy flavor.

Fresh Cheese (*requeijão/queijo fresco*)
Azorean and continental Portuguese make this semi-soft white cheese, which has a delicate texture and mild flavor. Traditionally it was made with sheep milk, but is also made with cow milk (page 225). It is also used to make sweet cheese tarts, *queijadas* (pages 277–278).

Goat Cheese of Palhais (*queijo de cabra—Palhais*)
This tangy and slightly salty semi-soft goat cheese is from Palhais on mainland Portugal.

CHILI PEPPERS

Portuguese cooking may not be as spicy as Spanish, but we like to add a zing to some dishes. The most commonly used Portuguese chili is *piri piri* (in Africa, spelled *peri-peri*), a *capsicum frutescens* cultivar. Portuguese explorers brought the small bushy plants from Brazil to the former Portuguese colony of Mozambique, where it was cultivated and eventually spread to other countries. Though the same chili, this pepper is known as *malagueta* in the Azorean islands (who use the term to refer to a number of chilies) and in Brazil. The term *piri piri* is more common in mainland Portugal, the island of Madeira, and in Mozambique.

The *piri piri* chili resembles the shape of a Thai bird's eye chili, varying in length depending on the harvest. The Scoville Heat Units of this chili is 50,000 to 175,000. In Portuguese cooking, these chilies are pickled, made into hot sauce, and also dried and crushed or ground into a powder. For the recipes in this book, you can use different varieties of chili peppers, and other forms of chili powder, paste, and sauce according to preference and availability.

Pickled Chili Peppers (*malagueta na vinagre*)
The smallest *piri piri/malagueta* chilies are trimmed of their caps and stems and pickled in a vinegar brine. Portuguese folks will eat these pickled chilies whole as an accompaniment to soup. The brine itself is never wasted—the cook will certainly find a dish to stir it in to. Find the recipe on page 221.

Hot Pepper Sauce (*molho de piri piri* or *molho picante*)
This thin hot sauce is sometimes called *piri piri* sauce in English. It is with chilies, vinegar, and salt. Tabasco sauce is a good substitute.

Dried Crushed Red Pepper (*piri piri moido* or *malagueta seca* or *malagueta moida*)
Dried crushed *piri piri/malagueta* chili flakes are sprinkled with a light hand into stews, seafood dishes, and used to season some Portuguese sausages.

Hot Pepper Paste (*massa de malagueta* or *massa de piri piri*)
Hot pepper paste varies slightly from one cook to another, but it is made primarily of chili peppers and salt. Some recipes include a touch of sweet red pepper, lemon juice, perhaps a small amount of garlic, and olive oil. The largest chilies in the *piri piri/malagueta* harvest are perfect for making *massa de malagueta* because they are fleshy. Find the recipe on page 220.

CITRUS

The flavors of lemon and orange go beyond enhancing the desserts of Portugal. Their juices are used to flavor pork roasts, tripe, and even the *farinheira* sausage of the Alentejo region. The zest (the colored portion of the peel) is traditionally used whole or grated, perfuming cakes, sweet breads, or puddings. Pure lemon or orange extract may be substituted in desserts.

CORNMEAL

Both yellow and white cornmeal is used in bread making. The grind can range from fine to coarse. Many supermarkets now sell corn flour, yellow or white, which is finer than fine cornmeal. The recipes in this book usually call for corn flour because the results are more pleasing to modern tastes. Cornmeal or flour must be "scalded"—combined with boiling water—before being incorporated into the dough.

FATS

In Portuguese cooking the traditional fats are salt pork, bacon, lard, olive oil, and butter. Each fat plays a special role. In the Alentejo area, for example, bacon fat and lard are commonly used in frying and stewing, while olive oil, rather than meat stock, provides the flavor in soups. The Azoreans, lacking readily available olive oil, traditionally used lard as their primary fat. When corn oil became available in the Azores, it grew in popularity, especially for frying; whereas olive oil is more commonly used for frying on the mainland. Butter, which at one time was considered to be a luxury reserved for the wealthy, is used moderately for frying beef, dotting the tops of pork roasts or chicken, and for cooking rice. Butter is used more widely in baking. Many Portuguese cooks continue to use lard or salt pork in certain dishes that would lose their original character otherwise—fat substitutions can be made, but with a loss of traditional flavor. Olive oil makes the best substitute.

Lard (*gordura* or *banha de porco*)
An animal fat, lard was once used extensively as a cooking medium and as a preservative. Lard imparts a distinctive flavor to sautéed dishes, but has fallen out of favor, because it is generally regarded as unhealthy. Olive oil, a healthier traditional cooking oil, preserves the Portuguese flavor of dishes and can be substituted.

Olive Oil (*azeite*)
Portuguese olive oil is aromatic, fruity, and as intensely flavored as it is rich in color. The imported Saloio and Victor Guedes brands are most readily found in international food markets. If you have difficulty finding Portuguese olive oil, Spanish and Italian extra-virgin and virgin olive oil are good substitutes.

Salt Pork (*toucinho*)
Pork fat, preserved in salt, was traditionally fried to render lard. The crispy fried rinds or cracklings, called *torresmos,* are considered a delicious snack, familiar in the southern United States. Pieces of raw salt pork are added to some stews and soups for flavor. Smoked bacon is considered an acceptable substitute.

HERBS

The following herbs are the ones used most often in Portuguese cooking. For the most part, they are readily available to cooks in North America.

Bay Leaves (*loureiro*)

Also known as laurel, this aromatic herb is used frequently in European cooking. In Portugal, where it grows profusely, it was often planted as a hedge to delineate property boundaries—a practice that continues in some areas. The dried leaves flavor soups, stews, and braises. Remove the whole leaf before serving.

Cilantro (*coentros*)

Fresh cilantro leaves infuse Portuguese seafood dishes, salads, vegetables, and rice dishes with a sweet lemony flavor. I find the dried form to be flavorless and strongly recommend using fresh cilantro whenever possible.

Garlic (*alho*)

Garlic is indispensable in Portuguese cooking. It imparts its flavor to soups and stews and is essential to *Escabeche* (page 224) or *Molhanga* (page 217), the garlic-flavored vinegar sauces served with fried fish. I recommend using only fresh garlic for the best flavor. When recipes in this book call for garlic, use large cloves. (One clove, finely chopped, equals a generous teaspoonful.) I recommend the purple-skinned Italian garlic variety, if you can find it.

Parsley (*salsa*)

This herb is available in two varieties—flat and curly. Flat-leaf parsley has a stronger flavor and is most likely found infusing stews, seafood, and vegetable dishes. Parsley is rich in vitamin C and is touted as a breath freshener. Use fresh whenever possible, but freezing retains the flavor and color better than drying.

LEAFY GREENS

Used primarily in soups, leafy greens provide the highest amount of vitamin K and give us vitamin C and folic acid. In most dishes, cabbage, spinach, kale, collard greens, chard, baby turnip greens—even mustard greens—can be used interchangeably.

Kale (*couve*)

When they came to this country, many Portuguese immigrants brought seeds to grow familiar crops, which they carefully cultivated in their backyard gardens. My father planted a variety of kale called *couve talo branco*, or "white-stalk kale," similar to collard greens. The broad, flat leaves, almost ten inches wide, are best in soups and salt-cod dishes, and is popular on the Portuguese mainland. *Galega*, a taller smooth, green-leaf kale, is used for Green Broth Soup, *Caldo Verde* (page 42). A wide, curly-leaf kale (*couve*), typical of the Azores, is similar to the curly kale you can find in most supermarkets. Along with collard greens, the narrow-leaf Italian Lacinato kale (*cavolo nero*) makes a good substitute for Portuguese curly kale.

Unless it is cut in a chiffonade for *Caldo Verde*, kale is usually torn, not cut. To do this the Portuguese way, take a stalk in one hand. Using your thumb and first two fingers of the other hand, pull off pieces of kale leaf about an inch or so from the main rib and between the fibrous branches of the leaf, until only the skeleton of the leaf remains. Repeat with the remaining leaves until enough has been torn for the dish you are preparing.

Cabbage (*repolho*)

When a Portuguese recipe calls for cabbage, Savoy cabbage, which we refer to as *lombarda,* with its crinkled leaves and sweeter taste, is preferred.

Wild Fennel or Anise (*funcho*)

This licorice-flavored, feathery-leafed green is especially prized by the Azorean Portuguese. A wild, bulbless variety is essential to the Azorean Fennel Soup, *Sopa de Funcho* (page 54). The fennel you can find in your local supermarket makes an excellent substitute.

TO WASH GREENS FOR COOKING

Place greens in a clean sink and rinse with several changes of cold water, with special attention to the underside of the leaves. Rinsing the kale greens thoroughly while rubbing the top side of the leaves against each other is a time-honored technique believed to remove not only the grayish-white bloom on the leaves, but also the bitterness. Lift the greens out to drain in a colander or on a kitchen towel. Any grit should fall to the bottom of the sink. To prevent any grit from settling back onto the greens, do not allow the sink to drain while greens are still in the water.

LEGUMES

Legumes are well represented in Portuguese cooking, not only in soups and stews, but in salads as well. Dried beans (*feijão seco*)—cranberry beans, black-eyed peas, roman beans, fava beans, butter beans, kidney beans, and chickpeas can be used interchangeably in many soups and stews. Dried beans are best for flavor, but in a pinch, good-quality canned beans are acceptable. While most dried beans require soaking in water for at least 8 hours, chickpeas and fava beans require a minimum of 15 hours, and a longer cooking time.

  1 cup (6 oz) uncooked dried beans = 3 cups cooked beans
  15 oz can of beans, drained = 1½ cups cooked beans, from about ½ cup (3 oz) dried beans
  28 oz can of beans, drained = about 3¼ cups cooked beans, from about 1 cup (6 oz) dried beans

(If you are using canned beans, do not drain and rinse them before using unless they are going into a salad.)

Note: Be especially careful with dried fava beans, which can be toxic unless cooked thoroughly. The beans contain vicine, which causes a toxic allergic reaction that can be fatal in rare cases.

OLIVES

Olives (*azeitonas*) accompany nearly every meal in a traditional Portuguese home. Regal olive groves dot the landscape of the Alentejo region, and much of the country produces black olives that are cured in water, salt, and wild marjoram or oregano. Three varieties are imported to the United States. A large, black, mild-tasting olive; a smaller black olive with a sharper bite, carrying a more traditional Portuguese flavor; and a green sharp-flavored olive.

ONIONS

It is no wonder that onions are cherished in Portugal. They are the main ingredient for the *refogado*, an aromatic, sautéed mixture which is the base of many stews and soups. All-purpose yellow and Spanish onions are common kitchen staples.

Refogado describes in one word both the method and the aromatic foundation on which stews, seafood dishes, and many soups are based. "*Faz um refogado*" (make a *refogado*) is an instruction understood as the first step to many Portuguese recipes. In that single step, the cook sautés onions in olive oil and may add one or all of the following: garlic, bay leaf, paprika, or tomatoes. In the recipes that follow, when I speak of cooking the tomato after it has been added to sautéed onions "until it is partially dissolved," I mean cooked down until the vegetables are softened and the flavors are married to each other. We often say that we know when we are in a Portuguese home because of the aroma of *refogado* that fills the kitchen.

PRESUNTO

Presunto is a lean, spice-and-salt-cured ham, very much like the Italian Prosciutto di Parma. It is cut into small cubes and added to soups and stews or simply sliced and eaten with bread, accompanied by wine. Other than in a Portuguese specialty store, it can be difficult to find in the United States. The very lean prosciutto is a perfect substitute.

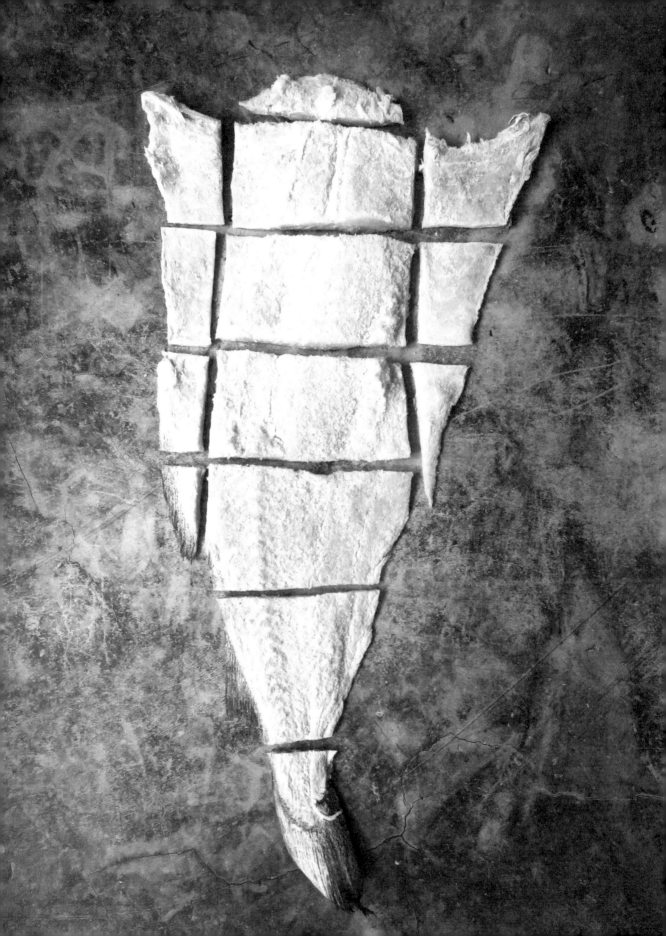

SALT COD

Salt cod (*bacalhau*) is dry, salt-cured codfish that must be reconstituted before use. Traditionally, cod was salted aboard the fishing boats; back on shore, the salted fish were laid out in the sun to dry. This method preserved the fish for a long time. Portuguese cooking makes frequent use of salt cod.

PURCHASING AND PREPARING SALT COD

The best salt cod comes from the cold waters of Norway, but it is becoming increasingly available in North American markets. Portuguese cooks prefer large fillets of salt cod, containing bones and skin, which are removed after the fish is soaked or cooked. These fillets give maximum flavor. Salt cod fillets are available boned and skinned. They can also be purchased in smaller pieces, packed either in wooden boxes or on foam trays, wrapped in plastic.

The day or two before the fish is to be used, rinse and cut the fillets into approximately 4-inch pieces or the size called for by your recipe. Place them in a large bowl and cover by at least 2 inches with cold tap water. Soak the cod in the refrigerator for 16 to 24, even 36 hours if need be, changing the water several times to re-hydrate the fish and remove some of the salt. To prepare a cod dish for tomorrow night's dinner, for example, start soaking the cod late this afternoon, changing the water 2 to 3 times before you retire for the evening and 4 more times tomorrow before using.

If you are preparing large fillets that have skin and bones, soaking make take as long as 48 hours. Frequent changes of water hasten the process. Smaller pieces of fish (about 8 oz) may take 16 to 24 hours or as few as 10 hours if you change the water frequently. Near the end of the soaking period, taste a small piece of the fish. If it is still too salty for your taste, change the water again and soak it longer. If you are soaking more than 2 pounds of fish, use more than one bowl. Remember that salt can always be added back in at the end of cooking, but if too much salt remains after the presoak, the finished dish will be irredeemably salty. At the end of soaking, the fish should have a mild taste of salt. There is a fine line between removing too much and not enough of the salt. If the fish is oversoaked, flavor is lost, resulting in a tasteless piece of fish. Bear in mind soaking times vary not only with the amount of fish but the degree of saltiness, which varies from batch to batch. The times are given merely as a guide.

Precooking Salt Cod

Some recipes call for the previously soaked salt cod to be precooked or poached before it is used in the dish. The following method is the one I prefer, and recommend, for most cod dishes.

1. Fill a pan large enough to accommodate the fish with water, and bring to a full boil. Turn off the heat.
2. Rinse the presoaked fish again and add to the pan. Cover and allow to sit for 15 to 30 minutes (depending on the thickness of the fish), until the cod is opaque or flakes easily. Remove the smaller pieces as they become opaque.
3. Drain the cod, discard bones and skin, if present, and place the fish in a bowl. Cover with scalded milk. Cover the bowl and set aside for 1 hour. Drain, taste again for salt, and use the fish as needed.

Note: Soaking the fish in scalded milk is a trick I learned in Portugal. The milk helps the fish retain its moisture and tenderness. Not all Portuguese cooks soak the cod this way, however. I do it both ways: I do not use milk when I make Salt Cod Cakes (page 88), but I find it improves baked salt cod dishes to which little or no extra moisture is added.

SAUSAGES

Flavorful smoked sausages are part of the fabric of Portuguese cooking. A variety of sausages, made with various cuts of pork and by-products, are popular any time of the year. Pork meat is cut into pieces and infused with a marinade or seasoning before being stuffed into casings and smoked. Sausages are commonly grilled, or added in slices or chunks to soups, seafood, poultry, and even beef dishes. Since the sausage is already cooked during smoking, it needs only to be heated through; overcooking can dry out sausage. Chapter 5 describes the common sausage types (page 168) and contains instructions for sausage-making with specific recipes.

SEAFOOD (SEE ALSO SALT COD)

The Portuguese have always taken advantage of the availability of different varieties of fish and shellfish. Many Portuguese Americans live near the coasts in the United States and still make a living from the sea. Others buy haddock, scrod, fresh tuna, halibut, and other white fish in fish markets.

Cockles (*améijoas*)

These tiny sweet clams from the waters off of Portugal are traditionally used in Alentejo-Style Pork with Clams (page 98). They are difficult to find in the United States. I suggest small littleneck clams, which make an excellent substitute. (For how to clean and purge clams, see page 82.)

Sardines (*sardinhas*)

Sardines are a naturally oily fish with a flavor similar to mackerel, but milder. They are a healthful source of calcium and beneficial fatty acids. Americans are generally only familiar with canned sardines, packed in olive or vegetable oil (now soy and canola oils, too). The canned sardines are great in sandwiches. Fresh sardines that are 2 to 3 inches in size are called *petingas.* They are easily pan-fried or baked and eaten bones and all. Larger sardines (5 to 6 inches) are baked or grilled over charcoal. Fresh (or fast-frozen) sardines are necessary for the recipes in this book; canned sardines cannot be substituted.

Tinker Mackerel (*carapaus*)

These little fish of the mackerel family are usually gutted, salted, and fried. Larger ones, called *chicharro,* are oilier and are usually grilled.

CLEANING OR DRESSING FISH

Using a pair of kitchen scissors, cut off the fins at the top, sides, and belly of the fish. With the edge of one scissor blade, scrape off the scales. Place the point of the scissors at the belly fin, and snip along the ridge of the belly to the vent, located midway toward the tail. With your index finger, reach inside the belly and pull out and discard the innards. Rinse the fish well and pat dry, ready for your recipe.

SEASONING METHODS

Throughout this book, you will notice certain recurring spice and seasoning combinations, although the amounts may differ or another variable may be added, giving each recipe its own character. The following are a few typical combinations of spices and seasonings.

Herb and Spice Paste

This heady, aromatic paste is used to season meat and poultry, and it is one of the first things I learned to make at my father's elbow. To make it, garlic is mashed with a mortar and pestle, blended with coarse salt, crumbled bay leaf, a light touch of *massa de pimentão* (Sweet Red Pepper Paste, page 219), parsley, olive oil, and freshly ground pepper. This blending of seasonings is the hallmark of Portuguese cuisine, especially in the Alentejo region. (Some regions use paprika and salt in place of *massa de pimentão*; other regions may include cumin, safflower, or other spices; and proportions vary.) Although the ingredients sound ordinary, they work together to produce something extraordinary. This is used in Alentejo-Style Pork and Clams (page 128), Roasted Pork Loin with Sweet Red Pepper Paste (page 131), Portuguese-Style Beef (page 150), and Roasted Potatoes (184).

Sweet Red Pepper Paste (*massa de pimentão*)

This is a paste made from sweet red peppers that have been cured in coarse salt. It is a traditional ingredient, most popular in the Alentejo province of Portugal. Often used to flavor meats, especially pork dishes, it is also an ingredient in the basic herb and spice paste (left) and in the Alentejo's *linguiça* sausage. Although there is no substitute for *massa de pimentão*, some regions use paprika in its place. Find the recipe on page 219.

Wine and Garlic Marinades (*vinho d'alho*)

Marinating is a common method of seasoning and tenderizing meats and fish. Amounts of wine and garlic vary according to individual preferences (recipes, pages 222–223). Sometimes a marinade is used in combination with a seasoning paste.

SPICES

When Portugal took to the sea centuries ago, its explorers had no idea what lay ahead. At that time, the spice trade depended on overland routes that were dangerous because of thieves and costly because of high tariffs at foreign borders. The discovery of an alternate route—by sea—that avoided the overland dangers, turned out to be more than the country had hoped for. Portugal became Europe's marketplace for spices. In those times, only the wealthy could afford the costly imports. Today, we have access to the widest range of spices imaginable in our global market. The following spices are traditional in Portuguese cooking.

Cinnamon (*canela*)

A sweet, spicy, and aromatic spice, cinnamon is used mostly in desserts. It comes in stick and powdered forms. The stick form is commonly used to scent puddings during the cooking process. The powdered version is blended into mixtures and sprinkled onto dishes. There are different varieties of cinnamon. Two of the most popular are Ceylon, a subtle-flavored cinnamon, and Cassia, which has a stronger flavor and darker color. For decorating Sweet Rice Pudding (page 258), I prefer the Ceylon cinnamon. When I rub the ground spice of Ceylon between my fingers, the release of the cinnamon is easier to control.

Cumin (*cominhos*)

This pungent spice is used in vinegar sauces and seafood and meat dishes. Sometimes it is used to season Portuguese blood sausages. Although it is traditionally used in seed form and ground with a mortar and pestle, ground cumin can be used instead, reducing the amount called for by half.

Curry Powder (*caril*)

This mixture of spices is used occasionally to season seafood and meat, giving color in addition to flavor.

Nutmeg (*noz-moscada*)

Nutmeg is used in moderation for seasoning meat stews, vinegar sauces, and *tortas* (a Portuguese omelet snack). It is not very often used in desserts. Best when freshly ground, only a small amount is needed to flavor a dish.

Paprika (*colorau*)

Hungarian sweet paprika is not Portuguese in origin, but it may as well be. Used for centuries by the Portuguese, paprika is typically used in some regions of Portugal in dishes that other regions flavor with red pepper paste, *massa de pimentão*. Sometimes, it is used in combination with *massa de pimentão*. Today Spanish and Portuguese paprika is also used.

Pepper (*pimenta*)

The fruit of tropical plants, white and black peppercorns are not related to chili peppers. Freshly ground pepper is best. White is preferred in white sauce and in fish dishes where black specks might be unattractive. White pepper gives a subtle but hotter flavor than black.

Safflower (*assafróa*)

Transplanted here with seeds from Portugal, *carthamus tinctorius* is an annual that grows in many Portuguese gardens in the United States. The plant has prickly-edged oval leaves on stalks that are two to three feet tall. The globe-shaped flower has maroon threadlike petals with yellow tips. Under the thin petals, a white sphere holds the seeds, promising next season's harvest. It is the petals, which are first dried and then crushed, that are used to flavor some Portuguese dishes. Safflower is high in linoleic acid, one of the essential fatty acids. Do not confuse safflower with saffron, which comes from a crocus flower. Those who are allergic to ragweed may be severely allergic to safflower as well. Saffron or paprika can be used as a substitute.

Saffron (*assafrão*)

The harvested stigmas of the crocus flower add yellow color and subtle flavor. Crumble and soak in a bit of water for 15 minutes before using.

Salt (*sal*)

Coarse sea salt or kosher salt will bring out the best flavor of ingredients. Coarse salt does not contain additives to keep it from caking. The amount of salt given in these recipes is based on the Portuguese palate. Also, equal measures of table salt and coarse salt are not equally salty, because the coarse salt is less dense. So be sure to adjust the amount of salt to your liking—smaller amounts if you're using table salt—and taste as you season. Salt should be added toward the end of cooking, after any juice or broth has had time to reduce. Dishes that contain sausages, salt cod, or canned substitutions should be tasted before you add salt. Reserve the table salt for baking.

TOMATOES

Another important ingredient in making a *refogado* (see page 24), tomatoes impart a distinctive flavor to the base of some stews and seafood dishes. Meaty, red, ripe, flavorful tomatoes that are peeled and chopped work well in most Portuguese recipes. It is not essential to remove the seeds. When flavorful tomatoes are not available, high-quality canned tomatoes or a small amount of tomato paste can be used instead.

Heart of the Ox/Bull (*coração de boi/toro*)
This tomato, named for its large heart shape, is a popular Portuguese variety. Like other varieties of vegetables grown in the homeland, *coração de boi* tomatoes were brought here by Portuguese immigrants and cultivated. A meaty tomato with outstanding flavor and minimal seeds, it is grown in many Portuguese-American home gardens. The familiar American favorite beefsteak or Italian plum tomatoes also yield good results in Portuguese dishes.

VINEGAR

Vinegar plays a part in salad dressings, marinades, and vinegar sauces. Both red wine vinegar and white wine vinegar are used. Apple cider vinegar, which my uncle Ilidio claims was introduced to Portugal after World War II, is now popular as well and used for salads as an alternative to wine vinegar.

WINE

Just as necessary as bread and soup, wine has its place in the Portuguese meal. However, wine is more than a beverage. It is intrinsic to the wine and garlic marinades (pages 222–223) that are used to flavor meats and fish. (See Chapter 10.)

Left: Safflower (page 29)

EQUIPMENT

Very few special items are needed for creating Portuguese dishes. I am one in a small group of Portuguese cooks who gather to prepare a dinner for about 200 people for our monthly social. Before we begin, someone asks if we are ready. With a sheepish smile, a fellow cook always replies, "I have my knife—that is all I need." As much as we joke about it, it is almost literally true. A Portuguese cook, it is said, needs little more than their hands and a sharp, trusty paring knife. The "knife" is nothing more than a squared-off, 1-inch wide by 4-inch long carbon blade with a round wooden handle. This style of paring knife, owned by many Portuguese, is a utility knife, commonly used by leather workers, like my father, to trim hides. I purchased mine in a local hardware store. A few pots, a mortar and pestle, sieve, and bowls, of course, make up the rest. The following items make Portuguese cooking a breeze. I encourage you to use the additional conveniences of food processors, mixers, and the like.

Food Mill

In the evolution of kitchen equipment, the food mill, which we call a *passador* ("pass through"), replaced the colander and fork for puréeing. It is a labor-saving tool when it comes to puréeing vegetables, especially legumes, in Portuguese soups. It has a perforated bottom and a blade that is cranked to press the ingredients, holding back seeds and skins. To use, simply place it over a pot or bowl, ladle cooked ingredients into it, and turn the hand crank, adding broth as needed.

Kale Cutter

This hand-cranked device is used mainly to cut kale into a fine chiffonade for *Caldo Verde* (page 42).

Meat Grinder

A hand-cranked meat grinder that clamps to the table or a grinder attachment to a freestanding electric mixer is very useful in making cod cakes and sausages. It is available in kitchen shops.

Mortar and Pestle

The mortar, a small bowl, and pestle, a short, dowel-shaped tool, are used to pound and blend ingredients such as spices together. They are made in various sizes. They are made in various sizes out of wood, stone, or marble. It is an indispensable tool. Mashing in a mortar and pestle produces a paste that is significantly different from what a food processor will whip up. The food processor, or the chef's knife, simply cuts the ingredients, but the pestle mashes one element into another, pulverizing them and releasing their essences, and then marrying the flavors thoroughly. It is the Portuguese cook's secret tool.

Tartlet Tins (fluted and smooth)

Fluted 2½-inch tart tins are used to make Pastry Tartlets (page 277). Smooth aluminum tins, also 2½ inches, are used to make Custard Cream Tarts (page 280) and mini Chicken Pies (page 124). You can find them in Portuguese online stores or baker's supply stores.

Clay Pots A glazed pot resembling a Portuguese clay roof tile (*telha*) is traditionally used to make *Salmão Assado na Telha* (Salmon Baked in a Clay Tile, page 96). *Alcatra* (Slow-Braised Beef Rump, page 154) is typically made in an unglazed clay pot resembling an inverted lampshade. These pots are traditional, but any unglazed clay baker, good braising pot, or ceramic baking dish will work fine.

LITTLE TASTES ~ *PETISCOS*

Appetizers, as we call them today, were not traditionally part of a Portuguese family meal. As my Uncle Ilidio would say, "What was an appetizer? The people were poor; there wasn't any such thing as an appetizer." After a hard day's work, appetites did not need stimulation. What was served were simple starters or accompaniments. In most Portuguese homes, bread and olives are still always on the table. Roasted peppers, marinated lupini beans (*tremoços*), sautéed *linguiça* sausage, or fresh cheese may be included. A few slices of *presunto,* a salt-cured ham like Italian prosciutto, might be served with bread or perhaps a wedge of melon. The following list are recipes that lend themselves to a light course or snack, and can be used as *petiscos*, "little tastes." Savory pastries, *salgados*, can also be included on the appetizer table.

2

SOUPS

Sopas

2 SOUPS
Sopas

Light or hearty, soup has always been a mainstay of the Portuguese diet. When I was growing up, soup and bread were served in our house every day. Sometimes, we had the same delicious soup for supper we had eaten for lunch. Created from the humblest ingredients, soups were the lifeline to survival for many of Portugal's poor and especially Portuguese immigrants. Soups in Portugal, especially the Alentejo region, began with bread, olive oil, water, and garlic. This became a bread soup known as *Açorda* (page 68). Variations were created by adding native wild plants gathered in the field. *Sopa de Pedra* (page 61), my grandfather told me, is a soup that actually began with a stone! (The story of stone soup is retold on page 61.)

In the peasant kitchen, it is unusual for stock to be made ahead. Any meat, poultry, or fish flavor is obtained when the ingredient is used as part of the dish itself. Water is the primary liquid ingredient. Sometimes wine is added. If by chance there is broth remaining from a stew or braise, frugal cooks use it for making soup. In the hands of my great-grandmother Ana, an ounce of necessity and a pinch of creativity would transform the aromatic broth remaining from a Portuguese boiled dinner, *Cozido à Portuguesa* (page 158), or the liquid from cooking beans, into a flavorful soup. Actually, many soups began as the "soup of the pot," or *sopa de panela* as my grandmother would call it. In the old days, the recipe was adjusted according to whatever ingredients were on hand—pasta, beans, diced leftover cooked vegetables, or diced fresh vegetables. Today, I chill leftover broth, remove and discard any solidified fat, and strain the liquid. The ingredients are then combined with the reserved broth, creating a satisfying meal; no additional seasoning is necessary. Nothing is wasted.

Preparations for some soups begin with soaking legumes or salting meats a day ahead. Some start with a base of potatoes, beans, or other vegetables puréed with water. The addition of chopped vegetables gives texture to the soup, and starches (potatoes, rice, bread, and beans) add body. It is very common for potatoes, rice, and beans to be served together in some combination, either in the same meal or even in the same soup, to make it more substantial.

We know that if our children are picky eaters when it comes to vegetables, they will at least get their nutrients from our soups. Vegetarians also enjoy these soups simply by eliminating any sausage or other meat.

For a satisfying and nourishing meal, ladle out a bowl of hearty soup and cut some thick slices from a crusty wheat bread or dense cornbread loaf. Add some regional olives and wine. *Boa apetite!*

Serves 6

VEGETABLE SOUP

Sopa de Legumes

Sopa de legumes, nicknamed simply Portuguese soup or *sopa à Portuguesa* by Portuguese-Americans, is one of the more popular soups served in our homes. This version is that of my friend Isaura Nogueira, who includes pork ribs with carrots, green beans, white kidney beans, cabbage, and kale. The ribs add depth of flavor, while the combination of vegetables deliver full texture to this nutritious soup. This soup can be easily transformed into a vegetarian dish by omitting the pork and adding an extra tablespoon of olive oil to the pot.

1¼ cups (8 oz) dried white kidney beans
1 lb meaty pork ribs
2 tablespoons coarse kosher salt

BROTH

2 medium starchy potatoes, such as Maine or
   Yukon Gold, peeled and cut into 1-inch cubes
1 carrot, peeled and coarsely chopped
1 large very ripe tomato, peeled, seeded, and
   coarsely chopped

SOUP

5 oz collard greens or flat-leaf kale, coarse stems
   discarded, chopped (about 4 cups)
3 cups (8 oz) Savoy cabbage, coarsely chopped
8 oz green beans, cut into ¼-inch pieces
1 large onion, finely chopped
1 medium carrot, peeled and coarsely chopped
½ cup (2 oz) small pasta, such as elbow macaroni
3 tablespoons olive oil
1 tablespoon coarse kosher salt, or to taste
Pinch freshly ground black pepper

A day ahead

1. Soak the beans overnight in enough water to cover by 2 inches (about 4 cups).

2. Rub the pork ribs with the salt, cover, and refrigerate for at least 8 hours.

Make the broth

3. Wipe excess salt from the meat and place in a 5-quart stockpot. Drain and rinse the beans. Add to the pot with 12 cups of fresh water, and the potatoes, carrot, and tomato. Cover and bring to a boil over high heat.

4. Reduce the heat and simmer for approximately 40 minutes or until the vegetables are very tender and the meat is nearly falling from the bones.

5. Transfer the pork ribs to a platter, cover, and set aside in a warm place. Using a food mill or immersion blender, purée the vegetables with the broth to a smooth consistency.

Finish the soup

6. Bring the puréed broth to a boil over medium-high heat. Add the kale, cabbage, green beans, onion, carrot, pasta, olive oil, salt, and pepper. Reduce the heat to medium-low. Cover and gently simmer for about 15 minutes, until the vegetables are tender and the pasta is cooked.

7. Remove the meat from the bones, cut into serving-size pieces, and serve on the side (or you can return it to the pot, if preferred). Serve with plenty of crusty bread to dip in the broth.

Serves 6

TURNIP GREEN SOUP WITH RICE

Sopa de Nabiça com Arroz

Very young, tender turnip greens are essential to this distinctive soup. Loaded with nutrients, the greens add a unique flavor. The *chouriço* sausage (see page 175) provides the right counterpoint for the slightly bitter leaves.

3 tablespoons olive oil

1 small onion, finely chopped

1 garlic clove, finely chopped

2 medium starchy potatoes, such as Maine or
  Yukon Gold, peeled and coarsely chopped

1 tablespoon short-grain rice

4 oz *chouriço* sausage, cut into ½-inch slices

2 teaspoons coarse kosher salt, or to taste

¼ teaspoon freshly ground black or white pepper,
  or to taste

½ teaspoon dried crushed red pepper (optional)

3 cups (3 oz) tender turnip greens, coarsely chopped

1. Heat the olive oil in a 4-quart stockpot. Add the onions and sauté over medium-high heat until soft and translucent, about 5 minutes. Toss in the garlic, cooking until slightly aromatic, about a minute.

2. Add 4 cups water and the potatoes. Cover and bring to a boil. Reduce the heat to medium-low and simmer until the potatoes are very tender, 20 to 30 minutes. Use a slotted spoon to transfer the potatoes to a dish. Coarsely mash the potatoes with a fork and return to the broth. Or, for a smooth consistency, purée the entire contents of the pot. A handheld immersion blender makes the job easy.

3. Return the soup to a boil. Add the rice, *chouriço*, salt, pepper, and crushed red pepper. Reduce the heat, cover, and simmer for 15 minutes, until the rice is not quite done.

4. Add the greens. Cover the pot and continue simmering until the rice is cooked and the greens are just tender, 7 to 10 minutes. Serve hot, accompanied by olives and plenty of crusty bread.

Variation: *Mustard greens and broccoli rabe make excellent substitutes for the turnip greens in this recipe. My father would harvest mustard greens from his garden in the spring when they were especially young and tender. Some of his friends used broccoli rabe. To use, rinse the greens well in cold water. Discard any mottled or older leaves. Chop and add when the rice is nearly done. Cover and simmer for just 5 minutes—these tender greens cook quickly.*

Serves 4 to 6

GREEN BROTH SOUP

Caldo Verde

Although oral history places the origin of this soup in the northern Minho province of Portugal, it is enjoyed throughout the country. The traditional ingredients—potatoes, *galega* kale (page 23), olive oil, and sautéed *linguiça* (a mild Portuguese smoked sausage)—mingle to create this classic soup, named for the color of the broth. The puréed potato broth with a very fine chiffonade of kale (see page 44) is the signature of this soup. Variations in the ratio of water to potatoes are evident from region to region and cook to cook, and you can adjust the amount of greens and potatoes to your preference as well. I prefer the soup to have a body like light cream. If it is too thick, thin it with a small amount of water. My family enjoys this dish with plenty of kale, but feel free to add less if you wish. Ladle the soup into bowls and serve, as tradition dictates, with a single slice of sautéed *linguiça* floating in the broth.

5 medium starchy potatoes, such as Maine or
   Yukon Gold, peeled and quartered

1 small yellow onion, finely chopped

1 tablespoon coarse kosher salt, or to taste

8 oz bunch flat-leaf kale or collard greens

5 tablespoons olive oil

4 oz *chouriço* or *linguiça* sausage (see page 44),
   cut into ¼-inch slices

Note: *Most Portuguese soups thicken as they cool because of the starch they contain. Once they are reheated, the broth loosens up. You can add a small amount of water, if necessary, to help it along.*

1. In a 4-quart stockpot, combine the potatoes, onion, and 6 cups of water. Cover and bring to a boil over high heat. Reduce the heat to medium-low, season with the salt, then simmer until the potatoes are very tender, 20 to 30 minutes.

2. Meanwhile, trim the kale of the thick central stem at the back of the leaf. Rinse the leaves well in a sink full of cool water. Lift out to drain. Read over the instructions on page 44 for how to easily cut the kale into thin, grass-like strips, no longer than 2 inches. You should have 6 to 7 cups. Set aside.

3. When the potatoes are cooked, purée the contents of the soup pot to a smooth consistency. Return to a boil.

4. Add the kale and olive oil. Simmer until the kale is bright green and tender, but not mushy, approximately 5 minutes.

5. In a frying pan, brown the sausage slices, turning to color both sides, and reserve.

6. Serve the soup in the traditional manner with one slice of the sausage added to each bowl. Any extra sausage is served on the side.

THE ART OF CHIFFONADE

One of the soups most associated with Portuguese cooking is Green Broth Soup, *caldo verde* (page 42). Equally important as the main ingredients of *caldo verde* is the chiffonade, greens cut into grass-like slivers—the signature of this soup. When my children were young, they would even ask for "grass soup," which raised an eyebrow or two when other parents learned from their children what Nancy and Marc were having for dinner.

I learned the art of chiffonade by watching my father. After rinsing the kale and trimming the thick middle rib, he stacked several leaves and rolled them up tightly, lengthwise. Holding this log-shaped bundle in one hand and taking up a sharp knife with the other, he cut very thin slivers of kale—as if paring an apple—until we had enough for the soup. In all the years that I have used this method, I have had innumerable green fingertips but I have never cut myself. I doubt any culinary instructor would encourage this method.

It does, however, give new meaning to the expression "green thumb." I recommend the safer use of a cutting board and a sharp chef knife or kale cutter (page 33). If you use a cutting board to cut greens into chiffonade, make diagonal cuts; otherwise, any long strands of greens will need to be torn or cut into 2-inch pieces. A kale cutter cuts the greens to just the right size.

Serves 8 to 10

KALE SOUP

Sopa de Couves

Sumptuous and heartwarming, this classic Portuguese soup hits the spot on a cold winter's night. In the Alentejo, where beef was scarce, my grandmother used the more plentiful lamb or pork for this dish. In the United States, she frequently alternated these with the beef shin I use here. The kale is traditionally torn (see page 44) but can also be chopped. My father always added yellow turnip (rutabaga) or you can use white turnips. My Aunt Ana likes to add carrots, too. My family uses Maine potatoes, which gives a looser texture; waxy varieties hold their shape better.

2½ cups (1 lb) dried red kidney beans, soaked overnight in enough water to cover by 2 inches

3 lb beef shinbone, trimmed of excess fat

1 medium onion, coarsely chopped

2 garlic cloves, finely chopped

1 bay leaf

1½ cups (7 oz) peeled and cubed yellow turnip

12 oz *salpicão* or *chouriço* sausage (see page 168)

1 lb waxy potatoes, such as Red Bliss or new potatoes, peeled and cut into 1-inch cubes

1 to 2 carrots, peeled and cut into ¼-inch slices (optional)

¼ teaspoon dried crushed red pepper (optional)

8 oz bunch kale or collard greens, trimmed of center rib, and into 1- to 2-inch pieces (about 7 cups)

¼ cup (1 oz) small pasta, such as elbow macaroni

¼ cup olive oil

1 tablespoon coarse kosher salt, or to taste

¼ teaspoon freshly ground black pepper

Notes: *Adding the kale about 5 minutes before adding the pasta will yield more al dente pasta, if that is your preference. Salpicão is the one sausage for which the casing is removed before serving. The reason seems to have been long forgotten; it is just one of those culinary quirks.*

1. Drain and rinse the beans. In a 5-quart stockpot, combine the beans, beef shin, onion, garlic, and bay leaf. Pour in approximately 12 cups of water or enough to cover the beef by about 1 inch. Cover, bring to a boil, then reduce the heat to medium-low. Simmer the beef and beans, occasionally skimming the broth of any impurities, for 1½ hours.

2. When the beans are very tender, transfer about 1 cup to a small dish. Mash the beans with a fork, adding some of the broth, then return the paste to the pot. (If preferred, you can pass these beans through a food mill, sieve, or colander fist, and discard the skins). Add the turnip, return the broth to a boil, then reduce the heat and simmer for 20 minutes.

3. If using *salpicão*, you may need to first trim the metal clip and the casing string from the ends. Add the sausage, potatoes, carrots, and dried crushed red pepper. Continue to simmer until the vegetables are almost tender, about 20 minutes.

4. Add the kale, pasta (see note), olive oil, salt, and pepper to the pot, and simmer for 15 to 20 minutes, or until the vegetables are tender. Remove the beef shin from the pot, trim away and discard any fat, along with the bone. Cut the meat into pieces. Remove the sausage from the pot. If using *salpicão*, peel and discard the casing. Cut the sausage into chunks. Serve the meat on the side, as part of a second course, or return it to the pot and heat through. Serve hot with plenty of crusty bread for dipping into the broth.

EGGS IN BROTH

Molho de Ovos

This dish is perfect for a Saturday-night supper. It is a welcome dish after a busy day when you just don't feel like making a complicated meal. My friend Manuel C. Silva made this, his grandmother's recipe, to feed the kitchen crew of Our Lady of Fatima Church in Peabody, Massachusetts, when they finished making 180 pounds of sausages for the church fair. The meat used that night for this stew happened to be marinated pork set aside before someone could stuff it into a casing, but Manny says, "The meat does not have to be marinated; use what you have—beef, pork, or smoked sausage."

¼ cup olive oil

1 medium onion, finely chopped

2 garlic cloves, finely chopped

1 bay leaf

¼ lb pork, beef, or sausage, cut into
   ½- to 1-inch pieces

½ cup white wine

2 large waxy potatoes, such as
   Red Bliss, peeled and cut into
   1-inch cubes

2 teaspoons coarse kosher salt,
   or to taste

1 teaspoon Hot Pepper Paste
   (page 220) or hot pepper sauce

⅛ teaspoon freshly ground black
   pepper, or to taste

2 eggs per person

1. Heat the oil in a 4-quart saucepan over medium-high heat. Add and sauté the onion until soft and translucent, about 5 minutes. Toss in the garlic and bay leaf. When the garlic becomes aromatic, put in the meat and sauté for 3 minutes. Pour in the wine and stir, scraping up any bits of caramelized juices from the bottom of the pan.

2. Add the potatoes with enough water to just cover them (about 2 cups). Season with the salt, hot pepper paste or hot sauce, and black pepper. Cover tightly and bring to a boil. Reduce the heat and simmer until the potatoes are just done, about 20 minutes.

3. One by one, crack the eggs into a shallow bowl and, nudging the potatoes aside, slide the eggs into the hot broth to poach for 3 minutes. Ladle into bowls and serve, accompanied with crusty bread to dip into the broth.

Serves 6

CHICKPEA SOUP WITH SPINACH

Sopa de Grão de Bico com Espinafres

Soups made with chickpeas are common in Mediterranean countries. This dish of the Alentejo area takes ordinary chickpeas and turns them into an extraordinary soup with a simple, comforting, and nutty flavor. This version is adapted from my grandmother's recipe as taught to me by my Aunt Ana. Chickpeas require longer soaking than most dried beans. I recommend soaking them for at least 15 hours before cooking.

2½ cups (1 lb) dried chickpeas, soaked for at least
   15 hours in enough water to cover by 2 inches

5 tablespoons olive oil

1 small onion, finely chopped

4 large garlic cloves, finely chopped

1 bay leaf

¼ cup (1¾ oz) white rice

1½ tablespoons coarse kosher salt, or to taste

¼ teaspoon ground white pepper

2 tablespoons finely chopped fresh cilantro

7½ cups (8 oz) coarsely chopped spinach
   leaves (optional)

8 oz *linguiça* sausage (see page 168), cut into
   ¼-inch rounds

Variation: *Omit the spinach leaves and serve as an elegant first course.*

1. Drain and rinse the chickpeas, then set aside. Heat 4 tablespoons of the oil in a 4-quart saucepan over medium-high heat. Add the onion and sauté until soft and translucent, about 5 minutes. Add the garlic and bay leaf, cooking until the garlic releases its aroma, about 1 minute.

2. Add the chickpeas to the pot with 12 cups of fresh water. Cover, bring to a boil over high heat, then reduce the heat to medium-low. Simmer until the chickpeas are very tender and easily mashed, 1½ to 2 hours.

3. Use the back of a fork or large spoon to press the chickpeas against the sides of the pot. They should mash easily, which will allow the skins to float to the surface of the broth. Remove the skins with a slotted spoon and discard.

4. Remove the bay leaf. Strain the chickpeas, reserving the broth. Remove any remaining skins.

5. Set a food mill, sieve, or colander over the soup pot. Press the chickpeas through the holes, adding a little of the broth to create a smooth consistency. Alternatively, you can use a blender: work in small batches, and then strain the soup back into the pot.

6. Return the soup to a boil. Add the rice, salt, and pepper. Cover, reduce the heat, and simmer, stirring frequently, until the rice is almost done, about 20 minutes.

7. Add the cilantro and the spinach. Stir well and simmer for another 5 minutes or until the rice is cooked.

8. Meanwhile, in a small frying pan, sauté the sausage with 1 tablespoon of the oil until lightly brown, turning to color both sides. Ladle the soup into bowls and garnish with a few slices of the sausage.

Serves 6

BEAN SOUP

Sopa de Feijão

The simple and traditional *sopa de feijão*, in the style of my father's hometown of Galveias, is one of the first soups my father taught me to make. He would set a colander over the soup pot and let me force the beans through the holes, using just a fork and some water. (Resist the urge to use a handheld immersion blender to puree the beans—the little pieces of bean skin do not feel particularly good in the mouth.) The lighter bean broth and the additional flavor of cilantro sets this soup apart from other kale soups.

1¼ cups (8 oz) dried red kidney or roman beans, soaked overnight in enough water to cover by 2 inches

8 oz bunch kale, trimmed of thick center rib

3 garlic cloves, finely chopped

1 bay leaf

¼ cup olive oil

1 tablespoon finely chopped cilantro

1 tablespoon coarse kosher salt, or to taste

½ teaspoon freshly ground black pepper

1. Drain and rinse the beans and place them in a 4-quart stockpot with 8 cups of water. Cover and bring to a boil. Reduce the heat to medium-low and simmer for 1 hour or until the beans are very tender and can be easily mashed with a fork.

2. Stack the kale leaves, a few at a time, on top of one another. Roll lengthwise like a cigar and slice crosswise into ½-inch-wide strips—like chiffonade but wider. Cut the strips again, crosswise, into shorter lengths, about 2 inches. You should have about 7 cups. Set aside.

3. Remove about half of the beans from the pot, along with some of the cooking liquid, and push them through a food mill, or a sieve or colander set over a bowl. You want to purée the beans, leaving the skins behind. Discard the skins and return the puréed beans to the pot, along with the garlic, bay leaf, and olive oil.

4. Return the soup to a boil. Add the kale, cilantro, salt, and pepper. Re-cover the pot, reduce the heat, and simmer 10 to 15 minutes, until the kale is tender, but not mushy. Serve simply with crusty country bread and olives.

Variations: *Use white kidney beans (my grandfather's favorite), in place of red kidney beans. Flouting tradition, my father often added a small chunk of sausage to the pot as well.*

Serves 4 to 6

BEAN SOUP WITH TOMATO

Sopa de Feijão com Tomate

Rich with fiber and flavor, this soup has a wonderful body to it, which thickens as it cools. When our children, Nancy and Marc, were young, they would always ask me to make this soup. The thickness of the soup made it easier for them to feed themselves without spilling very much broth. The beans can be prepared in advance, making short time of the remaining preparations.

1¼ cups (8 oz) kidney beans, soaked overnight in enough water to cover by 2 inches

¼ cup olive oil

1 small onion, finely chopped

1 small very ripe tomato, peeled, seeded, and coarsely chopped

1 teaspoon sweet paprika

1 bay leaf

1 garlic clove, finely chopped

1 large boiling potato, cut into ½-inch cubes

½ cup (2 to 3½ oz) rice or elbow pasta

1 tablespoon finely chopped parsley

2 teaspoons coarse kosher salt, or to taste

½ teaspoon freshly ground white or black pepper

1. Drain and rinse the beans, and place them in a 2-quart saucepan, along with 3½ cups of fresh water, or enough water to cover them by 2 inches. Cover the pot and bring to a boil over medium-high heat. Reduce the heat and simmer until the beans are very tender, about 40 minutes. Reserve with cooking liquid.

2. Heat the oil in a 3-quart stockpot and sauté the onion until soft and translucent, about 5 minutes. Add the tomato, paprika, bay leaf, and garlic. Cover and simmer until the tomato becomes soft and partially dissolved, about 15 minutes.

3. Set a food mill over the pot and purée half or all of the kidney beans into the pot, using the reserved cooking liquid and 3½ cups more fresh water. Add any unpuréed beans with the potatoes to the pot, cover, and bring to a boil.

4. Toss in the rice or pasta, parsley, salt, and pepper. Reduce the heat, cover, and simmer until the potatoes and rice or pasta are done, 25 to 30 minutes. Serve with plenty of crusty bread for dipping in the broth.

Variation: *My Aunt Ana would sometimes skip the rice or pasta and potatoes. Instead she would add 2 cups (1 lb) of coarsely cubed winter squash. I sometimes take this variation one step further and add coarsely chopped spinach in the last 5 minutes of cooking.*

CARROT SOUP

Sopa de Cenoura

Made with freshly harvested carrots, this is a truly wonderful soup that is easy to make and loaded with vitamin A. It's perfect in the fall and makes a delectable first course for Thanksgiving dinner. A friend from Torres Vedras, a town north of Lisbon, made this unique soup for my husband and me while we were honeymooning in Portugal. It is unique because a simple puréed soup—without other ingredients added to give it texture—is unusual in Portuguese cooking.

Regular white potatoes are typically used for this soup, but one day I found myself with only white sweet potatoes in my pantry. Taught to use what I have on hand, I added one to the pot. The result was wonderful. Since then, I use a white sweet potato for this recipe; I like the way it rounds out the flavors. Try it both ways and see which you prefer.

4 tablespoons olive oil

1 small onion, coarsely chopped

1 small very ripe tomato, peeled, seeded, and coarsely chopped (¼ cup)

1 garlic clove, peeled but left whole

1 lb carrots, peeled and coarsely chopped

1 small white sweet potato, peeled and cut into 1-inch pieces (1 cup)

1 medium yellow turnip, peeled and chopped (1 cup)

1 tablespoon coarse kosher salt, or to taste

Pinch ground white pepper

Heavy cream, for drizzling (optional)

1. Heat 2 tablespoons of the oil in a 4-quart stockpot over medium-high heat. Add and sauté the onion until light golden in color. Stir in the tomato and garlic. Reduce the heat to medium-low. Cover and continue to cook until the tomato is soft and partially dissolved, about 15 minutes.

2. Add the carrots, sweet potato, and turnip. Pour in 4 cups water, cover, and bring to a boil over medium-high heat. Reduce the heat and simmer until the vegetables are very tender, 30 to 40 minutes. Remove the pot from the heat and purée the soup (a handheld immersion blender works well).

3. Stir in the remaining oil and the salt and white pepper. Bring the soup back to a boil, reduce the heat, and simmer for 2 more minutes, then serve, drizzled with cream, if using.

Variation: *For a change in color and texture, add 12 oz fresh spinach, coarsely chopped, or 4 oz green beans, cut into ¼-inch pieces. Simmer for 5 minutes until the spinach or beans are just tender.*

Serves 6 to 8

FENNEL SOUP

Sopa de Funcho

The Azorean Portuguese speak with great delight of this dish. Licorice flavor dominates this soup, and it is the Azoreans' most common use for fennel. The slightly sweet flavor comes from the feathery fennel fronds. The variety of fennel found in most supermarkets has a large, somewhat flattened white bulb at the base of the leafy stems. This is a good substitute for the wild version. Unfortunately, some markets remove most of the leafy stalks from the plant. Shop around for bulbs with the most greens. If you have the benefit of a local farmers' market, you may find fennel bulbs with the fine leaves still intact. Lucia Rebelo, who is from Terceira (the "third" island to be discovered in the Azores), adds pig's knuckles for extra flavor. I prefer the less fatty ribs of pork. My uncle Joe Ortins says his mother, who was born on the island of Graciosa, added some carrots to the broth. You can also make this soup without any meat—just add two extra tablespoons of olive oil in its place. The following version was inspired by my husband's cousin, Evelyn Ortins Cunha, who is a natural cook.

1½ cups (8 oz) dried white kidney beans
1 lb pork ribs or pig's knuckle
2 tablespoons coarse kosher salt

SOUP

2 dense bunches feathery fennel fronds,
  or 2 fennel bulbs with fronds
1 medium onion, finely chopped
5 garlic cloves, finely chopped
1 bay leaf
⅛ teaspoon ground cloves
⅛ teaspoon freshly ground black pepper
1 cup (2½ oz) coarsely chopped
  Savoy cabbage leaves
1 lb starchy potatoes, such as Maine
  or Yukon Gold, peeled and cut into
  1-inch cubes
1 bunch scallions, dark green parts removed,
  thinly sliced (about ½ cup)
3 tablespoons olive oil
8 oz *linguiça* sausage (see page 168),
  cut into ⅛-inch slices

A day ahead
1. Soak the dried beans overnight in enough water to cover them by 2 inches. Rub the meat with the coarse salt and chill overnight.

The next day
2. Drain and rinse the beans and place them in a 4-quart stockpot. Wipe any excess salt from the pork and add it to the beans, along with 8 cups of water. Cover the pot, and bring to a boil. Reduce the heat, and simmer until the meat is tender and the beans are easily mashed with a fork, about 1 hour. Occasionally skim the surface of any impurities.

3. Meanwhile, trim and discard coarse stems from the fine feathery fennel fronds. Finely chop enough leaves to yield 2 cups. (If you are using fennel bulbs, discard the outer layer. Separate sections of the bulbs, rinse well, and coarsely chop.) Set aside.

4. Add the onion, garlic, bay leaf, cloves, and black pepper to the pot. Simmer for 5 minutes, then toss in the fennel fronds, and chopped bulb, if using, along with the cabbage, potatoes, scallions, olive oil, and sausage. Return the soup to a boil, reduce the heat to medium-low, and continue to simmer until the potatoes are done and the cabbage is tender, about 20 minutes. Usually this soup needs no additional salt, but taste and season to your preference.

Serves 4 to 6

ONION SOUP

Sopa de Cebola

My grandmother Teresa's tasty version of onion soup is lightly flavored with tomato and quite different from the French variety. She would fry the onions until just translucent, but I like to bring out the sweetness of the onions by sautéing them until they are golden.

3 tablespoons olive oil

3 medium onions, thinly sliced

1 small very ripe tomato, peeled, seeded, and finely chopped

½ teaspoon paprika

1 bay leaf

2 medium starchy potatoes, such as Maine or Yukon Gold, peeled and cut into ½-inch cubes

1 tablespoon finely chopped parsley, plus more to serve

1 tablespoon coarse kosher salt, or to taste

¼ teaspoon freshly ground white or black pepper

4 to 6 slices day-old Homestyle Bread (page 236) or crusty sourdough, toasted or fried in olive oil

4 to 6 eggs

1. Heat the olive oil in a 3-quart saucepan over medium-high heat. Add and sauté the onion until translucent or lightly golden, about 15 minutes.

2. Add the tomato, paprika, and bay leaf and cover the pot. Cook over medium-low heat, stirring occasionally, until the tomato becomes soft and mixture is partially dissolved, about 15 minutes.

3. Add 4 cups water, and the potatoes, parsley, salt, and pepper. Cover and bring to a boil. Reduce the heat and simmer until the potatoes are tender but not mushy.

4. Place a slice of toasted or fried bread into each soup bowl. Ladle the soup over the bread. Carefully break an egg into each bowl, allowing the eggs to poach in the piping hot broth. It takes 2 to 3 minutes for the eggs to cook.

5. Serve with an extra sprinkle of finely chopped parsley.

Tip: *Before adding the raw egg, you can break it into a small bowl to make sure there aren't any small pieces of shell in the bowl. Slide the egg into the soup. Alternatively, eggs may be softly poached separately and then added to the soup bowls.*

Variation: *Omit the tomato, eggs, and bread. Remove the bay leaf and puree the ingredients before adding ½ cup (2 to 3½ oz) short-grain rice or orzo pasta. Cook until tender. Garnish with finely chopped cilantro.*

Serves 4 to 6

GREEN BEAN AND LINGUIÇA SOUP WITH TOMATO

Sopa de Feijão Verde e Linguiça com Tomate

For the best flavor, use the freshest green beans you can find for this soup. My father-in-law took great satisfaction in adding his homemade *linguiça* sausage to this, his favorite soup.

3 tablespoons olive oil

8 oz *linguiça* sausage (see page 168), cut into
  ½-inch slices

1 large onion, thinly sliced

2 large very ripe tomatoes, peeled, seeded,
  and coarsely chopped (2 cups)

2 garlic cloves, finely chopped

2 large waxy potatoes, such as Red Bliss or
  new potatoes, peeled and cut into
  ½-inch cubes

½ cup red wine

1 tablespoon finely chopped parsley

1 to 2 teaspoons kosher salt, or to taste

Pinch freshly ground white or black pepper

1 lb fresh string beans, trimmed and cut into
  1-inch pieces (about 4 cups)

1. Heat the olive oil in a 4-quart stockpot over medium-high heat. Add and lightly brown the sausage slices, turning to color both sides. Remove the sausage from the pan and set aside.

2. Add the onion to the pot and sauté until light golden, about 15 minutes. Reduce the heat to medium-low. Add the tomatoes with the garlic. Stir, cover, and cook until the garlic is aromatic and the tomatoes are soft and partially dissolved, about 15 minutes.

3. Add 4 cups water, and the potatoes, wine, parsley, salt, and pepper. Re-cover the pot and bring to a boil over medium-high heat. Reduce the heat and simmer for 15 minutes.

4. Add the green beans and continue to simmer until the potatoes and green beans are tender, 10 to 15 minutes. Return the sausage to the pan. Heat through and serve with plenty of bread to dip in the broth.

Serves 6

KALE SOUP WITH PEAS

Sopa de Couve com Ervilhas

My friend Olinda Fernandes created this *sopa de panela* (soup of the pot) one day. It's an interesting twist on pea soup. Chicken and sausage flavor its broth, which tastes even better the next day. Many Portuguese cooks take advantage of what is on hand to create delicious soups. Tomorrow's *sopa de panela* most likely will be different.

1 whole chicken leg (drumstick and thigh) with skin

1 to 2 large waxy potatoes, such as Red Bliss, peeled and cut into 1-inch cubes

8 oz *linguiça* or *chouriço* sausage (see page 168)

2 large carrots, peeled and cut into 1-inch chunks

½ cup (3½ oz) dried green split peas

1 small onion, finely chopped

1 garlic clove, finely chopped

2 tablespoons rice

2 tablespoons small pasta, such as elbow macaroni

1 teaspoon coarse kosher salt, or to taste

¼ teaspoon freshly ground white or black pepper

8 oz bunch collard greens or kale, trimmed of thick center ribs and torn into 1- to 2-inch pieces (about 7 cups)

1. In a 5-quart stockpot, combine the chicken, potatoes, sausage, carrots, split peas, onion, garlic, and enough water to cover the ingredients by 1 inch (about 7 cups). Cover and bring to a boil over medium-high heat. Reduce the heat and simmer over medium-low heat until the chicken is nearly falling from the bone, 30 to 40 minutes.

2. Remove the chicken and sausage from the pot, and set aside to cool. Remove and discard the bones, and reserve the chicken meat. Cut the sausage into chunks and set aside.

3. Using a handheld immersion blender or food processor, purée the remaining contents of the pot, then cover and return the soup to a boil. Stir in the rice, pasta, salt, and pepper. Reduce the heat and simmer for 12 minutes.

4. Add the greens and simmer until they are tender and the macaroni is cooked, 10 to 15 minutes. Return the chicken and sausage to the pot in the last few minutes of cooking to heat through.

Serves 4 to 6

GALVEIAS-STYLE GAZPACHO
Gaspacho de Galveias

Made in the style of my father's hometown, Galveias, this simple soup is satisfying on a sultry summer evening. My grandfather enjoyed it very much, especially with fresh cilantro. This gazpacho is different from most because it doesn't include tomatoes. Make sure it is well chilled. For extra crunch, toast the bread cubes before adding them to the soup.

3 garlic cloves, finely chopped

2 teaspoons coarse kosher salt, or to taste

1 small onion, finely chopped

1 small cucumber, peeled, seeded, and coarsely chopped (about 1 cup)

1 green pepper, coarsely chopped (about 1 cup)

¼ cup red wine vinegar

¼ cup olive oil

3 cups very cold water

4 oz *linguiça* sausage (see page 168), cut into ¼-inch slices (optional)

3 to 4 cups (9 to 12 oz) chopped day-old Homestyle Bread (page 236) or crusty sourdough

2 tablespoons finely chopped cilantro

Coarse kosher salt

Note: *If you don't have any day-old bread, cut fresh bread into rough cubes and toast it in the oven.*

Using a mortar and pestle, mash the garlic with the salt to make a paste. Place the garlic paste in a large mixing bowl, along with the onion, cucumber, pepper, and vinegar.

5. Mix the ingredients together well then, continuing to mix, drizzle in the olive oil. Pour in the cold water until you reach your desired texture (the soup should be fairly thick). Taste and season with salt, if needed, stir, and chill well.

6. Just before serving, briefly sauté the sausage slices. To serve, ladle the soup into chilled soup bowls and top with the bread cubes and slices of sausage. Garnish with the cilantro.

Serves 6

CHICKEN BROTH

Canja

This simple chicken soup appeared frequently on our Sunday dinner table. My father always included chicken feet. When we sat down together to eat, we would make little deals about who would get the choice parts. Can you guess who got the feet? (Hint: Dad was easily charmed.) The name *canja* is East Asian (Concani or Malay), which suggests that the recipe was picked up by navigators during the Age of Discovery. Like other peoples, the Portuguese turn to chicken soup for comfort when they feel under the weather. The simplicity of the ingredients allows the full flavor of the chicken to come through. For a simple meal, my grandmother used chicken pieces, deboning the cooked meat and returning it to the soup. Sometimes she used a whole chicken. I can still see her, removing the partially-cooked chicken from her large white enamel soup pot. She would additional spices, drape the chicken with bacon, and finished roasting it in the oven. Her *canja* would be just the broth, a very small amount of pasta or rice, and the gizzard, heart, and feet of the chicken. The roasted bird served as the second course. A squirt of lemon juice often found its way to my father's bowl of *canja*. I didn't appreciate this practice until I was older, so this is optional.

2½ lb chicken pieces (legs, thighs, backs, necks),
   chicken gizzard, and heart

2 chicken feet, rubbed with kosher salt and rinsed well

½ cup (2 to 3½ oz) short-grain rice or small pasta,
   such as elbow macaroni (optional)

1 tablespoon coarse kosher salt, or to taste

¼ teaspoon ground white pepper

Sprigs of mint, to garnish

Lemon wedges (optional)

Note: *Chicken feet are a delicacy in many countries. Look for them, fresh or frozen, at ethnic food stores, or ask your butcher. They are usually sold with the outside skin removed, revealing a pale-yellow color, and with the nails trimmed. When cooked, the best part is the ball of the foot. Try it; you just might find it absolutely enticing.*

1. In a 4-quart stockpot, place the chicken pieces, gizzard, heart, and chicken feet, and add 6 cups of water, or enough water to cover the chicken by 1 inch. Cover and bring to a boil over high heat. Reduce the heat and simmer until the chicken is tender and nearly falling off the bone. Skim the broth of impurities as needed, about 25 minutes.

2. With the exception of the giblets and chicken feet, remove the chicken from the pot and set aside to cool.

3. Return the broth to a boil, then add rice or pasta, if desired. Season with the salt and pepper. Reduce the heat to medium-low and until the rice or pasta is cooked—about 20 minutes for rice; less time for pasta.

4. Meanwhile, remove the meat from the bones and hand-shred enough to yield about 1 cup. Reserve the rest of the meat to serve on the side, or use in another dish. When the pasta or rice is cooked, add the shredded chicken to the pot. Heat through and serve with a mint leaf and a wedge of lemon.

Serves 8 to 10

STONE SOUP

Sopa de Pedra

As a little girl, after listening to my grandfather tell the story of Stone Soup, I used to think of the whole beans as little stones. Use a different variety of dried beans if you prefer, but leave them whole. This version is loosely adapted from my grandmother's recipe, which my aunt taught me. The less spicy *chouriço* sausage may be substituted for the *salpicão*.

1 cup (7 oz) dried red kidney beans, soaked overnight in enough water to cover by 2 inches

8 oz *salpicão* or *chouriço* sausage (see page 168)

1 bay leaf

1 small white or yellow turnip (rutabaga), cut into ½-inch cubes (2 cups)

2 medium waxy or boiling potatoes, such as Red Blisss or Yukon Gold, cut into ½-inch cubes

1 medium onion, coarsely chopped

2 small carrots, peeled and coarsely chopped

¼ cup (½ oz) finely chopped parsley

2 garlic cloves, coarsely chopped

2 tablespoons coarse kosher salt, or to taste

½ teaspoon freshly ground black pepper

1½ cups (3½ oz) coarsely chopped Savoy cabbage

1. Drain and rinse the beans, then place in a 5-quart stockpot. Add 8 cups of water and the sausage and bay leaf. Cover the pot and bring to a boil over medium-high heat. Reduce the heat and simmer over medium-low for 15 minutes, skimming off any impurities. When the sausage pieces are tender, remove them from the pot. Remove the casings, cut the meat into medium cubes, and reserve.

2. Add the turnip, potatoes, onion, carrots, parsley, garlic, salt, and pepper. Re-cover the pot and simmer for 45 minutes.

3. Toss in the cabbage and simmer until tender, 10 to 15 minutes. Return the reserved sausage to the pot, heat through, and serve the soup hot with plenty of crusty bread.

Note: *Variations to the soup are as numerous as to the story itself. The addition of pig's feet or knuckles is one common version.*

THE STORY OF STONE SOUP

According to one Portuguese version of the universal folk tale, *sopa de pedra* was created by a monk who traveled the countryside in search of a meal. Knocking on door after door, he asked in vain for food. None of the villagers had a scrap to spare. Finally, in desperation, the monk approached one more family and asked to borrow a large kettle. A puzzled lady of the house complied. He took out a stone from his sack and placed it in the empty kettle. He asked if she could spare a little water. At once, the helpful villager brought a pot of water and added it to the empty kettle. "How much better this soup would taste if only I had an onion," cried the monk. Quickly, the woman gave him an onion for the pot. "What wonderful flavor garlic would add to my soup," the monk said. The women's daughter brought him a fistful of garlic. And so it continued, until the monk had filled his kettle with tasty ingredients provided by the unsuspecting family, and the enticing aroma of stone soup filled the air. Leaving them with the stone with which to make their own batch, he left.

Serves 6

SOUP OF THE HOLY GHOST

Sopa do Espírito Santo

As well as for the Feast of the Holy Ghost, this soup is also served at other times of thanksgiving when prayers have been answered. Edelberto Ataide, from Graciosa in the Azores, is the chief cook for our church gatherings. He shared this recipe with me. It can easily be doubled or tripled; he often prepares it for more than 200 people.

1 small onion, finely chopped

5 garlic cloves, peeled and left whole

1 bay leaf

½ cup white wine

2½ lb whole chicken or chicken legs
   and/or thighs

4 oz smoked bacon, roughly chopped

8 oz beef shoulder on the bone

8 oz beef brisket or chuck

8 oz *linguiça* sausage (see page 168)

4 oz beef liver (traditional, but optional)

1 lb waxy potatoes, such as Red Bliss,
   peeled and cut into 1-inch cubes

2 teaspoons coarse kosher salt, or to taste

3 allspice berries (Jamaican is best)

8 oz bunch kale or collard greens, trimmed of thick
   center ribs, leaves torn into 1- to 2-inch pieces
   (about 7 cups)

1 lb head Savoy cabbage, cored, cut into quarters

3 mint sprigs

5 to 10 oz day-old day-old Homestyle Bread
   (page 236) or crusty sourdough

Variation: *On the island of Terceira, cinnamon lightly spices their version of this soup, and potatoes and kale are omitted.*

1. In a 5-quart stockpot, combine the onion, garlic, bay leaf, wine, and 8 cups of water. Cover and bring to a boil over medium heat.

2. Add the chicken, bacon, beef shoulder bone, beef brisket, and sausage. Re-cover and return to a boil. Reduce the heat and simmer until the meats are just tender, about 1 hour, occasionally skimming off impurities. Check the pot frequently after 45 minutes and remove the meats and chicken from the pot as they become tender, set aside, and keep warm.

3. If including the beef liver, bring 2 cups of water to a low simmer in a separate pan. Poach the liver in the hot water until just tender and slightly pink in the center, about 5 minutes. Remove and set aside.

4. When all of the meats are tender and have been removed from the pot, strain the broth and return it to the pot. Add the potatoes, salt, and allspice and bring to a boil over medium-high heat. Reduce the heat to medium-low and simmer for about 10 minutes. Add the kale and cabbage, and gently simmer for another 15 minutes. Turn off the heat. Add one of the mint sprigs, cover, and let stand for 5 minutes.

5. Meanwhile, cut the reserved chicken into serving pieces. Cut the beef into serving pieces, discarding the bones and any fat or gristle. Arrange the chicken and beef on a serving platter. Dice the liver, if using, and place in a dish to serve separately.

6. To serve, place a few torn pieces of the bread in a soup tureen. Ladle in some of the broth and let it rest for 5 minutes so the bread absorbs some liquid. Fill the tureen with the rest of the soup. Garnish the top with the remaining mint. Place a bread slice in each soup bowl and ladle the soup over it. Serve the meat as a second course with buttered rice.

FEAST OF THE HOLY GHOST *Festa do Espírito Santo*

In the Azores, there are nearly as many religious celebrations as there are weeks in the year. When immigrants from the Azores came to the United States, they continued to celebrate the Feast of the Holy Ghost. It remains the quintessential festival of the Azores.

My earliest childhood memory is the taste of the Soup of the Holy Ghost, *sopa do Espirito Santo*. It was the meal of thanksgiving following the beautiful procession and Mass on the Feast of the Holy Ghost. I understood that the event had great significance as I walked in the procession, wearing a white gown and carrying a bouquet of red roses. Various groups, including children dressed as saints, were cordoned off with yards of red ribbon. One lucky young woman was chosen Empress of the Procession and reverently carried the crown of the Holy Ghost.

Oral tradition bases the Azorean festival on two religious experiences. In the sixteenth century, the king of Germany vowed to end poverty in Europe by feeding the poor. The king of Portugal refused to help. In secret, Queen (Santa) Isabella brought food to the poor against her husband's decree. When she was caught, her only recourse was a prayer to the Holy Ghost. She dropped the ends of her apron and the food miraculously transformed into red roses. Realizing the power of the Holy Ghost, she ordered that a silver dove, representing the Holy Ghost, be added to the top of her crown, thereby dedicating her royal symbol to the service of a higher power.

The second experience happened when Spain refused to give up control of the Azores. A nobleman, sent by Portugal to take charge of removing the Spaniards, was falsely accused of treason and jailed. His prayers to the Holy Ghost for exoneration were answered. Shoeless and having the appearance of a peasant, he offered a meal to the poor in thanksgiving, serving them himself.

Since then, the Portuguese, particularly those from the Azores, have continued to offer *novenas* and *promessas* (promises of pious offerings) to the Holy Ghost during the seven weeks following Easter. Pentecost Sunday, the feast of the Holy Ghost, concludes the season with a procession to the church, a Mass, and the crowning of individuals whose prayers have been answered, followed by the celebratory meal of thanksgiving.

The first time the feast was celebrated in Peabody, Massachusetts, was on May 16, 1916. It has been held there every year since. The meal begins with the time-honored *sopa do Espirito Santo*, a heady concoction of meats, greens, and stock perfumed with garlic and *linguiça* sausage. Some families have their meal of thanksgiving at home instead of eating at the church hall. Sometimes the soup is followed by *carne assada*, beef braised with tomato, wine, bacon, and allspice. Other families serve *alcatra*, a dish for which the island of Terceira is especially known. It is a delectable meal of marinated meat cooked in a special unglazed red-clay pot (see recipe on page 154). Either rice or *batatas assadas* (potatoes roasted with aromatic spices) are served alongside the meat with fresh crusty bread. Each island, town, and family has its own variation of the thanksgiving meal—the soup of the Holy Ghost is the constant component.

Serves 6

SHRIMP SOUP WITH WHITE BEANS

Sopa de Camarão com Feijão Branco

The fragrance and flavor of this soup excites the senses. This family favorite includes beans, which give the soup body. You can, however, completely eliminate the beans if you wish to have a lighter soup. Serve this dish as a first course or as a light meal.

¾ cup (5 oz) dried white kidney beans, soaked overnight in enough water to cover by 2 inches

12 oz small raw shell-on shrimp, peeled and deveined (reserve the shells)

¼ cup olive oil

1 small onion, finely chopped

1 bay leaf

1 large very ripe tomato, peeled, seeded, and finely chopped

2 garlic cloves, finely chopped

½ cup white wine (optional)

2 tablespoons finely chopped fresh cilantro

2 teaspoons kosher salt, or to taste

1 teaspoon hot pepper sauce

¼ teaspoon ground white pepper

4 thick slices Homestyle Bread (page 236) or crusty sourdough

Tip: *This soup can also be made ahead. After processing the beans, allow to cool and refrigerate. Just before serving, bring the soup to a boil, add the shrimp, and continue with the recipe.*

1. Drain and rinse the beans, and place them in a 2-quart pot with 3 cups of fresh water, or enough to cover the beans by 2 inches. Cover and bring to a boil over high heat. Reduce the heat to medium-low and simmer until the beans are easily mashed with a fork, 45 to 60 minutes. Set aside with the cooking liquid.

2. Meanwhile, briefly rinse the shrimp shells and combine with 3 cups of water in a 1-quart saucepan. Cover and bring to a boil over medium-high heat, then reduce the heat and simmer for 20 minutes. Strain the broth into another container, pressing the shells to extract the cooking water. Discard the shells.

3. Heat the oil in a 2½-quart saucepan over medium-high heat. Add and sauté the onion until soft and translucent, about 5 minutes. Add the bay leaf, tomato, and garlic. Cover and continue to cook over medium-low heat until the tomato pieces have softened and partially dissolved, about 15 minutes. Pour in the wine, if using, simmer for one minute, and remove the pot from the heat.

4. Set a food mill over the pot. Process the cooked beans into the pot, using their cooking liquid, as well as the reserved shrimp broth. (Alternatively, you can use a food processor to purée the beans, then pass them through a sieve.) Cover and bring to a boil, then reduce the heat to medium-low.

5. Add the shrimp, ½ tablespoon of the cilantro, and the salt, hot pepper sauce, and white pepper. Cover the pot and simmer gently for 3 minutes, until the shrimp are just opaque.

6. Place one slice of the toasted bread in each soup bowl. Ladle the soup over it. Garnish with remaining cilantro and serve immediately.

Variations: *For added texture, leave some or all of the beans whole and add 2 cups (2 oz) coarsely chopped spinach with the shrimp. Or, for a lighter soup, eliminate the beans entirely and cook the shrimp shells in 6 cups of water. Add the strained broth to the pot along with the wine, and bring to a medium simmer, before cooking the shrimp and continuing with the recipe.*

Serves 4

ALENTEJO-STYLE BREAD SOUP

Açorda à Alentejana

According to oral history, this very old and most basic of the bread soups goes back to the days when the Moors occupied the Alentejo region. Garlic, olive oil, and a fistful of chopped fresh cilantro season the water. Small broken pieces of day-old bread, the amount of which can be very little or quite a bit, are then added to the aromatic broth. The bread absorbs the flavorful broth and softens.

4 garlic cloves, coarsely chopped

1 tablespoon coarse kosher salt, or to taste

¼ cup olive oil

½ cup (1 oz) finely chopped cilantro

4 cups boiling water

4 cups (1 lb) torn day-old Homestyle Bread (page 236) or crusty sourdough (or to taste)

4 eggs

Note: *The eggs can be boiled or poached separately and added to the individual soup bowls if you prefer.*

1. Using a mortar and pestle, mash the garlic with the salt, forming a paste.

2. In a large, heatproof serving bowl, combine the garlic paste with the olive oil and cilantro. Gradually stir in half of the boiling water.

3. Toss in as little or as much of the bread as you wish. Set aside for about 5 minutes to soak up some liquid. If necessary, add more of the water so that the mixture is not dry. Mix gently. There should be a decent amount of broth, though the ratio of liquid to bread is a matter of preference.

4. Making sure the broth is still piping hot, break an egg into a small bowl, then slide it into the large serving bowl, making a space between the pieces of bread, and repeat with the rest of the eggs. Allow them to poach in the hot broth for about 5 minutes.

5. Ladle the soup into individual bowls, including an egg in each one. Serve immediately.

BREAD SOUPS AND PANADAS *Açordas and Migas*

My father once explained to me that, in Portugal, bread was usually baked once or twice a week. By the end of the week, any remaining bread would be hard. For many of the less fortunate Portuguese, sometimes this was all they had to eat by the week's end. It is understandable why wastefulness is not part of the Portuguese character. Taught by the Arabs, the Portuguese made stale bread into meager but tasty dishes known as *açordas* and *migas*. Eventually those who fared better added salt cod or shrimp to the *açordas*. Although *açorda* can be eaten any time of day, when I was growing up, we usually enjoyed it on Saturday or Sunday mornings as a late breakfast or a light meal, served with olives and maybe some wine.

Açorda is a soup of dense day-old bread moistened with boiling water or broth and flavored with garlic and cilantro (*coentros*). The bread soaks up most of the broth and becomes very wet. *Migas,* on the other hand, has a drier texture, like bread stuffing without the turkey. Although the finished result lacks a broth, it is made the same as the *açorda* in that the bread is moistened. A lot less liquid is used, however, and the seasoning is different. Some versions are even cooked in a frying pan to give the *migas* a golden crust. Too much liquid will cause excessive sticking to the pan.

When a dish calls for bread to be incorporated with liquid ingredients, typical American-style sliced bread should not be used. If you cannot obtain the Portuguese peasant-style bread known as *caseiro,* use other crusty European peasant-style breads—Italian, French, or Greek, for example. The texture should be somewhat dense with an open grain, not soft and fluffy. Today, many specialty bakeries sell delicious rustic European peasant-style breads and rolls.

Thinking about the *migas* and *açordas* brings back memories of my father going out to his garden and returning with freshly cut cilantro (*coentros*). When he picked this herb, he would enter the kitchen sniffing the wonderful leaves, and exclaim, "I love this!" or "Smell, smell!" as he waved the fresh herb under my mother's nose. My mother waved it off—she didn't like cilantro at all. Not everyone does, but if you do, you'll know what my father meant.

Serves 4

BREAD SOUP WITH SALT COD

Açorda de Bacalhau

After I was married, my father would often call me on the phone and ask in his broken English, "You get the smell?" He didn't need to explain. I would simply reply, "I'll be right there." There wasn't any doubt that I was about to enjoy an *açorda de bacalhau*. The aroma of the fresh cilantro and fish that filled the kitchen would greet me as I entered the house. Begin this dish one day ahead to soak the salt cod, and be sure to taste the soaked cod for salt before cooking—you may need to soak longer. Page 26 describes in detail how to prepare salt cod.

4 oz salt cod, soaked in several changes of cold water for 16 to 24 hours, refrigerated (see page 26)

4 garlic cloves, coarsely chopped

4 tablespoons olive oil

½ green pepper, coarsely chopped (optional)

½ cup (1 oz) finely chopped fresh cilantro

4 cups (1 lb) torn day-old Homestyle Bread (page 236) or crusty sourdough

4 eggs

Salt, if needed

Note: *Be sure to taste before adding salt to any dish that involves salt cod, waiting until the very end of cooking. Usually additional salt is not needed.*

1. Bring 4 cups of water to a boil in a medium pot and turn off the heat. Remove the fish from the soaking water, rinse, and add it to the hot water. Cover the pot and allow the fish to gently poach for 10 to 15 minutes, until it flakes easily.

2. Using a mortar and pestle, mash the garlic to a paste. In the bottom of a large heat-safe serving bowl, combine the garlic paste and the olive oil. Mix in the chopped green pepper and cilantro.

3. Transfer the cod to a dish, reserving the hot liquid. Remove and discard any skin and bones and break the fish into pieces. Add the fish pieces to the serving bowl.

4. Making sure it is piping hot, pour in 2 cups of the fish broth. Add the bread chunks to the bowl, letting the bread soak up the broth. Add a bit more liquid if the mixture is too dry, and stir gently. The mixture should be a fairly thick soup but not dry; there should be some broth.

5. Carefully break the eggs into the serving bowl. Spoon the hot liquid over the eggs and let them poach for 5 minutes. (Alternatively, you can poach or soft-boil the eggs separately and add one to each portion. Make sure to peel soft-boiled eggs carefully so as not to break them open.)

6. Ladle the *açorda* into individual bowls, including an egg in each. Serve immediately.

Serves 4

CAT'S PANADA

Migas Gatas

Although *migas* is often flavored with rendered bacon fat, spices, and *linguiça* sausage, there are versions like this one that are closer to an *açorda* (see page 68). My Uncle Ilidio Valente, who often prepares this dish when left to his own devices, shared his recipe. It is not quite clear how this dish got its name. Perhaps it came about because cats like fish, or the creator was in a whimsical mood. This version of *migas*, a garlic lover's delight, is not cooked over heat. The hot broth from cooking the fish brings the mixture together.

1 lb salt cod, soaked in several changes of cold water
   for 16 to 24 hours, refrigerated (see page 26)
1 round loaf (12 oz) day-old Homestyle Bread
   (page 236) or crusty sourdough, cut in 1-inch slices,
   heavy crusts removed
6 large garlic cloves, thinly sliced, or more if needed
Olive oil, to drizzle
Wine vinegar or cider vinegar, to drizzle
¼ teaspoon freshly ground black pepper, or to taste
Salt, if needed

1. Drain the fish and discard the soaking water. In a medium saucepan, bring 4 cups of fresh water to a boil and turn off the heat. Add the fish and poach for 15 minutes.

2. In the bottom of a 3-inch-deep 9- by 13-inch dish, place a layer of bread slices (about 2 large slices). Arrange slices of garlic fairly evenly over the bread, almost covering it. Make a second layer of bread and again cover with garlic slices. Follow with a third layer.

3. Remove the fish from the water and set it aside until it is cool enough to handle.

4. Meanwhile, gradually pour enough of the cooking liquid into the dish to just cover the bread slices (about 2 cups). Let stand, covered, for about 5 minutes, allowing the bread to absorb the water. Drain off any liquid that has not been absorbed. (If the bread seems to be too wet, add additional bread in small amounts, to absorb the liquid. It should not be sopping wet.) Using a fork, mash the bread and garlic.

5. Remove any skin and bones from the cod and shred the flesh. You should have about 2 cups. Scatter the fish on top of the bread mixture. Gently mix everything together, folding the ingredients to blend and form a ball. The texture should be like bread stuffing or thick mashed potatoes.

6. Drizzle with oil and vinegar and season with black pepper. Taste before adding any salt. Spoon into individual bowls and serve with olives and a green salad. This makes a tasty lunch.

When my grandfather came home from his morning errands, he liked to have what I would call an *açorda de café*, or "coffee soup." My grandmother would place some day-old bread in a large soup bowl and sprinkle the bread with sugar. Over this she poured milky coffee, being careful not to add too much. Sometimes my grandfather preferred to use just hot milk and sugar on his bread, which he would call *sopa de leite* or "milk soup."

Serves 4

ALENTEJO-STYLE PANADA

Migas à Alentejana

Pork ribs or cubed pork are flavored with the traditional sweet red pepper paste (*massa de pimentão*) in this old favorite of the Alentejo. Unlike the soupier texture of *Migas Gatas*, this *migas* has a firmer texture and a golden crust. A nonstick frying pan is wonderful for making *migas*, but a cast-iron skillet will impart extra flavor. Lard, salt pork, and bacon are traditional fats for this dish, but I find olive oil to be a good substitute.

1 lb pork tenderloin, butt, or ribs, or any combination

4 garlic cloves, coarsely chopped

1 bay leaf

1 tablespoon Sweet Red Pepper Paste (page 219)

½ cup olive oil, ¼ cup lard, or 4 oz lean salt pork or bacon

3 cups (12 oz) torn day-old Homestyle Bread (page 236) or crusty sourdough (heavy crusts removed)

2 cups boiling water, or more if needed (amount depends on the dryness of the bread)

Finely chopped cilantro, to garnish

A day ahead

1. If using pork butt or tenderloin, trim excess fat, gristle, and the thin silvery muscle called sinew. Cut the meat into 2-inch cubes. If using ribs, cut between the bones to separate them. Transfer a large bowl. Add the garlic, bay leaf, and sweet red pepper paste. Turn the meat to coat evenly with the seasoning. Cover and marinate overnight in the refrigerator.

The next day

2. Remove the meat from the refrigerator 30 minutes before you are ready to cook, and discard the bay leaf.

3. Heat the olive oil or melt the lard in a large cast-iron or nonstick frying pan. If you are using salt pork or bacon, fry it in the until the pieces are crisp and the fat has been rendered. Remove the solid pieces. Fry the meat, a few pieces at a time, over medium-high heat until nicely browned on all sides and cooked through, about 10 minutes. Transfer to a platter and keep warm. Drain off all but 2 tablespoons of fat and set the pan aside.

4. Place the bread in a large bowl and gradually add enough boiling water to just moisten it. It should not be sopping wet (too much liquid makes it stick to the pan, especially if you are using cast-iron). Lightly mash. It should be the consistency of bread stuffing. Reheat the frying pan. Add the bread to the pan and cook, mashing it again to incorporate the pan juices.

5. Using a wooden spoon, fold the mixture into itself, and cook it until the excess moisture has evaporated and the mixture comes together.

6. Shake the pan back and forth to form the mixture into a log shape, using the spoon to help it along. When the bread is a nice light golden color, roll it out of the pan (as you would an omelet) onto a serving platter and arrange the meat around the bread. Garnish with chopped cilantro and serve immediately.

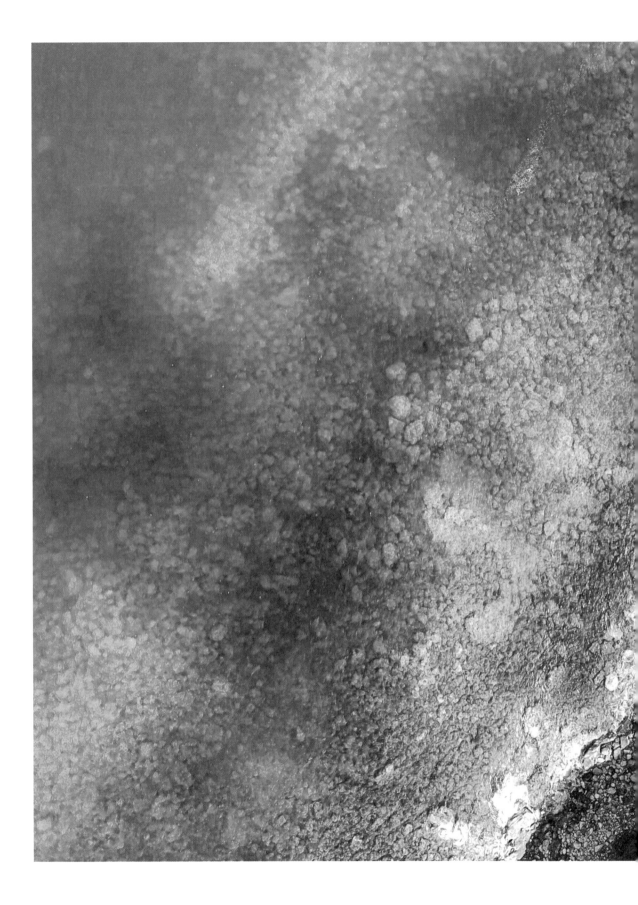

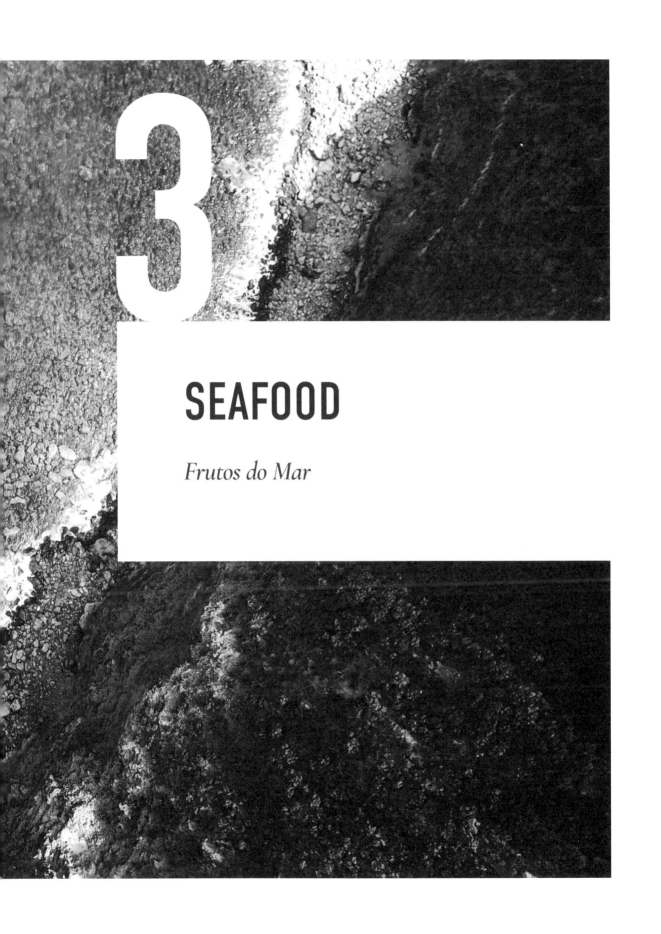

3

SEAFOOD

Frutos do Mar

3 SEAFOOD
Frutos do Mar

The location of Portugal and its Azores Islands, on the Atlantic, have for centuries provided the country with access to an abundant variety of seafood, especially along the coast. Portuguese cooks took advantage of bountiful catches and created unique and flavorful dishes. Today, many of these tasty recipes are made in the United States by Portuguese immigrants and their families in much the same manner.

Some types of fish used in Portugal are not readily available in the North America, and substitutions are made. In Portugal, *caldeirada*, a fish stew, might contain conger eel, mullet, skate, and sea bass. Here in the United States, I might use pollock, cusk, salmon, red snapper, and halibut. The one fish for which there is no acceptable substitute is salt cod—*bacalhau* in Portuguese. Ironically, cod, the most utilized fish in Portugal, is obtained outside Portuguese waters. Once viewed as fish of the poor, salt cod eventually became highly esteemed.

Seafood—especially salt cod, shellfish, and sardines—is fundamental to the Portuguese diet. There are countless dishes for salt cod. This versatile fish, after it is reconstituted in water, can be poached, fried, grilled, or baked in a casserole. A long-standing favorite of my family, as for many Portuguese, is *Bacalhau à Gomes da Sá* (page 92). This traditional dish combines poached salt cod with boiled potatoes and sautéed onions; it is baked and then garnished with black olives and slices of hard-boiled egg.

Other Portuguese favorites include *Améijoas na Cataplana* (page 81), which is typically made with sweet cockles in the Algarve region of southern Portugal. In North America, littleneck clams, soft-shell clams, or even mussels can be used to prepare this heady concoction of onions, white wine, sweet pepper, savory sausage, and lots of garlic, herbs, and spices. There are *Lagosta Fervida* (page 105), lobsters boiled in herb- and spice-infused water. The flavorful result leaves little need for melted butter.

Fillets of light fish like flounder and hake are likely to be quickly pan-fried then imbibed or drizzled with the tangy aromatic vinegar sauce *molhanga*, suggesting the Portuguese-Azorean influence. This treat is eaten hot or at room temperature.

Finally, sardines—fresh, not canned—that are simply cooked over a charcoal grill are always a hit whenever they are served. Sardines preserved in brine—originally to survive trips to the Portuguese interior—are a good source both of calcium and healthful fatty acids. They are often served with boiled potatoes and drizzled with oil and vinegar.

The dishes in this chapter can be accompanied by a simple green salad or sautéed greens, olives, crusty peasant bread, and of course, a chilled bottle of crisp *vinho verde,* Portuguese "green" wine (see Chapter 10). Some types of red wine go nicely with fish; the choice depends on the preparation of the dish. Whether they are grilled, baked, stewed, or fried, seafood dishes—made from whitefish, sardines, shellfish, or salt cod—are simply flavored with spices, scented with herbs like cilantro or parsley, and perhaps given a drizzle of oil and vinegar or splash of piquant *Molhanga* (Vinegar Sauce; page 217). Plan ahead for dishes that require marinating, soaking (of salt cod; see page 26), or purging (the process of removing sand from shellfish).

Left: Shrimp Rissoles (page 110)

Serves 4 to 6

PAN-FRIED FISH FILLETS

Filletes de Peixe Frito na Frigideira

Many Portuguese cooks fry their fish without flour or eggs. The oil is simply heated until it is hot (but not smoking) and the fish is quickly fried. Others fry their fish with a very light coating of seasoned fine yellow or white corn flour (not to be confused with cornstarch). My friend Olinda Fernandes, from Mangualda in northern Portugal, shares her simple marinade for fish. Here I have combined it with my father's seasoned corn flour, giving a flavorful twist to fried fish. I like the flavor of olive oil for frying fish, but if you prefer to use canola, corn, or other vegetable oil, keep in mind the difference in taste.

2 lb white fish fillets, such as
   flounder, hake, sole, or haddock,
   skins intact, cut into
   serving-size pieces

6 to 8 garlic cloves, finely chopped

1 cup lemon juice (white wine
   vinegar or white wine
   can be substituted)

1 cup (4 oz) yellow corn flour

1 tablespoon paprika

½ teaspoon coarse sea salt,
   or to taste

¼ teaspoon ground white pepper

2 eggs

2 tablespoons finely chopped
   fresh parsley or cilantro

Olive oil, for frying

1. Rinse the fish and pat dry. Place the fish fillets in a glass dish and season each side with the garlic. Pour the lemon juice over the fish and marinate it for 1 hour. Drain off the marinade and set aside

2. Meanwhile, on a shallow plate or a sheet of wax paper, season the corn flour with the paprika, salt, and pepper. Blend well and set aside.

3. In a small bowl, beat the eggs and mix in the parsley or cilantro. Set aside.

4. Making sure to wipe off any marinade, dip the fish into the seasoned flour, lightly coating it. Shake off any excess flour and then dip the fish into the beaten eggs.

5. In a large frying pan, add olive oil to a depth of ¼ inch and place over medium-high heat. When the oil is hot, but not smoking, pan-fry the coated fish for little more than 1 minute per side for flounder (a little longer for thicker fillets), until golden. Serve with hot Tomato Rice (page 192), Sautéed Greens (page 198), and Vinegar Sauce (*Escabeche*, page *224*, or *Molhanga*, page 217).

Serves 4

MARINATED FISH

Pescada em Vinho d'Alhos

Adding cider vinegar to the marinade gives this dish extra zing. Marinate no more than 1 hour before cooking. This dish can be pan-fried in fillets, as below, or grilled (see Variation). In Portugal, when the fish is fresh off the boat, it is sometimes cleaned and cut into chunks before being seasoned as below, and deep fried. Boiled potatoes drizzled with vinegar sauce are a traditional accompaniment.

6 garlic cloves, finely chopped

1 teaspoon coarse kosher salt

1 cup white wine or lemon juice

2 tablespoons cider vinegar

2 tablespoons olive oil

1 bay leaf

¼ teaspoon ground white pepper

2 lb hake or red snapper fillets, skins intact
   (use halibut or swordfish, if grilling)

2 teaspoons paprika

1 cup (4 oz) yellow or white corn flour

2 eggs, lightly beaten (optional)

Olive or corn oil, for frying

Vinegar Sauce (*Escabeche*, page 224;
   or *Molhanga*, page 217), to serve

1. Using a mortar and pestle, mash the garlic with the salt, forming a paste. Transfer the paste to a 9- by 13-inch ceramic or glass baking dish and whisk in the wine or lemon juice and cider vinegar, followed by the olive oil, bay leaf, and pepper.

2. Rinse the fish and pat dry. Add the fish to the marinade, turn to coat, and refrigerate, covered, for 1 hour, turning occasionally.

3. Drain the marinade from the fish. If you are grilling the fish, reserve the marinade (see Variation). Mix the paprika and corn flour on a plate. Coat the fish with the corn flour mixture, shaking off any excess. Dip the fish into the beaten eggs, if using.

4. In a large frying pan, add olive oil to a depth of ¼ inch and place over medium-high heat. When the oil is hot, but not smoking, pan-fry the fish until golden and cooked through, about 2 minutes per side, depending on the thickness of the fish. Transfer to a serving platter, cover lightly, and keep warm. Serve with the vinegar sauce on the side.

Variation: *If you prefer to grill your fish, use steaks that are 1-inch thick. Cook over very hot charcoal and baste periodically with the reserved marinade heated in a saucepan. Cook for about 5 minutes per side, turning only once.*

Serves 4 to 6

BAKED SARDINES

Sardinhas no Forno

Before baking sardines, scale and gut them and remove the fins (see page 27). I first prepared sardines this way—guided by my father—when I was eight. It is very easy to do. The following recipe for sardines can be used for baking other fish as well. For an even simpler version, you can omit the egg and just give the fish a thin coating of corn flour followed by a drizzle of olive oil.

2 cups (8½ oz) yellow corn flour

2 tablespoons paprika

¼ cup (½ oz) finely chopped parsley, plus extra to garnish

½ tablespoon finely chopped garlic

½ tablespoon coarse kosher salt

12 large sardines, fresh or previously frozen, scaled, and gutted (see page 27)

3 eggs, lightly beaten (optional)

Olive oil, for drizzling

1. Preheat the oven to 350°F.

2. On a shallow dish or a piece of wax paper, combine the corn flour, paprika, parsley, garlic, and salt.

3. Rinse the fish and pat dry. Dip the fish in the corn-flour mixture, shaking off excess. Dip the fish into the beaten egg, if using, and immediately place on a lightly oiled baking sheet. Repeat with remaining fish, placing head to tail on the pan. Drizzle the tops of the fish with olive oil.

4. Bake until cooked through and medium golden, 20 to 30 minutes. Garnish with parsley. Serve with boiled potatoes, Vinegar Sauce (page 217), and Sautéed Greens (page 198).

SARDINES AND BABIES

Most cultures have a particular method for predicting the sex of unborn children. I was sixteen years old when I first witnessed the Portuguese method. My family was attending an outdoor summer dance held at our social club, the Club Luis de Camões. On this summer's night, grilled sardines were guaranteed to be served. Dining with us on this particular evening was a dear family friend, Elena, who was very much in the family way. As soon as she finished eating her sardine, my father snapped up the fish's skeletal remains and threw them onto the grill. His friends explained that if the skeleton jumped, Elena would be sure to have a girl. Well, the fish's skeleton jumped, and a few weeks later Elena gave birth to a beautiful baby girl.

Serves 4 to 6

GRILLED SARDINES

Sardinhas Assadas na Brasa

Grilled sardines have always been one of my favorite dishes. Eating grilled sardines *al fresco* on a warm summer's night with friends is a very simple and pleasurable way to wind down. We even like to bring a brazier along on picnics lunches so we can cook sardines. Grilled sardines are commonly served with a salad of tomatoes, onions, and peppers, drizzled with oil and vinegar or a vinegar sauce, a dish of black olives, bread, and boiled potatoes or *Feijão Frade* (page 197). Pick them apart with your fingers and eat them with bread.

An oily fish, sardines are similar to large smelt but moister and more flavorful, though not as strong as mackerel. Fresh sardines are best, of course, but frozen ones can be substituted (see page 27).

1 lb fresh or frozen sardines (usually found in international food shops if your fish market doesn't have them), thawed overnight in the refrigerator if frozen
Coarse kosher salt

Tip: *If you plan to grill additional items like chicken or beef, grill the sardines last so that the flavor does not affect the other foods. We usually reserve a small cast-iron grill specifically for cooking sardines.*

Variation: *You can marinate grilled sardines as follows: fillet the cooked fish, remove the center bones, and transfer the fillets to a shallow dish. Add Escabeche (page 224) and refrigerate. Serve chilled or at room temperature.*

1. There isn't any need to gut sardines for charcoal grilling, and there are different opinions about scaling them. I don't scale sardines unless I bake them. Rinse sardines with cold water and salt them with a coating of salt, layering them in a colander or slanted plate to allow water to drain off. Let the salted sardines sit for an hour in the refrigerator. Wipe off excess salt.
2. Preheat your grill until white-hot: the coals should be covered with white ash. Using a clean, preheated grill rack will make the fish easier to turn. Grill the sardines over white-hot coals until the skin blisters and is somewhat charred and the eyes are opaque, about 3 minutes on each side. Watch for flames flaring up. A spray bottle of water can help, and judicious rearrangement of the fish usually solves this problem.

Special occasions are not a prerequisite for enjoying cooking and eating *al fresco*. I remember a particular summer when we were putting cedar shingles on the house. Several of my father's friends came over to help. At the day's end, my father showed his appreciation in typical Portuguese manner by feeding his helpers. To the strains of Portuguese music playing on his Motorola, he grilled fresh sardines and an assortment of meats. The feast was rounded out with sautéed spinach, bread, boiled potatoes, delicious fresh corn from the garden, wine, cheese and pears picked fresh from our tree. A day of shared work ends in a day of shared feasting.

Serves 4 to 6

CLAMS CATAPLANA

Amêijoas na Cataplana

There are many versions of this mouth-watering dish, which originated on the southern coast of Portugal, the Algarve. It is fairly simple, and very flavorful. Mussels and other shellfish can be prepared the same way.

This dish is traditionally made in a *cataplana*, a deep bowl-shaped pan of copper or aluminum with a hinged lid that makes it resemble a clam shell. The copper *cataplanas* are usually lined with tin. The lid has clamps to keep it closed tightly. Until recently, the pans were not imported to the United States. Now, *cataplana* pans are available through some kitchen specialty stores and online. If you don't have one of these traditional pans, a deep pot with a tight lid will work well. Chilled *vinho verde* goes extremely well with this dish.

2 tablespoons olive oil

1 large onion, thinly sliced (about 1½ cups)

1 bay leaf

3 garlic cloves, mashed

1 tablespoon paprika

Hefty pinch crushed red pepper flakes

¼ cup (½ oz) finely chopped cilantro

½ ounce *presunto* ham (see page 24), or
   Prosciutto di Parma, coarsely chopped

4 to 8 oz *chouriço* sausage (see page 168),
   cut into ½-inch slices

36 cockles or count littleneck clams (4 lb),
   scrubbed (see page 82)

1 cup white wine

4 tablespoons (2 oz) butter, softened

Salt, if needed

Lemon wedges, to garnish

1. Heat the oil in a medium-sized lidded frying pan over medium-high heat and sauté the onion until a light golden color, 7 to 10 minutes.

2. Add the bay leaf, garlic, paprika, crushed red pepper, and half of the cilantro. Cover and simmer for an additional minute or two.

3. In a *cataplana* pan or a deep 5-quart pot with a lid, combine the onion mixture with the meats and shellfish. Gently turn to distribute the ingredients. Pour the wine over the top.

4. Cover and cook over medium-high heat until the clams open, 10 to 12 minutes (or up to 25 minutes for littlenecks). Check after 8 minutes to be sure they don't overcook. Using a slotted spoon, lift the opened clams, meats, and onion onto a serving dish and cover. Discard any unopened clams.

5. Boil over medium-high heat to reduce the liquid by half, then remove from the heat. Let the broth cool for 1 minute before whisking in the butter. (If the broth is too hot when the butter is added, it will not emulsify.) Taste before adding any salt. Pour the broth over the clams or serve on the side as a dipping sauce. Garnish with lemon wedges and the remaining cilantro and serve immediately.

Variations: *Add ½ cup (3 oz) finely chopped tomato (1 small), along with the garlic and paprika. Cover and cook until the tomato is soft and partially dissolved, about 15 minutes, before continuing with the recipe. Mussels can be used in place of the clams.*

Serves 4

BULHÃO PATO CLAMS

Amêijoas à Bulhão Pato

Oral history holds that this dish was created in honor of the Portuguese poet Bulhão Pato, who lived during the 1800s. It is simple and flavorful and makes a great appetizer. Cilantro is traditional, and my preference, though parsley can be used. Either way, this dish is sure to please. Purge the clams in advance (see below).

¼ cup Portuguese or extra-virgin olive oil

3 garlic cloves, finely chopped

1 cup (2 oz) finely chopped cilantro, or to taste

1 cup *vinho verde* or other light white wine

1 teaspoon Hot Pepper Paste (page 220)

1 teaspoon coarse kosher salt

¼ teaspoon ground white pepper

36 small littleneck clams (3 lb), scrubbed

Lemon wedges, to serve

1. In the bottom of a deep 4-quart pot with a tight lid, heat the butter or oil and lightly cook the garlic, just until it becomes aromatic. Toss in the cilantro and stir in the wine, pepper paste, salt, and pepper.

2. Add the clams, gently turn to coat, and cover tightly. Cook over medium-high heat until the clams have opened, 15 to 20 minutes, depending on the size of the clams. Discard any unopened clams. To serve, ladle the clams, with some broth, into shallow bowls. Serve with lemon wedges for squeezing, and plenty of crusty bread to soak up the juices.

Variations: *Soft-shell clams or mussels can be substituted for the littlenecks in this recipe. The cooking time varies depending on the size of the clams. To substitute wine in seafood recipes, use ½ cup of water and the juice of 1 lemon per 1 cup of wine.*

PURGING AND CLEANING FRESH CLAMS

When I can get freshly dug clams from a clam digger, or if I dig them myself, I grab a bucket of fresh seawater and soak the clams overnight or for several hours so that they purge themselves of sand and grit. Saltwater works fastest and best. I then refrigerate the clams until needed. To those cooks who have access to fresh saltwater, I recommend this method whether the clams are freshly dug or purchased from a fish market. You will be amazed at how well it works.

Another popular method is to soak the shellfish in a large bowl of cold salted fresh water along with mustard powder or hot pepper sauce. Use about 1 tablespoon of table salt and 1 tablespoon of mustard powder or hot pepper sauce per 2 lb clams and soak for half an hour.

Some cooks add cornmeal to the water instead of salt and mustard or hot sauce. If you use cornmeal, add ½ cup (2 oz) fine cornmeal per 2 lb clams. Try each method and see which you prefer. After soaking, scrub the clams with a stiff brush and rinse with cold water several times. Discard any shellfish that are open. Drain and refrigerate.

Serves 6

CLAMS WITH POTATOES AND CHOURIÇO

Amêijoas com Batatas e Chouriço

There are times when I wonder who is the host and who is the guest. Whenever we invite our cousins Tony, Noelia, Evelyn, and Manuel to join us for the day at our home in Maine, they insist on bringing food, since we provide the location. They come bearing covered pots and dishes that emit enticing aromas. It is what I call Portuguese cooperative hospitality. Tony brings his passion for cooking good food and enjoying it to the fullest, alongside good conversation with family and friends. His infectious enthusiasm overflows into my kitchen in a way that makes me happy to step aside and watch him create. This recipe of Tony's is a wonderful first course to a seafood dinner—it makes an easy light meal as well. Purge the clams in advance according to the instructions on page 82.

48 to 60 soft-shell clams (8 lb), scrubbed

1 lb waxy potatoes, such as Red Bliss or new potatoes, scrubbed, skins intact, cut into ¼-inch rounds

8 oz *chouriço* sausage (see page 168), sliced into ½-inch rounds

1 small onion, finely chopped

2 large garlic cloves, mashed

2 teaspoons wine vinegar

½ teaspoon Hot Pepper Paste (page 220)

½ teaspoon cumin

¼ teaspoon coarse kosher salt

¼ teaspoon freshly ground black pepper

1½ cups wine or beer, or a combination

1. In a 5-quart stockpot, combine all of the ingredients, except the wine or beer, and gently mix. Pour the wine or beer over the ingredients, cover the pot, and cook over medium-high heat until the clams have opened, 12 to 15 minutes. Discard any unopened clams and serve immediately.

Serves 4

BAKED STUFFED LITTLENECK CLAMS

Amêijoas Recheados no Forno

These are wonderful as an appetizer. They can be made up the morning ahead, chilled, and then brought to room temperature 15 minutes before baking. Purge the clams in advance according to the instructions on page 82.

24 large littleneck clams (about 2½ lb), scrubbed

4 tablespoons (2 oz) butter

4 tablespoons olive oil

1 small onion, finely chopped

4 garlic cloves, finely chopped

2 oz *linguiça* sausage (see page 168), coarsely chopped

2 tablespoons finely chopped cilantro

½ teaspoon hot pepper sauce (optional)

¼ teaspoon ground white pepper

3 cups (9 oz) fresh breadcrumbs, without crusts

Paprika, for sprinkling

Tip: *Use an ice-cream or cookie dough scoop to fill the shells. The spring-tension kind come in different sizes, and are also a great time-saver for filling muffin tins, stuffing shrimp, and making drop cookies of uniform size.*

Note: *Pre-shucked clams can be purchased from fishmongers, usually in 1 lb bags. You will need 8 oz pre-shucked clams for this recipe. Scallop shells, sometimes sold in fish markets and kitchen specialty stores, also work well for stuffing.*

1. Preheat the oven to 375°F.

2. Fresh clams, littlenecks especially, can be difficult to open when they're raw. Placing them in a pan of slightly hot water or cooking them just enough to make the shells open a crack makes the job easier. Carefully shuck the littlenecks using a clam knife. Watch for tiny chips of shell that may break off. Reserve 12 of the shells. Transfer the clam meat to a cutting board and chop coarsely, reserving any juices. Set aside the chopped clams and reserved juice.

3. Heat the butter and oil in a small frying pan over medium-high heat, until hot but not smoking. Add and sauté the onion until lightly golden. Mix in the garlic, sausage, cilantro, hot pepper sauce, and white pepper. Cook, letting the sausage and garlic sweat with the onions, for 2 minutes. Remove the pan from the heat.

4. In a medium bowl, combine the onion mixture with the chopped clams and clam juice.

5. In a small bowl, just moisten the breadcrumbs with up to ½ cup water. Do not soak it. Gently squeeze the bread to remove any excess water. Using your hands thoroughly mix the breadcrumbs into the bowl of clams and clam juice.

6. Place a heaped tablespoon of the filling onto a clam shell half, press firmly, and sprinkle with paprika. Place the stuffed shells on a baking sheet. Bake until they turn a rich golden color on top, 15 to 20 minutes. Serve hot.

Serves 4

POACHED COD WITH VEGETABLES

Bacalhau de Consoada

This traditional dish is served most anytime, but particularly on Christmas Eve. My grandmother Teresa made this dish in a big white enamel pot. Her version included green beans, potatoes, and cauliflower, and it was the only way I would eat cauliflower when I was young. Some recipes use kale, cabbage, and carrots instead of green beans. Whatever vegetables you choose, simply adjust cooking times to suit. Leafy greens (mustard greens, broccoli rabe, and spinach) take 5 minutes to cook, while kale and cabbage take 10 to 15 minutes.

1 lb either kale, green beans, mustard greens, broccoli rabe, spinach, or a small head of cabbage

4 medium boiling potatoes, such as Yukon gold, skins intact, scrubbed

4 medium carrots, peeled and left whole (optional)

1 lb salt cod with skin, soaked in several changes of cold water for 24 to 36 hours, refrigerated (see page 26)

Hard-boiled eggs, peeled, 1 or more per person

Wine or cider vinegar, to drizzle

Extra-virgin olive oil, to drizzle

2 tablespoons finely chopped parsley

8 large garlic cloves, coarsely chopped, to serve

Coarse kosher salt and freshly ground black pepper

1. Trim the greens. If using cabbage, trim and cut it into quarters.

2. In an 8-quart pot, combine the whole potatoes, carrots, and any hearty greens like kale (if using), with enough water to cover by 2 inches. Cover and bring to a boil, reduce the heat, and simmer gently for 15 minutes.

3. Drain the cod from the soaking water, rinse, and add it to the pot. Cover and return to a boil. Reduce the heat to medium-low and simmer for about 15 minutes (depending on the thickness of the fish), until the fish is tender, opaque, and just starting to flake. If you are using green beans, cabbage, or more delicate leafy greens, like spinach, broccoli rabe, or mustard greens, add them after the cod has been cooking for 5 minutes.

4. Remove the fish and vegetables from the pot as they become cooked. Peel the potatoes and arrange on a serving platter with the fish, vegetables, and hard-boiled eggs. Drizzle with oil and vinegar to taste and sprinkle with the parsley.

5. Provide decanters of additional extra-virgin olive oil and cider vinegar, as well as chopped garlic, salt, and pepper alongside. Serve with Portuguese or other crusty bread and olives.

Serves 4 to 6

SALT COD STEW

Bacalhau Estufado

This aromatic broth complements salt cod wonderfully well. We eat this family favorite year-round. The presoaked salt cod is gently cooked in a cilantro-infused tomato and onion broth, along with rice and potatoes, creating a flavorful one-pot meal.

8 oz salt cod, soaked in several changes of cold water for 16 to 24 hours, refrigerated (see page 26)

⅓ cup Portuguese or extra-virgin olive oil

1 medium onion, coarsely chopped

1 bay leaf

½ teaspoon paprika

3 large very ripe tomatoes, peeled and coarsely chopped

2 garlic cloves, coarsely chopped

¼ cup white wine (optional)

2 medium all-purpose potatoes, such as white or Yukon Gold, peeled and cut into 1-inch cubes

¾ cup (5 oz) medium-grain rice

1 to 2 tablespoons finely chopped cilantro or parsley

½ teaspoon coarse kosher salt, or to taste

¼ teaspoon freshly ground black pepper

1. Taste the fish for salt and let it soak a little longer in fresh water if it is still too salty. Drain, rinse, and cut the fish into 2- to 3-inch pieces. Set aside.

2. Heat the olive oil in a 5-quart pot over medium-high heat. Sauté the onion until soft and translucent, about 5 minutes. Stir in the bay leaf and paprika. Add the tomatoes and garlic. Reduce the heat to medium-low, cover, and cook until the tomatoes start to break down, about 15 minutes. Pour in the wine, if using, and simmer for 1 minute.

3. Add the potatoes and 6 cups of water. Cover and bring to a boil. Toss in the rice and reduce the heat. Simmer until the potatoes and rice are almost tender, 15 to 20 minutes.

4. Add the cilantro or parsley, salt, pepper, and the salt cod. Continue to simmer until the fish is opaque and the potatoes are cooked, 10 to 15 minutes more. Ladle the stew into bowls and serve with plenty of bread to dip in the fragrant broth.

Variation: *You can add 8 oz (about 25) bay scallops and 8 oz (U 26/30) peeled and deveined shrimp to this dish. After the cod has cooked for 10 minutes, and the rice and potatoes are just about done, add the scallops and shrimp and simmer for 3 more minutes (be careful not to overcook them).*

Makes about 40

SALT COD CAKES

Bolinhos de Bacalhau

This easy continental-style recipe for cod cakes can be served as an appetizer for a party, as a snack, or as part of a simple meal with rice and greens. Cod cakes are served throughout the year and always on Christmas Eve. As a young girl, I enjoyed learning how to form the cakes into their somewhat flattened egg shape, but this technique does take a little practice! Allocate about 4 per person as a party appetizer, but they go fast!

1 lb boneless salt cod, soaked in several changes of cold water for 24 hours, refrigerated (see page 26)

1 lb starchy potatoes, such as Yukon Gold, skins intact

¼ cup (1½ oz) finely chopped onion (optional)

2 to 3 large eggs, lightly beaten, as needed

¼ cup (½ oz) finely chopped parsley

½ teaspoon hot pepper sauce (optional)

¼ teaspoon white pepper

Olive oil, for deep frying

Coarse kosher salt, if needed

1. Taste the fish for salt. When the fish is ready, drain the cod from the soaking water and rinse. Place the fish in a 5-quart pot with the potatoes, onion, and enough water to cover the ingredients completely. Cover and bring to a boil, reduce the heat to medium-low, and simmer for 15 minutes.

2. Using a slotted spoon transfer the cod to a dish, leaving the potatoes and onion in the pot. When the fish is cool enough to handle, remove any bones and skin and set aside. Continue to cook the potatoes until easily pierced with a fork. Drain the potatoes and onion, and set aside until cool enough to handle. Peel the potatoes.

3. If you have one, use a meat grinder to process the cooked cod, onion, and potatoes. Alternatively, shred the cod by hand and mash the potatoes and onions with a masher or fork. Do not use a food processor.

4. Place the mixture in a bowl and add 2 of the beaten eggs. Mix in the parsley, hot sauce, and white pepper. The mixture should be fairly thick, but not stiff. Add an extra egg if the mixture seems dry and isn't binding together.

5. Form the cod mixture into slightly flattened egg-shaped cakes using two teaspoons: with one hand, take a spoonful of the mixture, and with the other hand and a rotating motion, insert the bowl of the second spoon behind the mixture, scooping it out of the first spoon. Repeat several times, back and forth, to obtain an oval shape and smooth finish. Try to keep them uniform in size.

6. Heat 5 to 6 inches of olive oil in a 2½-quart saucepan until it is very hot, but not smoking (about 350°F on an oil thermometer). Cook a small amount of the mixture and taste for salt.

7. Fry the cod cakes, a few at a time, until the outside is medium golden and center is hot, 4 to 5 minutes. They should be fairly light and puffy. Drain on paper towels. Transfer to a serving platter and garnish with parsley.

Note: *The mixture can also be made ahead, shaped, tightly wrapped, and refrigerated or frozen. Deep-fry just before serving (do not defrost).*

Variation: *For a lighter, fluffy interior, some Portuguese cooks separate the eggs and beat the egg whites to soft peaks before adding them, along with the yolks, to the mixture. Either way, they're like eating potato chips—you can't stop with just one.*

Serves 6 to 8

SALT COD WITH CREAM

Bacalhau com Nata

On one of our visits to Portugal, we had the pleasure of dining with family friends in their flat in the older section of Lisbon. Ismailde, who is a wonderful cook, prepared a cod dish for us while Jose poured his homemade wine. Our son isn't a big eater but considers this his favorite dish. Ismailde thought he didn't care for the meal since he ate only a small amount. In Portuguese, she said to him, "*Passarinho, passarinho, quando eu for tua casa, eu não vou comer também.*" I translated for him: "Little bird, little bird, when I go to your house, I won't eat either." He then surprised us all by replying in Portuguese, with perfect timing, "*Mais fica,*" literally "more stays," meaning "more for me," which set everyone laughing.

In this dish, cod is first poached in water, then milk, before it is combined with sautéed vegetables and a rich cream sauce. The sauce can also be made using the broth from poaching the fish. This dish takes time to prepare and uses a number of pans, but it is so luscious that it is really worth the effort.

1½ lb boneless salt cod, soaked in several changes of cold water for 24 to 36 hours, refrigerated (see page 26)

4 cups hot milk

½ cup (1½ oz) fresh breadcrumbs

1 small carrot, peeled and cut into thin strips, to garnish (optional)

VEGETABLE MIXTURE

3 tablespoons olive oil, plus more for deep frying

1 large onion, thinly sliced

1 bay leaf

1 large carrot, peeled and shredded or finely sliced

1 garlic clove, finely chopped

1 tablespoon finely chopped parsley, plus more to garnish

Scant ½ teaspoon coarse kosher salt

3 large potatoes, peeled and cut into thin slices (like shoe strings)

Prepare the fish

1. Taste the fish for salt and let it soak longer if needed.

2. Pour 8 cups of water into a large pan and bring to a boil over high heat. Turn off the heat. Remove the cod from the soaking water, rinse, and add it to the pan, making sure that the fish is completely covered by the hot water (add more boiling water if needed). Cover the pan and poach the fish for 15 minutes or a little longer if the pieces are thicker than 1 inch.

3. Drain the fish (reserve the broth if you are using it in the sauce). In a large bowl, hand-shred the fish, removing any remaining bones or skin. Pour the hot milk over the fish, cover, and let stand for 30 minutes to 1 hour.

Prepare the vegetable mixture

4. While the fish is poaching in the milk, heat 3 tablespoons of the oil in a large, deep frying pan over medium-high heat. Sauté the onion with the bay leaf until the onion is soft and translucent. Stir in the carrots and garlic, and cook for one minute. Toss in the parsley, season with the salt, and set aside.

5. Pour olive oil in a deep pan to a depth of 5 inches. Place over medium-high heat until hot, but not smoking (about 375°F), and deep-fry the potatoes in small batches until golden. Transfer to a plate lined with paper towels and reserve.

SAUCE

5 tablespoons (2½ oz) butter

5 tablespoons all-purpose flour

1¾ cups milk

1¾ cups heavy cream (for a lighter sauce, use light cream or the salt cod cooking broth)

¼ teaspoon white pepper, or to taste

¼ teaspoon nutmeg

2 egg yolks, lightly beaten

Juice of ¼ lemon

Scant 1 teaspoon coarse kosher salt

Tip: *The vegetable mixture can be made ahead, combined, refrigerated, then assembled with the fish and sauce later.*

Make the sauce

6. Melt the butter in a medium saucepan over medium-low heat. Add the flour, stirring constantly to make a roux. Let it cook on low heat for 2 to 3 minutes to cook the starch. Pour the cool milk slowly into the hot roux, stirring constantly to avoid lumps. Still stirring constantly, add the cream or fish broth. Bring to a low simmer, then remove from the heat and add the pepper and nutmeg.

7. In a medium bowl, stir a small amount of the sauce into the egg yolks, to temper them. Then transfer the egg mixture into the cream sauce, stirring constantly. (If you add the eggs to the sauce without tempering them first, they will not blend with the sauce.) Whisk in the lemon juice and any additional salt. Simmer, stirring, for an additional minute, then remove from the heat and set aside.

To assemble

8. Preheat the oven to 350°F.

9. Drain the cod from the milk and transfer to a large bowl. Add the onion and carrot mixture and the potatoes. Toss lightly to mix the ingredients thoroughly. Fold half of the cream sauce into the mixture and gently blend.

10. Gently spread the mixture evenly in the base of a baking dish measuring approximately 9 by 13 inches. Pour the remaining sauce over the top and sprinkle with breadcrumbs.

11. Bake at 350°F for about 20 minutes or until the top is lightly golden and bubbly. The ingredients should be heated through. Garnish with parsley and a fine julienne of carrot sticks.

Serves 6 to 8

GOMES DE SÁ-STYLE SALT COD

Bacalhau à Gomes de Sá

This popular traditional dish is extremely simple to prepare, beginning a day ahead with the soaking of the salt cod. After poaching the cod in water, soaking it in hot milk keeps it tender, but this step can be omitted. The recipe was created by Gomes de Sá, of Oporto's famous Restaurante Lisbonense. There are different versions of it; which is the original is a subject of debate. This version is the one I learned as the youngest cook in the family.

1 lb thick salt cod pieces, skin intact, soaked in several changes of cold water for 24 to 36 hours, refrigerated (see page 26)

4 cups hot milk

1½ lb boiling potatoes, skins intact

½ cup olive oil

2 large onions, peeled and thinly sliced

3 garlic cloves, finely chopped

1 teaspoon coarse kosher salt, if needed

3 hard-boiled eggs, peeled and sliced

¼ cup (½ oz) finely chopped parsley

Handful of briny pitted black olives

1. Pour 6 to 8 cups of water into a 4-quart pot and bring to a boil. Turn off the heat.

2. Drain and rinse the fish and add it to the boiling water, making sure it is completely covered. Cover the pot and let the fish poach for 15 to 20 minutes, until opaque and almost starting to flake.

3. Drain the fish, place it in a bowl, and break it into medium-sized pieces, discarding any bones or skin. Pour the hot milk over the fish and let stand for 30 minutes.

4. Meanwhile, boil the potatoes in their skins until they are tender. Cool, peel, and slice the potatoes into ½-inch rounds.

5. Preheat the oven to 350°F. Heat 2 tablespoons of the oil in a large frying pan over medium-high heat. Add and sauté the onions until golden, 10 to 15 minutes. Add the remaining oil and the garlic, and stir to just heat through.

6. Drain the milk from the cod. In a 9- by 13-inch baking dish, alternate layers of cod, potatoes, and onion sauce, ending with a layer of sauce on top. Season with salt only if needed.

7. Bake for about 20 minutes, until heated through and lightly golden on top.

8. Garnish the dish with a row of egg slices in the middle, a sprinkling of parsley, and black olives along the edges. Serve with a simple green salad.

Serves 4

BRAS-STYLE SALT COD

Bacalhau à Brás

If there were leftovers from *Bacalhau à Gomes de Sá*, my father-in-law would make a quick version of *Bacalhau à Brás*. In the traditional method, potatoes are cut into fine strips and fried, then combined with presoaked salt cod, then sautéed with garlic. The mixture was then "embraced," or coated, with lightly beaten eggs. My father-in-law's shortcut is a great way to use leftover *Bacalhau à Gomes de Sá*.

2 tablespoons olive oil

2 cups (about ¼ recipe) leftover
  Bacalhau à Gomes de Sá (see opposite)

4 eggs, lightly beaten

½ teaspoon coarse kosher salt, or to taste

¼ teaspoon freshly ground black pepper, or to taste

2 tablespoons finely chopped parsley

1. Heat the oil in a medium frying pan over medium-high heat. Add and thoroughly heat the leftover cod mixture for about 5 minutes.

2. Add the beaten eggs. Season with salt and pepper, if needed, and cook just until the eggs are done, stirring occasionally, as if cooking scrambled eggs. (Be careful not to overcook the eggs; they should still be a little creamy.)

3. Garnish with parsley and serve immediately.

Serves 4

COD BAKED WITH ONION SAUCE

Bacalhau no Forno com Cebolada

The rule of thumb for this tasty dish is one onion per person. If you have onion lovers in the family, use large ones. This is adapted from a recipe that is particularly popular in Portugal, especially for wedding feasts, and has made its way to the United States. It is typically made with salt cod that has the skins and bones intact, which can usually be found in Portuguese or Italian markets. Traditionally, the fish is cooked skin side up and coated with mayonnaise. I prefer using boneless and skinless fish for this dish, especially if I am serving it to guests. A drizzle of olive oil replaces the mayonnaise.

1 lb boneless, skinless salt cod, thick center cut, soaked in several changes of cold water for 24 to 36 hours, refrigerated (see page 26)

½ cup olive oil, plus more to drizzle

4 large onions (one per person), thinly sliced

2 garlic cloves, coarsely chopped

1 bay leaf

1 large very ripe tomato, peeled, seeded, and coarsely chopped

1 teaspoon hot pepper sauce

1 cup white wine

3 sprigs of parsley

¼ teaspoon ground white pepper

2 eggs, lightly beaten

1 cup (4 oz) plain dried breadcrumbs

Chopped parsley, to serve

1. Preheat the oven to 350°F.

2. In a large frying pan, heat the olive oil over medium-high heat and sauté the onions until golden, 10 to 15 minutes. Reduce the heat to medium-low, add the garlic and bay leaf, and cook until the garlic is aromatic and lightly colored.

3. Mix the chopped tomatoes and hot sauce into the pan, cover, and simmer until the tomatoes become soft and partially dissolve into the onions, about 15 minutes. Pour in the wine and add the parsley and white pepper. Simmer until the liquid is reduced by half; the sauce should have the consistency of oatmeal. Remove from the heat, discard the bay leaf and parsley sprigs, then transfer the sauce to a 9- by 13-inch baking dish.

4. Drain and rinse the cod and cut it into 4 serving pieces.

5. Dip the fish into the beaten eggs and then into the breadcrumbs, coating all sides. Place the pieces of fish on top of the onion sauce. Drizzle a small amount of olive oil on top of each piece of fish. Bake for 35 minutes or until the breadcrumbs are a light golden color. Garnish with fresh parsley and serve with Punched Potatoes (page 184).

PAN-FRIED SARDINES WITH GARLIC AND LEMON

Sardinhas Fritas com Alho e Limão

Who said singers can't cook? A fado singer, Lourdes Silva, shared her special way of preparing sardines with me. In between her frequent trips back and forth to Portugal, she enjoys cooking her family favorites. This is a satisfying appetizer or light meal. Serve with boiled potatoes or Tomato Rice (page 192) and a salad for a flavorful lunch.

12 sardines (preferably fresh, but frozen will do, thawed)

Juice of 1 lemon

1 teaspoon coarse kosher salt, or to taste

½ teaspoon freshly ground black pepper, or to taste

2 garlic cloves, finely chopped

1 bay leaf

¾ cup (3 oz) dried breadcrumbs, for coating

Corn oil, for frying

1. Cut the heads and fins off the sardines. Slice the sardines lengthwise on the belly side. Open each fish up and lay it flat. Fillet the fish: grab the tail bone with your fingers and, with the other hand pushing the flesh in the opposite direction, carefully lift out the main bone. The smaller rib bones should come out with it. It is ok if the fish separates into two sections. You can have your fishmonger do this for you.

2. Place the fish fillets in a shallow glass or ceramic dish. Sprinkle with the lemon juice, salt, pepper, garlic, and the bay leaf. Cover and marinate for 30 minutes in the refrigerator.

3. Spread the breadcrumbs on a sheet of wax paper, which makes cleanup easier. Pour the oil into a frying pan to a depth of ¼ inch and heat over medium-high heat. Coat the fish with the breadcrumbs, shaking off the excess, and pan-fry in small batches until lightly golden on both sides, adding more oil if needed. Drain on paper towels or a brown paper bag and serve.

Serves 4

SALMON BAKED IN A CLAY TILE

Salmão Assado na Telha

The Portuguese are known for making multiple uses of most anything. In Portugal, this dish is cooked in a *telha*, a clay "roof tile." Of course, in cooking, the curved clay tiles are not taken from a roof, but are rather created in the same curved shape—about 7 inches long and 4 inches wide—except with closed ends. They make for a great presentation, but can be hard to find here. For the best flavor, I recommend using an unglazed clay baker or deep-dish pizza stone, at least 2-inches deep (sold at kitchen specialty stores). You can use a metal, glass, or glazed dish, but the flavor will not be as scrumptious. Follow the directions for pre-soaking your clay baker so that it doesn't crack.

Rich Nunes adapted this recipe from one he enjoyed in the Azores. He uses salmon in place of *lidio*, a fish found in Portuguese waters and not available in American markets. The method is unusual, but the result is a very tasty dish that is not greasy. This recipe is almost guaranteed to win over any who are not fond of salmon. Ask your fishmonger to remove the thin rib bones from the fish or do it yourself using needle-nose pliers to pull them out.

20 garlic cloves, finely chopped

½ cup olive oil, or as needed

Two 1-inch thick salmon steaks (1 lb total), halved lengthwise, center bone removed

2 strips lean bacon or thinly sliced prosciutto, halved crosswise

4 thin crosscut onion slices

8 oz *chouriço* sausage (see page 168), cut into ¼-inch slices

Coarse kosher salt, as needed

Freshly ground black pepper

Finely chopped parsley, to serve

Note: *Instead of salmon, you can use any equally flavorful type of fish steaks; a mild tasting fish does not work well in this recipe. Using salmon fillets instead of steaks (arranged skin side down, with the other ingredients on top) results in an oilier taste.*

1. Preheat the oven to 350°F. Scatter the garlic over the bottom of a pre-soaked unglazed clay baker in an even layer, making a bed. Pour the olive oil over the garlic. It should barely cover the garlic; add more if needed.

2. Remove any tiny bones from the salmon. Place each steak-half skin side up on top of the bed of garlic in the baker, spaced at least 1½ inches apart.

3. Place one half-strip of bacon against and slightly pressing into one side of each piece of salmon. Because the fish steaks are upright, not flat, the bacon flavor is imparted to the salmon while the bacon fat drips to the bottom of the baker. Press one slice of onion against the opposite side of each piece of fish.

4. Scatter the sausage slices around the outside edges of the baker. Sprinkle the fish skins with coarse salt and season all over with ground black pepper.

5. Place the baker on a baking sheet and bake for 25 to 30 minutes or to desired doneness. Garnish with finely chopped parsley, and serve with Punched Potatoes (page 184).

Serves 4

BROILED SALMON
Salmão Grelhado

Many good cooks have come to America from the island of Faial in the Azores. Among them is Leonia Clarimundo, whose method for preparing salmon is simple and delicious. The butter and lemon become one with the flavor of cilantro, creating a stimulating aroma that is very special (though you can use parsley). Second only to the people from the Alentejo region, the people of Faial are great lovers of fresh cilantro. This may be explained by the fact that many of the early settlers of Faial came from the Alentejo and Algarve regions of the mainland.

4 salmon steaks, ¾-inch-thick, skins intact

1 tablespoon coarse kosher salt, or to taste

½ cup (4 oz) butter

Juice of ½ lemon, or to taste

4 garlic cloves, finely chopped

¼ teaspoon freshly ground white or black pepper

¼ cup (½ oz) finely chopped cilantro

1. Season the fish with salt on both sides. Broil or grill over a hot flame for 4 to 5 minutes on each side, until opaque or to desired doneness.

2. Meanwhile, in a 1-quart saucepan over medium-low heat, melt the butter, and then add the lemon juice, garlic, and pepper. Cook briefly, just until the garlic becomes aromatic. Toss in the cilantro and heat through for 2 minutes.

3. Transfer the salmon to a serving dish, drizzle with the sauce, and serve immediately.

Serves 2 to 4

PERIWINKLES WITH GARLIC

Caracois/Caramujos com Alho

Warm summer nights bring back memories of sitting outside with my father and some of his friends, sharing a bowl of periwinkles delicately flavored with garlic, onion, herbs, and spice. Equipped with pins or toothpicks, we carefully pried the periwinkles from their shells, savoring every bite. Anyone who enjoys escargot should try this recipe! It makes for an interesting appetizer or snack.

4 lb saltwater periwinkles (about 5 cups)
1 tablespoons finely chopped parsley or cilantro
1 small onion, peeled, left whole
1 scant tablespoon coarse kosher salt
3 garlic cloves, peeled and smashed
1 tablespoon hot pepper sauce
1 tablespoon finely ground black pepper
1 bay leaf
2 cups cold water, or as needed

A day ahead

1. Rinse the periwinkles and soak in enough water to cover with 1 tablespoon salt for 1 hour. Drain, rinse, and sprinkle with 2 tablespoons of parsley or cilantro. Refrigerate overnight.

The next day

2. Rinse the periwinkles in several changes of water. Combine the remaining ingredients with the periwinkles in a 3-quart saucepan with sufficient cold water to just cover them.

3. Cover the pan and bring to a boil over medium-high heat. Once the water begins to boil, reduce the heat and simmer for 20 minutes. The disk-like flaps at the opening of the periwinkles will separate easily when they are cooked. Drain the liquid and transfer the periwinkles to a serving bowl.

4. Serve hot with toothpicks or pins. To eat, insert pins or toothpicks into the shell, discard the thin round flap, and remove the curly meat.

Serves 8

FISH STEW WITH SHELLFISH

Caldeirada com Mariscos

Typically, a *caldeirada* contains only fish, usually more than one kind, in an aromatic broth. Fishermen used whatever fish they caught, even conger eels. Some *caldeiradas* are made with a bottom layer of bread instead of potatoes. This version is enriched with clams and shrimp, and is prepared in the traditional method: All the ingredients are assembled raw in a single pot and are not stirred during the cooking process. Instead, the pot is moved back and forth across the burner, shaking the ingredients, to "stir" without disturbing the layers. With only a single cup of white wine and no additional water, the delicious broth comes from the ingredients themselves. The secret is slow-cooking with a tight cover. To complete this meal, serve with chunks of crusty bread to soak up the broth, flavorful black olives, and plenty of *vinho verde* or other crisp white wine. It is perfect for casual summer entertaining.

½ cup olive oil

3 large onions, thinly sliced

2 large Red Bliss potatoes, scrubbed,
  skins intact, cut into ½-inch slices

4 large, ripe tomatoes, peeled and chopped (4 cups)

4 garlic cloves, coarsely chopped

2 bay leaves, torn in half

1½ large sweet green peppers, thinly sliced

¼ cup (½ oz) finely chopped cilantro

½ teaspoon crushed red pepper flakes

2 tablespoons sweet paprika

1 teaspoon coarse kosher salt, plus more if needed

½ teaspoon freshly ground black or
  white pepper, plus more if needed

24 small littleneck clams (about 2¼ lb),
  scrubbed (see page 82)

2 lb firm white fish, such as halibut, monkfish,
  or a combination, cut into 3-inch chunks

8 oz medium shrimp, peeled and deveined

½ teaspoon saffron, crushed

1 tablespoon warm water

1 cup white wine

Dry or toasted slices of Homestyle Bread (page 236)
  or crusty sourdough, to serve

1. Pour the olive oil into a heavy-bottom 8- or 10-quart pot. Arrange the onion slices in the pot in a thick single layer, followed by a layer of potatoes, overlapping the slices as necessary.

2. In a large bowl, combine the tomatoes, garlic, bay leaves, sweet peppers, cilantro, crushed red pepper, paprika, salt, and ground pepper. Mix well.

3. Scatter one-third of the tomato mixture over the potatoes. Add the littleneck clams in one layer, followed by the fish. Layer on another third of the tomato mixture. Top with a single layer of shrimp, and then a final layer of the tomato mixture.

4. In a small bowl, combine the saffron and warm water and set aside for 15 minutes. Mix with the wine and pour over the layered ingredients in the pot. Cover tightly and place over medium-high heat for 5 minutes, or until you hear the liquid start to boil. Quickly reduce the heat to medium-low.

5. Simmer gently, without uncovering, for 30 minutes, gently shaking the pot back and forth from time to time to stir. When ready, the shrimp should be opaque and tender and the peppers cooked (simmer for an additional 5 minutes or so if needed). Add more salt or pepper, if needed.

6. Place the pot in the center of the table. Divide the bread among individual soup bowls. Serve, making sure to scoop up some of each layer.

FISHERMEN'S STEW OF GRACIOSA

Caldeirada à Moda do Pescador da Graciosa

With limited kitchen equipment on-board, Portuguese fishermen still manage to create fish stews with magnificently seasoned broth. Each member of the crew takes part in preparing the ingredients, using some of the fish from their catch. A stew can contain anywhere from one to many kinds of fish, including sardines and eels. This recipe is that of Azorean Portuguese fishermen and their descendants. It is associated with the island of Graciosa (meaning "gracious"), one of the nine islands in the Azores. In this version, the fish is poached rather than stewed. Spices and seasonings are added to the poaching liquid, creating a spicy broth that is ladled over the fish.

4 lb dressed cusk, cut into 1-inch steaks (or thick
  fillets, cut into serving pieces; see Note)

3 parsley sprigs

2 medium onions, thinly sliced

3 bay leaves

1½ tablespoons coarse kosher salt

1 tablespoon olive oil

SEASONING PASTE

7 garlic cloves, coarsely chopped

2 teaspoons coarse kosher salt

1½ teaspoons cumin seeds, or
  ½ teaspoon ground cumin

1½ tablespoons finely chopped parsley

2 pickled chili peppers (page 221), each
  about 1 inch, finely chopped

1 teaspoon ground safflower (see page 29) or
  paprika, or 1 teaspoon saffron threads, crushed

3 tablespoons tomato paste

1 tablespoon sugar

¼ teaspoon ground nutmeg

½ cup olive oil

¼ cup red or white wine vinegar

1. In the bottom of an 8-quart pot, arrange the fish in layers. Pour in enough cold water to barely cover the fish (about 4 cups). Add the parsley, onions, bay leaves, salt, and olive oil.

2. Cover tightly, place over medium-high heat, and bring to a boil. Reduce the heat and simmer gently until the fish is opaque, about 20 minutes.

3. Meanwhile, make the seasoning paste: Using a large mortar and pestle, mash the garlic with the salt to form a paste. Mash in the cumin, parsley, chili peppers, and safflower. Stir in the tomato paste, sugar, and nutmeg. Drizzle in the olive oil, followed by the vinegar. Stir to blend the ingredients well. (If you do not have a mortar and pestle or yours is not large enough, make the paste in a medium bowl using the back of a spoon or a fork.)

4. Using a slotted spoon, transfer the cooked fish to a serving dish. Cover and keep warm.

5. Whisk the seasoning paste into the fish broth, making sure it is well dispersed. Simmer for about 5 minutes over medium-low heat.

6. Ladle some of the seasoned broth over the fish and serve the remaining broth on the side. Or place generous pieces of fish in individual soup bowls and spoon the broth over it. Serve with plenty of bread to dip in the broth.

Note: *Cusk steaks yield a gelatinous substance that gives the broth a rich body that is lacking when skinless, boneless fillets are used.*

Serves 4

GRILLED SHRIMP WITH GARLIC AND CILANTRO

Camarão Grelhados com Alho e Coentros

One of the best ways to eat shrimp is when it is simply grilled. The lemony tang of cilantro works so well with shrimp—they are truly a well-matched pair. If you use wooden skewers, be sure to soak them in warm water for about 30 minutes before grilling. Serve these with a salad and Tomato Rice (page 192). Portuguese *vinho verde* is also perfect with shrimp.

8 garlic cloves, finely chopped

½ teaspoon coarse kosher salt, or to taste

½ cup (1 oz) finely chopped cilantro

1 teaspoon hot pepper sauce

½ cup white wine or lemon juice

16 jumbo shrimp, peeled, deveined, tail on

Piri piri sauce (page 20) or other
  hot pepper sauce (optional)

1. Using a mortar and pestle, mash the garlic with the salt, forming a thick paste. Blend in the cilantro and hot pepper sauce. Transfer to a medium bowl, then stir in the wine. Add the shrimp, turning gently to coat. Cover and refrigerate for 30 minutes.

2. Remove the shrimp from the marinade and thread onto presoaked skewers.

3. Preheat your barbecue and grill the shrimp over hot charcoal for 1½ to 2 minutes on each side. Hot pepper sauce for dipping adds a zesty touch.

Serves 4

BOILED LOBSTER

Lagosta Fervida

In this dish, fresh lobsters absorb the aromatic and flavorful seasoning, making melted butter unnecessary. The succulent and sweet soft-shell lobsters of early summer are my favorite. Lobster and *vinho verde*, Portuguese "green" wine, are well matched.

10 large garlic cloves, coarsely chopped

1 tablespoon coarse kosher salt

2 teaspoons Hot Pepper Paste (page 220)

½ teaspoon cumin seed

1 bay leaf

3 parsley sprigs, coarsely chopped

1 small onion, coarsely chopped

4 live chicken lobsters (about 1¼ lb each)

Melted butter, for dipping (optional)

1. To kill the lobsters humanely, put them in the freezer for 20 minutes before cooking.

2. Using a mortar and pestle, mash the garlic with the salt to form a paste. Add the remaining ingredients—except for the onions and lobsters—mashing well after each addition, to open up the essence of the spices.

3. Fill a 12-quart stockpot three-quarters full of water (about 10 quarts). Add the seasoning paste and the onion, cover, and bring to a boil over medium-high heat.

4. Remove the rubber bands from the lobsters and add the lobsters to the pot. Return to a boil. Boil, uncovered, for 10 minutes (longer for larger ones), until bright red, and the flesh is opaque. Remove from the pot and let stand for 5 minutes before serving, with or without melted butter for dipping.

Variation: *For a spicy alternative, you can use a mixture of hot pepper sauce and olive oil for dipping instead of melted butter.*

Serves 4 to 6

CURRIED SHRIMP

Camarões de Caril

This recipe is adapted from a dish I enjoyed at a Portuguese function many years ago. It is one of my favorite dishes, especially for guests. The shrimp is gently sautéed in a spicy tomato and onion—based curry sauce, then served over rice. Coconut milk can be used in place of the heavy cream.

1½ lb large shrimp, peeled and
   deveined, shells reserved

4 cups cold water

1 cup white wine

1 small onion, finely chopped, divided

1 bay leaf

1½ cups (10 oz) long-grain rice, rinsed and drained

1 teaspoon coarse kosher salt, or to taste

1 tablespoon butter

1 tablespoon olive oil

1 large very ripe tomato, peeled,
   seeded, and finely chopped

1 garlic clove, finely chopped

1 teaspoon hot pepper sauce

½ teaspoon paprika

1 tablespoon curry powder, dissolved
   in ¼ cup warm milk

½ cup heavy cream

1. In a 2½-quart pot, combine the shrimp shells, cold water, wine, half of the onion, and the bay leaf. Cover and bring to a boil over high heat. Reduce the heat to medium-low and simmer for 15 minutes. Strain and reserve the broth, discarding the shells.

2. In a separate medium saucepan, bring $3\frac{1}{3}$ cups of the shrimp broth to a boil. Add the rice and salt. Reduce the heat to medium-low, cover, and simmer until the rice is tender and the liquid is absorbed, 20 to 25 minutes. Keep warm.

3. Meanwhile, in a medium skillet or sauté pan, heat the butter and oil over medium-high heat. Add the shrimp and sauté for 2 minutes until just pink. Transfer the shrimp to a plate and cover.

4. Add the remaining onion to the same pan and sauté until lightly golden, about 10 minutes. Mix in the tomatoes, garlic, hot pepper sauce, and paprika. Reduce the heat to medium-low, cover, and simmer until the tomato has broken down and is partially dissolved, about 15 minutes.

5. Stir in the curry mixture, blending well, and continue cooking for another minute.

6. Pour in the remaining broth, stir, then quickly reduce by half. Remove from the heat and whisk in the cream. Return to medium-low heat and, without boiling, simmer until slightly thickened. Return the shrimp to the pan for 1 minute to heat through.

7. Fluff the rice with a fork and spread on a serving platter. Arrange the shrimp on top and spoon some of the curry sauce over it. Serve any extra sauce on the side.

Serves 4 to 6

PORTUGUESE-STYLE PEEL-AND-EAT SHRIMP

Camarões à Portuguesa

I can still see my father standing at the stove preparing this shrimp-lover's delight. Besides being a perfect light lunch, this dish makes a great appetizer. Sometimes my father would add coarsely chopped sweet green peppers to the pot. He never puréed the broth, but I occasionally do. Serve the broth, puréed or not, on the side as a dip for the shrimp.

¼ cup olive oil

1 small onion, thinly sliced

1 large very ripe tomato, peeled, seeded, and coarsely chopped

1 bay leaf

3 garlic cloves, crushed

¼ teaspoon crushed red pepper flakes

½ cup *vinho verde* or other white wine

1 tablespoon finely chopped fresh cilantro

2 lb fresh shrimp, in their shells

½ teaspoon coarse kosher salt, or to taste

2 tablespoons (1 oz) butter

1. Heat the olive oil in a 3-quart saucepan over medium-high heat and sauté the onion until lightly golden. Stir in the tomato, bay leaf, garlic, and red pepper flakes. Cover and cook over medium-low heat until the mixture is soft and the tomatoes are partially dissolved, about 15 minutes.

2. Pour in the wine, stir, cover, and bring to a boil over medium-high heat. Reduce the heat to medium-low, and add the cilantro, shrimp, and salt. Lightly mix and cover tightly. Simmer for 3 minutes or until the shrimp is just tender. Be careful not to overcook, or the shrimp will be tough.

3. Using a slotted spoon, transfer the shrimp to a serving dish and cover. Melt the butter into the broth, then strain or, using a handheld blender, purée the broth. Serve on the side as a dip for the peeled shrimp.

Makes 2 to 3 dozen

SHRIMP RISSOLES

Rissóis de Camarão

These delectable savories can be served as a single course, snack, or appetizer. Although they are most often made with shrimp, a filling of chicken is tasty as well. They can even be made with shredded poached salt cod (see Variations). This is adapted from a recipe from my friend Isaura, who uses olive oil to fry the onions and corn oil to fry the assembled turnover. Cornstarch is used to bind the filling. These rissoles freeze well, too (see Note). When you have unexpected guests, just pull as many as you need from the freezer and fry them up. Make them smaller or make them a bit larger, but make them. Serve with your favorite wine. (Pictured on page 74.)

PASTRY

2 cups milk

4 tablespoons (2 oz) butter

1 teaspoon salt

2 cups (9 oz) all-purpose flour

FILLING

2 tablespoons (1 oz) butter

½ small onion, finely chopped

1 cup milk, water, or shrimp broth

½ tablespoon finely chopped cilantro or parsley

1 to 2 teaspoons hot pepper sauce, to taste

½ teaspoon coarse kosher salt, or to taste

½ teaspoon ground white pepper

¼ teaspoon nutmeg

2 tablespoons cornstarch

8 oz shrimp, peeled, deveined, cooked, well drained, and coarsely chopped (about 1½ cups)

3 large eggs

2 cups (8 oz) plain dried breadcrumbs

Corn oil, for deep-frying

Make the pastry

1. In a 2-quart saucepan, combine the milk, butter, and salt. Warm over medium-high heat until the milk is scalded, not boiling. Reduce the heat to medium-low.

2. Using a wooden spoon, vigorously stir the flour into the milk. Keep stirring over medium-low heat until it forms a dough. When the dough pulls away from the sides of the pan and forms a ball, remove the pan from the heat.

3. Turn the dough out onto a lightly floured workspace. Using a plastic dough scraper or wooden spoon, turn the warm dough to knead briefly just until it is smooth and springs back slightly when pressed with your finger (be careful not to overwork the dough). Divide the dough in half, forming two balls, and cover with an inverted bowl. Set aside to cool to nearly room temperature.

Make the filling

4. Melt the butter in a 1-quart saucepan. Sauté the onion over medium-high heat until a light golden color, about 10 minutes.

5. Reduce the heat to medium-low, pour in the milk, and heat to scalding, not boiling. Stir in the cilantro or parsley, hot pepper sauce, salt, pepper, and nutmeg.

6. Combine the cornstarch with 2 tablespoons water. Stir this into the milk and simmer over medium-low heat, stirring constantly, until it thickens, 1 to 2 minutes. (Don't overcook or the cornstarch will break down and the mixture will loosen.) Stir in the chopped shrimp, heat through for 1 minute, and remove from heat. Set aside to cool completely.

To assemble

7. Line a baking sheet with plastic wrap or parchment paper. Beat the eggs with ¼ cup water.

8. On a lightly floured work surface, roll out one-half of the dough to ⅛-inch thickness. Using a 3½- to 4-inch cutter, cut out circles of dough.

9. Place 1 teaspoon of filling in the middle of a circle. Brush the edges with some of the beaten egg. With lightly floured fingertips, fold the dough over the filling to form a half circle, pressing the edges together to seal. Set aside on the lined pan. Repeat until all the filling is used, setting the leftover beaten egg aside.

To fry

10. Spread the breadcrumbs on a plate. Dip the pastries in the reserved beaten egg, then quickly into the breadcrumbs, shaking off any excess. Set aside.

11. Pour the oil into a deep pot to a depth of 5 inches. Place over medium-high heat until hot but not smoking (350°F). Fry the rissoles, two or three at a time, turning them over until golden, about 5 minutes. Transfer to paper towels to drain. Serve hot or at room temperature.

Note: *To freeze: Line a baking sheet with plastic wrap and arrange the uncooked pastries in a single layer without overlapping. Cover well with plastic wrap, smoothing out as much air as possible. Freeze. Thaw for about 10 minutes before frying. They will keep for at least a month, but you will most likely use them before then.*

Variation: *Substitute 1½ cups finely chopped cooked chicken, rabbit, or shredded poached salt cod for the shrimp. Stir briefly, add 1 tablespoon finely chopped celery, stir, and assemble.*

For a crisper pastry, use broth from cooking shrimp (or other proteins) in place of the milk.

Serves 4

MADEIRA-STYLE TUNA

Atum á Moda da Madeira

When I was growing up, I worked in a jacket factory after school. It was a culinary learning experience for me, as well as a manufacturing one. New England Sportswear, where I worked, was a melting pot of cultures. At lunch breaks, food was always a topic of conversation. It seems that when the canneries were built in Portugal, they enabled rural inland areas to add some fish to their diets—canned sardines and canned tuna. Canned tuna was eaten only on the mainland, however. On the island of Madeira, fresh tuna steaks are the standard. A coworker from the island of Madeira, Adelaide Figueira, taught me her method for preparing fresh tuna. I take liberty with this dish and use cilantro instead of parsley. To my taste, the cilantro complements the flavor of the tuna especially well, but the choice is yours. You'll want to serve this with crusty bread to soak up every drop of sauce.

2 garlic cloves, coarsely chopped

1 tablespoon coarse kosher salt

1 teaspoon Hot Pepper Paste (page 220)

4 fresh tuna steaks, ¾ to 1-inch thick,
    rinsed in ice-cold water

1 cup red wine vinegar, or more if needed

Olive oil

1 tablespoon finely chopped cilantro or parsley

1. Using a mortar and pestle, mash the garlic with the salt, to form a paste. Blend in the hot pepper paste. Use this mixture to coat both sides of the tuna steaks and transfer them to a baking dish large enough to accommodate the fish in a single layer.

2. Pour the vinegar and an equal amount of water into a medium bowl or large measuring cup. Blend well and pour over the fish, making sure there is enough marinade to cover the fish completely. (The amount varies according to the size of the dish you use.) Cover and marinate in the refrigerator for several hours or overnight.

3. Reserving the marinade, transfer the fish to a platter and blot with paper towels.

4. Pour in enough oil to cover the bottom of a medium frying pan (about ¼ cup) and place over medium-high heat until very hot, but not smoking. Fry the slices of tuna briefly, about 3 minutes on each side (be careful not to overcook them). Transfer to a serving platter.

5. Pour the reserved marinade into the same pan, bring to a simmer, reduce the heat to medium-low, and cook for 2 minutes, stirring occasionally. Add the cilantro or parsley and heat through. Pour the sauce over the fish and serve.

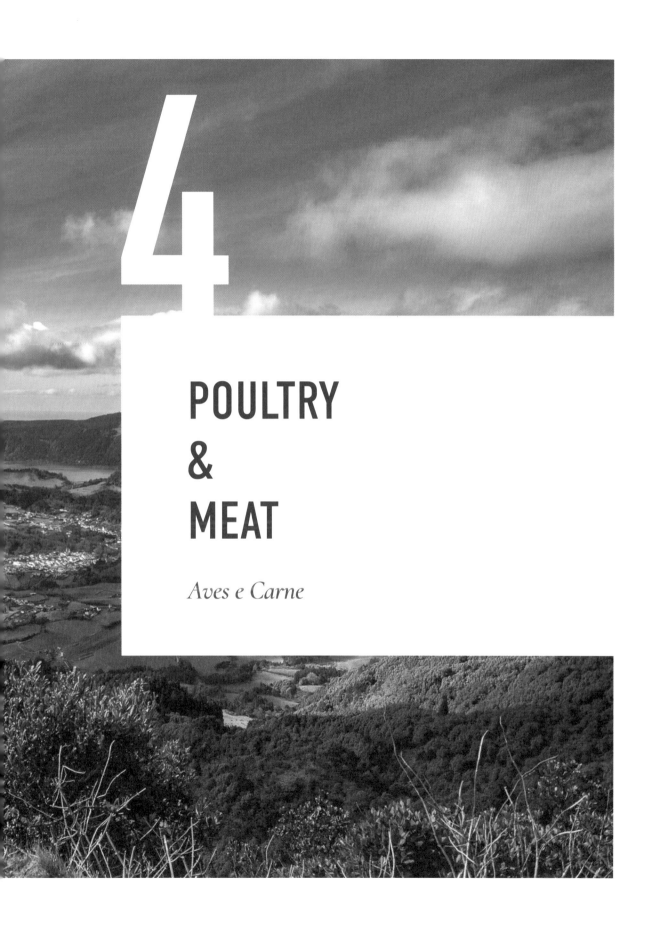

4

POULTRY
&
MEAT

Aves e Carne

4 POULTRY & MEAT
Aves e Carne

In the past, only the wealthy Portuguese could enjoy meat every day; the poor of the country made their soups hearty to fill and sustain themselves between meat meals. Portuguese immigrants, who brought these habits with them, often lived on soups all week long, as they scrimped and saved to make a better life in their new homeland. As families fared better, traditional meat dishes became increasingly visible.

When the nights get chilly, signaling the coming of fall and Old Man Winter, I look forward to the heartier meals of my heritage. Though fish is always on the table, during the colder months, there is something that is soul-comforting and heartwarming about stews and braises of chicken, rabbit, beef, and pork. Poultry and meat are quite often steeped in a wine-and-garlic marinade overnight before they are stewed or braised. Lamb and liver are not left out, you can be sure. A simple meal, *Cozido à Portuguesa* (page 156), almost mirrors the New England boiled dinner. Depending on what meats are available, this boiled dinner can be very simple or very extravagant. Preparation for some of the dishes begin a day or two ahead; plan accordingly.

Left: Chicken Pies (page 124)

Serves 4 to 6

STEWED CHICKEN

Galinha Estufada

This one-pot meal is tasty enough to serve to guests. When I make it with potatoes instead of rice (see Variation), I save any broth left over from the stew to use when I cook shrimp and scallops. The combination of tomatoes cooked with onions and garlic in olive oil is an aromatic marriage that entices the palate.

4 tablespoons olive oil

1 medium onion, coarsely chopped

1 large very ripe tomato, peeled, seeded,
  and chopped

½ tablespoon paprika

2 garlic cloves, finely chopped

1 bay leaf

½ cup white wine (optional)

1 whole chicken (2½ to 3 lb), cut into pieces

1½ cups (10 oz) long-grain rice, rinsed and drained

2 teaspoons coarse kosher salt, or to taste

¼ teaspoon freshly ground black pepper, or to taste

½ cup (2½ oz) shelled peas, frozen or fresh

2 tablespoons finely chopped parsley

Tip: *If, like my children, you do not like soft chicken skin, you can transfer the chicken pieces to a baking dish just before adding the rice or potatoes to the pot. Finish cooking the chicken in a 350°F oven for 15 minutes, which gives it a nice crisp skin. Serve on a platter surrounded by the rice or potatoes.*

1. Heat the oil in a 5-quart Dutch oven or heavy-based pot over medium-high heat. Sauté the onion until a light golden color, 10 to 15 minutes.

2. Add the tomatoes, paprika, garlic, and bay leaf. Reduce the heat, cover, and simmer until the tomatoes are soft and partially dissolved, about 15 minutes.

3. Pour in the wine, if using, and simmer for 2 more minutes. Add the chicken and enough water to just cover it (about 3½ cups). Tightly cover the pot and bring to a boil over medium-high heat. Reduce the heat and simmer for 15 minutes.

4. Toss in the rice, salt, and pepper. Stir, re-cover, and continue to simmer for another 20 minutes, until the rice is tender and the liquid has mostly absorbed. Stir in the peas and 1 tablespoon of the parsley. Simmer for 5 minutes more or until the chicken is nearly falling from the bone. Remove the pot from the heat and let the stew rest for 10 minutes before serving. Garnish with the remaining parsley.

Variation: *Add 4 medium potatoes, peeled and quartered, instead of the rice and peas. The potatoes are done when easily pierced with a fork.*

Serves 4

GRILLED CHILI-BASTED CHICKEN

Frango Piri Piri

In Portugal, Cornish hen-size chickens are very popular. As usual, the marinades for this dish vary, but the one constant in all of them is the use of *malagueta* or *piri piri* pepper sauce (see page 20). If you can't find Portuguese hot pepper sauce, you can use your favorite available hot sauce. This is how I make mine, but feel free to ad lib. I serve this with boiled or fried potatoes and a salad drizzled with oil and vinegar.

2 whole Cornish hens or small broiler chickens
   (1½ to 2½ lb each), split in half down the
   middle and butterflied

½ cup olive oil

1 tablespoon coarse kosher salt, or to taste

6 garlic cloves, finely chopped

4 tablespoons either white wine,
   lemon juice, cider, or wine vinegar

1 tablespoon paprika

1 bay leaf

2 tablespoons Portuguese hot pepper sauce
   (*molho picante* or *molho de piri piri*)

Crushed red pepper flakes, to taste

1 tablespoon finely chopped cilantro or parsley

¼ cup Bagaceira brandy, *aguardente* (see page 177),
   or grappa (optional)

1. Lay the butterflied birds in a glass container. Mix the remaining ingredients thoroughly. Coat the chicken on all sides. Cover and marinate for several hours in the refrigerator, turning from time to time. Remove the bay leaf.

2. Grill or broil the chicken, turning occasionally, for 45 to 55 minutes. If you have a rotisserie, use that. Cook the chicken until the juices run clear and the internal temperature is 165°F.

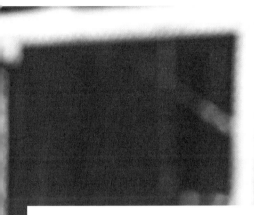

WALTER THE CHICKEN MAN

Growing up in an multiethnic neighborhood, we were used to seeing chickens running around fenced-in backyards. Although less common today, with the convenience of supermarkets, it still occurs. We never bought a chicken in a supermarket. Instead, we went to see Walter the Chicken Man, who received live chickens in cages from poultry farms. When we had selected our chicken, he broke its neck and hung it by its feet over a barrel. After cutting its throat, he drained the blood and dipped the chicken into hot water, then brought it to a machine where a rotating belt pulled out the feathers. Walter's wife gutted and washed our future dinner in the sink. She even trimmed the toenails. The chicken was then packaged up, gizzards, feet, and all.

My younger brothers and sisters were not old enough to have seen the chicken man in action, but they were not spared other chicken experiences. One year my father decided to raise chickens. Naturally my sisters quickly gave them names and treated them as pets. When my sisters discovered that one of their pets was our Sunday dinner, they were understandably very upset, and my mother quickly declared that there would be no more edible pets in our house. After that, we returned to Walter the Chicken Man and used his services until he retired. That same flock of chickens yielded a greater-than-average number of roosters. While this did not please some of our neighbors, those who came from Portugal and Poland loved the roosters, whose predawn crowing reminded them of the old country. Somehow, the eggs and chickens in markets today never taste quite as good as those fresh from the chicken coop.

Although turkeys were raised on our cousin Margaret's farm in Portugal, they seldom were here in America. Before the turkeys in Portugal were slaughtered, they were fed brandy until they were drunk, in hopes of tenderizing the meat. Turkeys were customarily served for dinner on Christmas, Easter, special occasions—and in America, on Thanksgiving. Today, except at Thanksgiving, the focus of festive meals has shifted from turkey to roast beef, lamb, and pork.

Makes about twenty 2½-inch pies

CHICKEN PIES

Empadas de Galinha

Edite Biscaia, who comes from the Alentejo region where these little pies are commonly made, shared her recipe with me. She lines small tart or muffin pans with circles of dough, adds the filling and a top crust, and creates these little pies. I prefer the more flavorful dark meat of chicken legs and thighs for this recipe. These little pies are great as appetizers, snacks, and at picnics. The filling can be made a day ahead. I use unfluted tart tins, 2½-inches in diameter and 1 inch deep, but you can also use mini muffin pans with openings of a similar size (for larger openings, you will need to adjust the size of your pastry circles). (Pictured on page 116.)

FILLING

2½ to 3 lb chicken pieces (legs and thighs)

2 garlic cloves, peeled

2 large sprigs of parsley

1 bay leaf

1 cup white wine, or ½ cup wine vinegar
   and ½ cup white wine

2 tablespoons olive oil

4 strips lean bacon

1 small onion, coarsely chopped (about ½ cup)

4 oz *chouriço* or *linguiça* sausage (see page 168),
   casing removed, coarsely chopped

2 teaspoons coarse kosher salt, or to taste

1 teaspoon ground marjoram

½ teaspoon ground white pepper

2 egg yolks, lightly beaten

PASTRY

1½ cups (6¾ oz) all-purpose flour,
   plus more for dusting

½ cup (2 oz) cake flour

1 teaspoon table salt

4 tablespoons (2 oz) cold butter, firm but
   pliable, cut in pieces, plus more for greasing

2 egg yolks, lightly beaten

½ cup cold water or milk

For the filling

1. In a 4-quart soup pot, place the chicken, garlic, parsley, and bay leaf. Pour in the wine or vinegar mixture, and just enough water to cover the top of the chicken (about 4 cups). Cover and bring to a boil over medium-high heat. Reduce the heat and simmer until the chicken is nearly falling from the bone, about 50 minutes.

2. Using tongs, remove the chicken, reserving the broth. When the chicken is cool, remove the meat from the bones. Coarsely chop or shred the meat and place it in a medium bowl (you should have about 2 cups). Set aside.

3. In a small frying pan, heat the oil with the bacon until hot, but not smoking. Sauté the bacon until the fat is rendered. Remove and the solid pieces and set them aside. Add the onion to the pan and sauté until nearly golden, about 8 minutes. Mix in the sausage, salt, marjoram, and pepper. Cook for 2 to 3 minutes or until the sausage lightly browns and releases some of its juices. Add to the bowl containing the chicken. Crumble in the crisp bacon and mix well.

4. Strain the broth. Whisk about ½ cup of the broth into the egg yolks to emulsify. Mix the egg mixture, 2 to 4 tablespoons at a time, into the chicken mixture until it comes together into a loose ball, somewhat like loose meatballs. You should have about 3 cups of filling.

For the pastry

5. Sift the flours and salt together into a bowl, along with the butter. Using a fork or pastry cutter, cut the butter into the flour until coarse lumps appear throughout.

6. Pile the flour-butter mixture onto a work surface. Make a well in the center and pour in the beaten yolks, along with 1 tablespoon of the water or milk. Using a fork, blend the eggs with the water or milk, gradually pulling in more of the flour. Slowly add the remaining liquid to the middle, simultaneously mixing in more flour. When the mixture is too thick to mix with the fork, turn it with your hand until it starts to form a dough. Lightly dust with flour and gently knead until pliable but not sticky, but be careful not to overwork the dough.

7. Dust lightly with additional flour, cover, and let the dough rest for 15 minutes.

To assemble

8. Preheat the oven to 400°F.

9. Divide the dough in half. Roll out one-half to about ⅛-inch thick and cut into 3-inch circles. Repeat with the second portion of dough. You should have about 40 circles in total. Grease about twenty 2½-inch diameter tart tins with butter, and line them with half of the dough circles.

10. Place 1 tablespoon of the filling in the center of each dough circle in the tins. Place a second circle on top, press the edges together, and turn them upwards to seal. Repeat until all the filling is used.

11. Bake for 25 minutes, or until golden. Serve hot or room temperature.

Tip: *You may find it easier and quicker to do all of one operation at a time: first line all the individual tins with a circle of dough, fill each one, and then top each one with a second circle of dough.*

Shortcuts: *I find that the following method is easy, especially if I am in a hurry. I use a ravioli mold that has open round pockets. Assemble the pies as you would ravioli. After sealing the filling with the top crust, separate the individual "pies," placing the flat side down and pinching up the edges. Bake on a parchment-lined baking sheet. The mold makes 12 pastries at a time. The shape, of course, is not traditional, but it works well if you are pressed for time. Another speedy method, also not traditional, is to cut rolled out sheets of dough into squares, place a small amount of filling in the middle, and fold the dough over into triangles.*

There is also a filling shortcut: With the exception of the yolks, combine all of the filling ingredients in the pot, leaving the sausage whole, and cook until the chicken is very tender. Remove the meats. Cut the sausage and bacon into small pieces and shred the chicken meat. Strain the broth, and continue with the remaining two steps to complete the filling.

CUTTING TECHNIQUES

The cutting techniques I learned from my father require skill, good eye-hand coordination, and much practice. To finely chop an onion, for example, I cut it in half and hold one section, cut-side up, in my left hand. Using a sharp paring knife, I make controlled crosshatch cuts half an inch deep as I turn the onion. Then I cut a slice horizontally beneath the cross-hatch cuts, releasing pieces of minced onion. I learned young, and constant practice made this method second nature to me, so I can honestly claim to be accident-free. However, my dear father-in-law was horrified when he first saw me cutting onions this way, and actually scolded me! I will add that a sharp knife and a cutting board yield the same results with greater safety.

Serves 8

ROASTED CHICKEN

Galinha Assada

The secret to this recipe is browning the chicken pieces in a cast-iron pan, instructs Senhorina Bettencourt, who has made many gatherings noteworthy by serving her garlic-and-wine-marinated chicken dish. The recipe can easily be doubled for picnics, buffet tables, and Super Bowl parties. It is a guaranteed hit. Chicken wings also make flavorful appetizers when prepared this way (add hot pepper sauce for extra zing).

8 to 10 chicken legs, halved at joint

2 tablespoons coarse kosher salt, or to taste

1 tablespoon white or black pepper, or to taste

10 garlic cloves, finely chopped

1 large onion, thinly sliced

½ cup olive oil

MARINADE

1 cup red wine

3 tablespoons tomato paste

1 cup water

3 garlic cloves, mashed

1 tablespoon Hot Pepper Paste
  (page 220, optional)

1. Using a sharp knife, remove excess fat from each piece of chicken, including any under the skin. Blot with a clean towel. Season each piece with salt, pepper, and chopped garlic, seasoning all sides and under the skin. Place the chicken in a glass or ceramic bowl and top with the onion slices.

2. Prepare the marinade in a separate bowl: mix the red wine with the tomato paste. Slowly stir in the measured water, mashed garlic cloves, and hot pepper paste, if using. Mix well and pour over the chicken. Marinate in the refrigerator for several hours or overnight.

3. About 1½ hours before serving, use tongs to transfer the chicken to a separate dish to drain, reserving the marinade. Preheat the oven to 350ºF.

4. In a black cast-iron skillet, heat the olive oil over medium-high heat, so that it is very hot, but not smoking. Add the chicken, a few pieces at a time, and brown on all sides.

5. Place the browned chicken in a covered roasting pan, preferably of dark enamel. Roast, basting frequently with the marinade, for 1 hour or until the chicken is nearly falling from the bone. Remove the cover during the last 15 minutes of roasting.

Serves 6

GRILLED PORK CUTLETS

Febras de Porco Grelhadas

Backyard chefs enjoy grilling these tasty cutlets. Easy to prepare, they are perfect as a light meal; you can serve them in crusty rolls alongside soup and a salad. They are also great topped with sautéed onions and Roasted Sweet Peppers (page 204).

2 garlic cloves, finely chopped

½ tablespoon Sweet Red Pepper Paste (page 219)

2 tablespoons olive oil

6 lean boneless pork cutlets, ½-inch thick

1. Using a mortar and pestle, mash the garlic and blend well with the sweet red pepper paste. Add the oil and mix well. Spread this mixture over the cutlets, coating both sides evenly.

2. Preheat your barbecue and grill the cutlets over hot flames, for about 3 minutes each side. Be careful not to overcook.

Serves 6

ALENTEJO-STYLE PORK WITH CLAMS

Carne de Porco à Alentejana

The name of this popular dish implies origins in the province of Alentejo. According to some, however, it originated in the Algarve region. It is traditionally made with tiny sweet cockles, which are difficult to find here. Instead, I use the smallest littleneck clams that I can find (no bigger than 2 to 3 inches) or steamer clams, if that is all I can get. The pork is traditionally browned in lard or bacon fat, but olive oil can be used instead. It will have a slightly different flavor, but still definitely Portuguese. I prefer to use a lean pork tenderloin, but less expensive pork butt can be used alone or in combination with more expensive cuts of pork, especially if you're cooking for a large crowd. Keep in mind that pork tenderloin takes less time to cook than the butt end. The boiled potatoes traditionally served with this dish have given way to the popular fried potatoes.

DAY AHEAD

1½ lb pork tenderloin, trimmed of
   the silvery tendon or sinew

1 lb pork butt, trimmed of visible fat,
   gristle, and sinew

8 garlic cloves, or to taste, coarsely chopped

1 tablespoon paprika

¼ teaspoon freshly ground black pepper

1 bay leaf, crumbled

¼ cup (½ oz) finely chopped cilantro

1 tablespoon Sweet Red Pepper Paste (page 219)

2 teaspoons hot pepper sauce

1 cup white wine

3 lb count littleneck clams, 2 to 3 inches in diameter,
   (about 6 per person)

Continued

A day ahead

1. Cut the pork into cubes no greater than 1½ inches. Place in a chilled ceramic or glass bowl.

2. Using a mortar and pestle, mash the garlic. Blend in the paprika, black pepper, and bay leaf, forming a paste. Mix in the cilantro, red pepper paste, and hot pepper sauce, blending well.

3. Blot the cubes of pork with a paper towel to absorb any excess moisture. Using clean hands, rub the garlic mixture onto the pork, coating the pieces thoroughly.

4. Pour the wine over the pork. Mix gently, cover, and marinate for 24 hours in the refrigerator, turning the meat occasionally.

5. Purge the clams, following instructions on page 82.

The next day

6. About 30 minutes before cooking, remove the pork from the marinade and transfer to a separate bowl, reserving the marinade. Allow the meat to drain well.

7. Heat ¼ cup of the olive oil in a 2-quart saucepan over medium-high heat until very hot, but not smoking. Add the onion and sauté until golden, about 15 minutes. Reduce the heat to medium-low and stir in the tomato. Cover, and simmer until

NEXT DAY

½ cup olive oil

1 medium onion, finely chopped

1 large very ripe tomato, peeled, seeded, and coarsely chopped

Reserved marinade

3 large cilantro sprigs, finely chopped, plus extra to garnish

1 tablespoon tomato paste (optional)

1 cup white wine

Finely sliced sweet red pepper, to garnish

Tips: *You can make the sauce earlier in the day and refrigerate until needed: remove the pork from the marinade, transfer to another bowl, cover, and refrigerate until 30 minutes before cooking. Make the onion and tomato sauce as directed and refrigerate until needed.*

If deep-red flavorful tomatoes are not available, substitute good-quality canned tomatoes or add a tablespoon of tomato paste to the sauce along with the chopped tomatoes.

When we cook for a huge crowd, we steam the clams separately and incorporate some of the clam juice into the onion-and-tomato sauce, to which the browned meat is eventually added.

the tomato is soft and partially dissolved, about 15 minutes. Strain the reserved marinade, then add it to the tomato mixture. Blend in the chopped cilantro and tomato paste. Stirring occasionally, continue to simmer gently, uncovered, for 30 minutes or until mixture has reduced by one-third. Set aside.

8. Heat the remaining ¼ cup olive oil in a large heavy frying pan over medium-high heat until very hot, but not smoking. In small batches, without crowding, gently brown the drained pork until golden, about 10 minutes per batch. (Crowding and excessively damp meat will prevent proper browning.) Using a slotted spoon, transfer the browned meat to a plate, cover, and keep warm.

9. Pour off any excess fat from the pan, and then add the tomato mixture and the wine. Bring to a simmer over medium-low heat and cook for 2 to 3 minutes, scraping up caramelized drippings from the bottom of the pan, and stirring to blend well. Return the pork to the pan and continue to simmer gently for 15 minutes. Do not allow the mixture to boil.

10. Place the clams on top of the meat and cover the pan. Continue to simmer until the pork is fork-tender and the clams have opened, 10 to 15 minutes, depending on the size and type of shellfish used. Discard any unopened clams. Transfer to a serving platter and garnish with the remaining cilantro and the red pepper slices. Surround with small boiled potatoes or top with fried potato cubes, if desired.

Variations: *Friends who are originally from northern Portugal use paprika and salt instead of sweet red pepper paste; others marinate with lemon juice instead of wine. I have even seen some Portuguese cooks add a small amount of coarsely chopped* linquiça *or* chouriço *sausage and a tablespoon or two of butter to the sauce, leaving traditionalists shaking their heads.*

Serves 6

SAUTÉED MEDALLIONS OF MARINATED PORK

Bifanas de Porco

Bifanas are medallions of pork or beef marinated with wine and garlic and then pan-fried. Served with caramelized onions in crusty rolls called *papo-secos* (page 238), they make perfect sandwiches.

DAY AHEAD

3 garlic cloves, coarsely chopped

1 teaspoon coarse kosher salt

1 teaspoon Hot Pepper Paste (page 220), or to taste

3 teaspoons paprika, divided

12 pork loin medallions, ¼- to ½-inch thick (about 1¼ lb total)

2 cups white wine, or more if needed

NEXT DAY

Olive oil, for frying

3 large onions, thinly sliced

6 *Papo-secos* (page 238), or other crusty rolls, to serve

Dijon mustard, to serve (optional)

A day ahead

1. Using a mortar and pestle, mash the garlic with the salt, forming a paste. Blend in the hot pepper paste and 1 teaspoon of the paprika.

2. Coat the medallions evenly with the paste and place in a shallow dish.

3. Pour in the wine, adding more if necessary, to just cover the meat. Marinate the medallions in the refrigerator overnight.

The next day

4. Remove the medallions from the marinade and drain, discarding the marinade.

5. Heat ½ cup of oil in a medium frying pan over medium-high heat. Add the onions and sauté until nearly golden, about 7 minutes. Add the remaining paprika and cook for 3 minutes more. Cover and set aside, keeping them warm.

6. Pour enough oil into a large frying pan to cover the bottom by ½ inch. Heat the oil over medium-high heat until very hot, but not smoking. In small batches so as not to crowd the pan, quickly fry the medallions until brown, about 1 minute each side. Serve in crusty rolls with the onions, mustard, and an ice-cold beer.

ROASTED PORK LOIN WITH SWEET RED PEPPER PASTE

Lombo de Porco Assado com Massa de Pimentão

This was—and still is—a popular dish in our home, especially with potatoes roasted with traditional seasonings (*Batatas Assadas*, page 184). This style is of the Alentejo.

2 large garlic cloves, finely chopped

1 bay leaf, crumbled

1 teaspoon paprika

1 tablespoon Sweet Red Pepper Paste (page 219)

2 tablespoons olive oil, plus more for oiling

3 lb boneless pork loin roast

Tip: *If you are planning to serve roasted potatoes with this dish, you can roast them in the same pan as the pork.*

1. Preheat the oven to 350°F and lightly oil a roasting pan.

2. Using a mortar and pestle, mash the garlic, bay leaf, and paprika. Blend in the sweet red pepper paste. Slowly drizzle in the olive oil and mix.

3. Cut crosshatches on the surface of the pork. Rub the paste all over the meat, pushing some of the paste into the crosshatches. Place in the prepared roasting pan.

4. Roast until the pork reaches an internal temperature of 150°F, about 1 hour. Let the meat rest for 10 to 15 minutes before carving. The roast will continue to cook during the standing time. Slice and transfer to a serving platter.

Serves 4 to 6

BEIRA ALTA–STYLE ROASTED PORK LOIN

Lombo de Porco à Moda da Beira Alta

Teresa Cunha Mendonça, a friend and neighbor, who is originally from the Beira Alta region, uses citrus juices to marinate pork. The orange and lemon juices marry nicely with the white wine to give the meat an extraordinary flavor.

2 garlic cloves

1½ tablespoons coarse kosher salt

½ teaspoon ground white pepper

3 lb boneless pork loin roast

Juice of 1 lemon (about ¼ cup)

Juice of 1 orange (about ½ cup)

1 cup white wine

1 medium very ripe tomato, peeled, seeded, and finely chopped

1 tablespoon red wine vinegar

4 tablespoons (2 oz) butter, cut into pieces

1 orange, cut into thin wedges

1 lemon, cut into thin wedges

1. Using a mortar and pestle, mash the garlic with the salt and pepper to form a paste. Wipe excess moisture from the meat. Rub the paste all over the meat, pushing it into any crevices and coating all sides.

2. Place the pork in a roasting pan and pour the citrus juices over it. Add the wine, tomato, and vinegar. Marinate for 1 to 2 hours in the refrigerator, turning occasionally.

3. Preheat the oven to 350°F. Remove the pan from the refrigerator and dot the roast with the butter, distributing the pieces evenly over the top. Roast, basting occasionally with the pan juices, until a meat thermometer indicates an internal temperature of 150°F, about 1 hour. Let the roast rest for 10 to 15 minutes before carving. Slice and arrange the pork on a serving platter and garnish with the orange and lemon wedges.

Serves 4 to 6

TRIPE

Dobrada

Although *dobrada* originated in Oporto, north of Lisbon, this version is adapted from a dish that graces the dinner table of Isaura Nogueira, who is originally from Beira Alta in the Azores. This adventuresome dish is made by cooking tripe, beans, and meat separately, then bringing them together in a lightly spiced sauce. In mainland Portugal, this stew is traditionally made with lima beans. In the Azores, however, white kidney beans were historically more plentiful, so Azoreans tend to use them in this stew still. The sauce of this continental version is paler than the red Azorean version. And here, the juice of oranges is used in place of the more common lemon juice. Simple preparations begin two days ahead, so plan accordingly.

The tripe available in markets today is of good quality, white, and clean. Nonetheless, I suggest the additional cleaning procedure that follows.

ONE TO TWO DAYS AHEAD

2 medium meaty pig's hocks

5 tablespoons coarse kosher salt, or as needed

DAY AHEAD

2½ cups (1 lb) dried lima or white kidney beans

2½ lb tripe

1½ cups coarse kosher salt, or as needed

½ cup white vinegar

Juice of 1 large orange (reserve the peel)

NEXT DAY

½ small onion

¼ cup white wine

3 garlic cloves

1 bay leaf

Continued

One to two days ahead

1. Rinse the hocks and pat dry. Heavily salt the hocks on all sides, place in a shallow dish, cover, and refrigerate for up to 2 days.

A day ahead

2. Place the beans in a large bowl and rinse with water. Pick through the beans, removing any stones and shriveled, deformed, or floating beans. Drain and rinse again. Soak the beans overnight in enough water to cover them by 2 inches (6 to 8 cups).

3. Next, clean the tripe: Using a sharp paring knife, remove any excess fat from the side opposite the honeycomb; the fat is whiter than the creamy color of the tripe.

4. Rub the coarse salt completely and thoroughly over the tripe and into the crevices on both sides, as if you are scrubbing it. Rinse several times with water. Place in a dish and pour the vinegar over it, coating both sides. Let stand for 30 minutes, then rinse well.

5. Place the tripe in a medium bowl and pour orange juice over it, tossing in the peel. Turn the tripe in the juice to make sure it is coated all over. Cover and refrigerate overnight, or for a minimum of 6 hours.

SAUCE

3 tablespoons olive oil

2 oz slab bacon, cut into ½-inch cubes

8 oz *chouriço* sausage (see page 168),
  cut into ¼-inch slices

1 large onion, finely chopped

3 garlic cloves, coarsely chopped

1 small very ripe tomato, peeled, seeded, finely
  chopped, or 2 tablespoons tomato paste

½ cup white wine

1 tablespoon hot pepper sauce

1 bay leaf

The next day

6. First, cook the tripe: Discard the orange juice and peel and rinse the tripe. Put it in a 4-quart saucepan with enough water to barely cover the meat. Cover tightly and bring to a boil over medium-high heat. Reduce the heat and gently simmer the tripe for 2½ to 3 hours, to your desired tenderness. (Some Portuguese like the tripe to be tender but with some chew to it; while others like to cook further, until it is very soft.) Drain the tripe well, discarding the cooking water. Cut into 1-inch pieces. Cool, cover, and refrigerate until needed.

7. Meanwhile, cook the hocks: Rinse the hocks of the salt and place in a 2-quart saucepan with the onion, wine, garlic, bay leaf, and enough water to cover it completely. Cover and bring to a boil over medium-high heat. Reduce the heat and simmer until the meat is falling from the bone, about 1 hour. Reserving the liquid, remove the hocks and set aside to cool. Remove the meat, fat, and skin and cut into 1-inch cubes. Discard the bone. If desired, strain the broth. Cool and refrigerate the meat and broth until needed.

8. Cook the beans: Once the hocks are cooking, drain and rinse the beans. Place them in a 4-quart pot with enough fresh water to cover them by about 2 inches (6 to 8 cups). Cover and bring to a boil, then reduce the heat and simmer, stirring the beans occasionally, for 45 minutes to 1 hour, until tender but not mushy. Transfer the cooking water and the beans into separate containers to chill until needed.

Make the sauce

9. Heat the oil in a 4-quart saucepan over medium-high heat. Add and sauté the bacon, cooking until the fat has been rendered. Remove the solid pieces and reserve. Toss in the *chouriço* and briefly sauté until lightly browned, then remove and reserve. Add the onions to the pan drippings and sauté until golden.

10. Add the garlic and cook until it becomes aromatic. Reduce the heat to medium-low and stir in the tomato. Cover and simmer until the tomato is partially dissolved, about 15 minutes. Pour in the wine, hot pepper sauce, and bay leaf. Simmer for 2 minutes.

Assemble the stew

11. Add the drained beans, the hock meat, tripe, sausage, and bacon, stirring to mix. Pour in equal amounts of the cooking liquids from the beans and the hocks, starting with 1 cup of each, until you reach the desired texture—the stew should be slightly thicker than a soup but not as thick as chili. Simmer for 10 minutes. If the stew is too thick, thin it with additional broth. Serve in deep bowls with bread on the side or spoon over hot boiled white rice.

Serves 4 to 6

SPICY TRIPE

Dobrada Picante

Originally from Graciosa, John Silva is the quiet bartender at the Portuguese Veterans Post #1 in Peabody, Massachusetts. Though he insists he is not a cook, his recipe for tripe says otherwise. The basic preparations are essentially the same as in the preceding recipe, except the bacon and *chouriço* are boiled whole with the hocks instead of fried separately. For his sauce, John uses lard to fry the onions, but he says you can use olive oil. His Azorean touch makes for a spicier sauce—one that attracts customers on Saturdays at noon. Here is his secret recipe, which he was generous enough to share. Read through the recipe for tripe on page 134, and plan ahead.

Ingredients for Tripe (page 134), except for
   the sauce ingredients

SAUCE

1½ tablespoons olive oil or lard

¾ cup (4 oz) finely chopped onion

8 garlic cloves, coarsely chopped

Scant ½ cup canned tomato sauce or
   homemade *Tomatada* (page 216)

Scant ½ cup hot pepper sauce

5 tablespoons tomato paste

1 teaspoon paprika

Scant ½ teaspoon ground cumin

1. Using the same measurements, follow the instructions to clean and cook the tripe, beans, and hocks in the tripe recipe on page 134, except add the bacon and sausage whole to the pot with the hocks, instead of frying them. When the hocks are done, remove the bones from the hocks and chop the meat and fat into ½-inch cubes. Cut the bacon into ½-inch cubes, and slice the sausage into ¼-inch rounds. Set aside, with the broth.

2. Next, make the sauce: Heat the olive oil or lard in a 5-quart saucepan over medium-high heat. Sauté the onion until translucent. Toss in the garlic and sauté until it is aromatic. Stir in the tomato sauce, hot sauce, a scant ½ cup water, the tomato paste, and paprika. Reduce the heat and simmer until the paste is dissolved, then add the cooked tripe, boiled sausage, bacon, and hock meat (reserving the broth).

3. For this version, drain the beans (discarding the cooking liquid) before adding them to the pot. Pour in just enough of the broth from cooking the hocks (about 8 cups) so that the stew is the right consistency: not as thick as chili, but not as thin as vegetable soup. Sprinkle the ground cumin over the top, stir, then simmer for about 10 minutes. Serve with bread or rice.

Serves 8 to 10

STUFFED PORK LOIN

Lombo de Porco Recheado

In this recipe, *chouriço* sausages and caramelized onions make a perfect stuffing without overpowering the pork. Have the butcher butterfly the loin or cut it yourself so it will lie open to be stuffed. I do not recommend a roast made from two loins tied together, simply because the slices do not hold together well during carving. The length of the roast determines the amount of sausage used. For instance, if the roast is 8 inches long, I cut a link of sausage the same length. If the sausage is left whole and surrounded by the onions, the carved servings have a charming bull's-eye effect. Not only is this recipe easily adaptable for larger roasts, but the simplicity and flavor of this dish makes it perfect for entertaining.

½ cup olive oil

2 large onions, finely chopped (about 3 cups)

1½ links (10 oz) *chouriço* sausage (see page 168), casings removed, coarsely chopped or left whole

6 oz São Jorge cheese (see page 19), or other semi-soft cheese, such as Havarti, shredded (about 1½ cups)

4 tablespoons finely chopped parsley

4 lb boneless pork loin roast, butterflied

3 garlic cloves, coarsely chopped

2 teaspoons coarse kosher salt

2 teaspoons paprika

¼ teaspoon freshly ground black pepper

1 bay leaf, crumbed

1. Preheat the oven to 350°F.

2. Heat ¼ cup of the oil in a medium-sized frying pan over medium-high heat until it is hot, but not smoking. Add the onions and sauté until quite golden. Add the sausage and sauté for 3 minutes. Transfer the onions and sausage to a medium bowl. Set aside to cool for about 15 minutes.

3. Add the shredded cheese and 1½ tablespoons of the parsley to the onions and sausage and mix well.

4. Open the roast flat on a work surface and spread the sausage mixture over the meat, leaving a 1-inch border around the edges. Roll the meat up like a jelly roll, and tie securely with butcher's twine, enclosing the ends. (If you are leaving the sausage whole, first spread the cooked onions and cheese over the meat, then place the sausage along the length of the roast, roll the roast around the sausage, and tie with butcher's twine so it is fully enclosed.)

5. Using a mortar and pestle, mash the garlic with the salt, paprika, and pepper. Mix in 1 tablespoon of the parsley, the crumbled bay leaf, and 2 tablespoons of the olive oil. Rub the paste over all sides of the meat and into the crevices, and place in a lightly oiled roasting pan.

6. Roast in the preheated oven for 1 hour, or until the internal temperature is 150°F. Remove from the oven and let the meat rest for 10 to 15 minutes before carving. Serve with rice or potatoes.

Variations: *You can add 1 to 1½ cups lightly cooked, well drained, chopped spinach to the stuffing. You can also use* presunto *or* prosciutto *in place of the sausage, or use fillet of beef in place of pork.*

Serves 4

ALENTEJO-STYLE PIG'S FEET

Pés de Porco à Alentejana

Elvira Covil came from the same area as my father—the Alentejo—where pork recipes are plentiful. The pig's feet can be used alone in this recipe or combined with hocks, which have more meat. My father would use his pocket knife to eat this dish, scraping the bones, to get every last bit of meat. Elvira cooks the meat with the sauce, but I suggest that you cook the meat separately to eliminate much of the gelatin and strong flavor.

DAY AHEAD

2½ cups (1 lb) dried lima or white kidney beans

4 small pig's feet or hocks

About ½ cup (4 oz) coarse kosher salt

NEXT DAY

1 small onion, peeled, left whole

¼ cup olive oil

2 large onions, thinly sliced

2 garlic cloves, coarsely chopped

1 scant tablespoon paprika

2 teaspoons coarse kosher salt, or to taste

¼ teaspoon pepper, or to taste

1 bay leaf

1 large very ripe tomato, peeled and coarsely chopped

½ cup white wine

½ tablespoon apple cider vinegar

1 tablespoon finely chopped cilantro or parsley

A day ahead

1. Soak the beans overnight in enough water to cover them by 2 inches (6 to 8 cups). Coat the pig's feet or hocks with the coarse salt and refrigerate them overnight.

The next day

2. Rinse the salt from the pig's feet or hocks, then place them in a 4-quart pot. Add the whole onion and enough water to cover the ingredients. Cover tightly and bring to a boil over medium-high heat. Reduce the heat to medium-low and simmer until the meat is nearly falling from the bone, about 1½ hours, though cooking may take longer depending on the age of the pig and size of the feet. When done, drain and discard the cooking water and set the feet or hocks aside.

3. Meanwhile, drain and rinse the beans. Place the beans in a separate 3-quart saucepan and add enough water to cover them by 2 inches (6 to 8 cups). Cover and bring to a boil. Reduce the heat and simmer until the beans are tender, about 45 minutes. Turn off the heat and reserve the beans, in their cooking liquid.

4. After the beans are cooked, heat the olive oil in a 4-quart pot over medium-high heat. Add and sauté the onions until they are a light golden color. Stir in the garlic, paprika, salt, pepper, and bay leaf, and cook for 1 minute, or until the garlic is aromatic. Mix in the tomatoes and cover the pot. Reduce the heat and simmer until the tomatoes have broken down with the onions and you have a sauce-like consistency, about 10 minutes.

5. Pour in the wine and apple cider vinegar, then stir in the beans, along with their cooking liquid, and the cilantro. Cover and simmer for another 10 minutes. Add the pig's feet or hocks, turn to coat them with the sauce, heat through, and serve.

Serves 8

MILK-BRAISED PORK LOIN

Lombo de Porco Assado com Leite

I have to admit I was skeptical when my friend Ester Mendonca told me about this very old method of cooking pork loin from the Azorean Island of Pico. However, I gave it a try and I was not disappointed. The loin was extremely moist and very tender. The milk became subtly infused with the flavor of the meat. I wanted to take advantage of the milk and so I thickened it with a cornstarch slurry, creating a savory white sauce, giving it a personal touch. This is best cooked in a clay roasting pot, but you can use a roasting pan or casserole dish.

3 lb boneless pork loin roast

1 tablespoon coarse kosher salt

½ teaspoon ground white pepper

1 medium onion, sliced

3 tablespoons olive oil or butter

2 garlic cloves, peeled and smashed

2 tablespoons (1 oz) butter, cubed

1 large bay leaf

3 cups whole milk, or more if needed

2 tablespoons cornstarch, mixed with
    2 tablespoons water

Note: *During the cooking time the milk will form a skin and slightly balloon. The traditional use of a clay pot helps to absorb excess moisture, concentrating the flavor and allowing the surface of the meat to caramelize. In a clay pot, there may be very little milk left for the sauce, so you will need to supplement with fresh milk, and the flavor may not be as intense.*

1. Preheat the oven to 350°F.

2. Season the pork all over with the salt and pepper. If you wish, pan-sear the roast in a cast-iron pan to give it a golden color (though it will further brown in the oven). In a separate pan, sauté the onions in the olive oil or butter, until nicely golden.

3. Place the roast in a presoaked unglazed clay roasting pot or a small nonreactive (stainless steel or ceramic) roasting pan or casserole dish with deep sides. Top the meat with the onions, garlic, butter, and bay leaf. Pour in enough milk so that it comes about three-quarters of the way up the sides of the roast.

4. Roast until the internal temperature of the pork reaches 150°F, about 2 hours, turning the meat periodically as the top of the roast browns, so that the browned part becomes submerged in the milk. As you continue doing this, eventually the whole roast will brown and its flavor will infuse the milk.

5. Transfer the roast to a cutting board (reserving the milk), cover, and let rest while you make the sauce.

6. Measure 2 cups of the flavored milk (adding fresh milk, if needed to make 2 cups) and pour it into a small saucepan. Place over medium-low heat. Stir in the cornstarch slurry and continue stirring until the milk becomes the consistency of heavy cream. You can strain the sauce into a gravy boat or serving bowl if you wish.

7. Slice the pork into serving pieces and place onto a serving platter. Ladle some of the sauce over and serve with extra sauce on the side.

Serves 4 to 6

GRILLED RABBIT

Coelho Grelhado

This recipe takes outdoor grilling beyond the everyday burgers and hot dogs. Poultry, rabbit, sausages, lamb, or seafood are more likely to appear on my grill—to the delight of eager eaters. Start this recipe one day ahead.

2 garlic cloves, finely chopped

1 teaspoon coarse kosher salt, or to taste

2 tablespoons finely chopped parsley

1 tablespoon paprika

¼ teaspoon ground white pepper

1 small onion, finely chopped

2 cups dry white wine

¼ cup olive oil

One 3 to 4 lb rabbit, cut into serving pieces

1. Using a mortar and pestle, mash the garlic with the salt, forming a paste. Blend in the parsley, paprika, and pepper. Transfer to a small bowl and add the onion. Stir in the wine. Pouring slowly, whisk in the olive oil.

2. Place the rabbit in a bowl or deep dish. Pour the marinade over the meat, cover, and refrigerate overnight.

3. The next day, transfer the rabbit to a bowl, reserving the marinade. Grill or broil the rabbit, basting with the marinade, until tender. Serve hot.

Serves 4 to 6

HUNTER-STYLE RABBIT

Coelho à Caçador

Hunters, like fishermen, did not carry much cooking equipment with them. Of all the rabbit stews, this one, my favorite, could not be simpler. Everything is added at once and, like the one-pot fishermen's stew, *Caldeirada com Mariscos* (page 100), it is cooked very slowly. This dish is traditionally served with potatoes and red wine.

One 4 lb rabbit, cut into serving pieces

1 large onion, coarsely chopped

1 large very ripe tomato, peeled, seeded, and coarsely chopped

2 strips bacon, coarsely chopped

4 tablespoons olive oil

¼ cup (½ oz) finely chopped parsley

4 garlic cloves, coarsely chopped

1 tablespoon coarse kosher salt, or to taste

1 teaspoon paprika

1 teaspoon Hot Pepper Paste (page 220)

¼ teaspoon freshly ground black pepper

1 bay leaf

1 cup red wine

1. In a heavy-bottom, 4-quart pot, combine all the ingredients except for the wine. Turn to mix thoroughly.

2. Pour the wine over the top, cover tightly, and place over medium-high heat. Listen carefully for the sound of boiling, immediately reduce the heat to medium-low, and simmer, covered, for about 1 hour or until the rabbit is tender, and easily pierced with a fork. Serve with boiled potatoes.

Note: *If you are using an electric stove, remove the pot when the ingredients start to boil, until the heat of the burner has cooled down a bit.*

Tip: *To cut rabbit in serving pieces, sever behind the front legs and in front of the back legs, cutting straight across. Separate the upper pieces in half, along the backbone. The middle can be cut crosswise in two, if it is large enough.*

In his eagerness to teach his children the ways of our culture, my father's methods sometimes backfired. During one "lesson," Dad was demonstrating to my older brother Joe how to prepare a live rabbit for dinner. With some reluctance, Joe quietly watched my father kill and skin a rabbit, and followed him into the kitchen, where my father prepared his tasty dish. After adding the last of the seasoning to the pot, my father turned to Joe and asked whether he would like to try some. Pensively, without much hesitation, Joe replied, "I, uh, don't think so." My father couldn't comprehend his reluctance. The rest of the family had no trouble enjoying the meal.

Serves 4 to 6

BAKED RABBIT WITH ONION SAUCE

Coelho com Cebolada

At one time, freshly killed rabbits were readily available from friends or neighbors. Now there are not as many people raising rabbits in their backyards, but rabbit is more often available in supermarkets. This recipe has origins in my father's hometown of Galveias. The flavor of the onion sauce is absorbed by the meat, resulting in a flavor worth savoring. It surprises many that rabbit prepared in the Portuguese manner does not have a gamey taste. It is customary to use rendered pork fat in this recipe, but I prefer butter. As with any of the rabbit recipes in this book, this can be easily prepared with chicken.

One 3½ to 4 lb rabbit, cut into serving pieces
4 garlic cloves, finely chopped
¼ cup (½ oz) finely chopped parsley
1 teaspoon coarse kosher salt, or to taste
½ teaspoon freshly ground black pepper
½ teaspoon Hot Pepper Paste (page 220)
  or crushed red pepper flakes
1 bay leaf
2 cups white wine
4 tablespoons (2 oz) butter or olive oil
3 large onions, thinly sliced
1 medium tomato, peeled and coarsely chopped,
  or 1 tablespoon tomato paste
Parsley sprigs, to garnish

A day ahead

1. In a large bowl, combine the rabbit with the garlic, parsley, salt, black pepper, hot pepper paste, and bay leaf. Turn to mix. Add the wine, adding more if needed, to just cover the rabbit. Cover and refrigerate overnight.

The next day

2. Preheat the oven to 350°F. Reserving the marinade, transfer the rabbit to a separate dish.

3. Melt the butter or oil in a large frying pan over medium-high heat until it starts to sizzle. Add the rabbit and lightly brown on all sides. Transfer the rabbit to a 9- by 13-inch baking dish.

4. Add the onions to the same pan and sauté over medium-high heat until light golden, about 6 minutes. Stir in the tomato, and the garlic and bay leaf from the marinade (reserving the rest of the marinade). Reduce the heat, cover, and simmer until the tomatoes have broken down, about 10 minutes. Stir in the reserved marinade and simmer for about 5 minutes, until slightly thickened. Ladle the sauce over the rabbit.

5. Bake in the preheated oven until tender, about 1 hour. Garnish with parsley sprigs and serve with boiled potatoes.

On our son's seventh birthday, while he and his friends were playing in another room, a freshly killed, skinned rabbit was brought to me by a friend. I immediately placed the rabbit in a colander in the kitchen sink to rinse and drain. There the rabbit sat, upright in the colander, until our daughter noticed it and ran to tell her brother and his friends. What a commotion followed! Before I knew it, ten children were crowded around my kitchen sink, staring at the rabbit, which stared silently back at them! Some of the parents, hearing this story, called to tease me about what else I might be cooking up.

I usually saved the head of the rabbit for my father who, like many Portuguese, considered rabbit brains a delicacy. Unless you can find freshly killed rabbit, most rabbits you will find in supermarkets are headless which, I must admit, pleases me.

Recording recipes for this book, I found myself asking silly questions like, "How much rabbit blood do you use for the rice?" I shook my head and chuckled as soon as I asked the question because I knew the obvious response from my friend Isaura would be "whatever blood is in the rabbit."

When Portuguese cooks get together for a social event, it is more than just preparing a meal for a lot of people. While the potatoes are being peeled or clams scrubbed, levity is in abundance. Perhaps it is the Portuguese sense of humor, but I find jokes and wisecracks funnier when told in Portuguese. Everyone is part of a big kitchen machine, each picking a task, knowing what needs to be done, and helping without waiting for someone else to pick up the slack.

Fernanda Simões is always dubbed "the Boss" or "Bossa." This little 70-plus-year-old woman is as delightful as she is petite, gentle, and unpretentious. I guess we are so fond of her because she takes ribbing so well. We offer her a kitchen stool to sit on while she works, and she keeps an "eye" on the crew from the boss's chair as she shakes her 2-foot wooden spoon in a comical gesture. Someone always responds with a remark that cracks everyone up.

We don't skimp on our lunch breaks at these gatherings. Someone always prepares a noontime meal that is a feast in itself—a sit-down meal of grilled fish, pork, or steak, boiled rice, or perhaps fried or boiled potatoes, vinegar sauce, crusty bread, olives, and of course, wine. We usually end the break with an *expresso com cheirinho,* an espresso with a tiny drop of brandy. The well-fed crew now is fortified for the remaining 8 or 9 hours of cooking, serving, and cleanup.

Serves 4

BRAISED RABBIT WITH RICE

Coelho com Arroz de Cabidela

When Fernanda Simões came to this country, she arrived in New Jersey. She met her husband when she made a return visit to Portugal and eventually found her way to Massachusetts. She told me that this dish is older than she is, older than her mother before her. It traditionally includes the liver, kidneys, and blood of the rabbit, which is drained when the rabbit is freshly killed and immediately mixed with vinegar to prevent coagulation (the same method is used for chicken and pig blood). I usually don't include the liver and kidneys when I make this dish. When I cannot get a freshly killed rabbit, I use frozen rabbit, which of course does not include the blood. The flavor of the stew is slightly different but still delicious. The rice in this dish should not have absorbed all the liquid, leaving it somewhat saucy.

DAY AHEAD

3 garlic cloves, coarsely chopped

1 teaspoon salt

1 teaspoon paprika

1 teaspoon hot pepper sauce

½ cup white wine

¼ cup olive oil

One 4 lb rabbit, cut into serving pieces

NEXT DAY

¼ cup olive oil

1 medium onion, finely chopped

1 small very ripe tomato, peeled,
  seeded, and coarsely chopped

1 bay leaf

2 tablespoons finely chopped parsley,
  plus extra to garnish

2 cups boiled water

1 cup (7 oz) long-grain rice, rinsed and drained

Rabbit blood (optional)

1. Using a mortar and pestle, mash the garlic with the salt, forming a paste. Mix in the paprika, hot pepper sauce, and wine. Transfer to a ceramic or glass dish, whisk in the oil, and add the rabbit, turning to coat all sides. Cover and marinate overnight.

The next day

2. Heat the olive oil in a 5-quart stockpot over medium-high heat, until it is very hot, but not smoking. Sauté the onion until light golden in color, 10 to 15 minutes. Add the tomato and bay leaf and stir to blend. Reduce the heat to medium-low, cover, and simmer until the tomato is soft and partially dissolved, about 15 minutes.

3. Transfer the rabbit to the pot along with its marinade. Toss in the parsley, stir, and cover tightly. Bring to a boil over medium-high heat, then reduce the heat and simmer gently for 30 minutes.

4. Pour in the hot water, re-cover, and continue to simmer for another 30 minutes, until the rabbit meat is nearly falling from the bone.

5. Stir in the rice. If you are using rabbit blood, add it with the rice. Cover and simmer for 20 minutes or until the rice is cooked. The liquid will not be totally absorbed. Transfer to a serving platter and garnish with additional parsley.

Serves 4 to 6

OVEN-BRAISED RABBIT

Coelho Assado

This is an Azorean-style oven-braised rabbit. Like many other Azorean stews and braises, it has a hot-spicy flavor and uses nutmeg as an interesting counterpoint. Rabbit is a very good, high-protein alternative to poultry, for those who do not eat red meat and are looking for something different. The braising sauce is so flavorful, you might ask for a spoon. See the recipe for *Alcatra* (page 154) for details about braising in a clay cooker.

One 4 lb rabbit (or ask a butcher to
  remove the head)
4 to 6 large Red Bliss potatoes, peeled and halved
¼ cup olive oil, or as needed

MARINADE

4 garlic cloves, coarsely chopped
2 teaspoons coarse kosher salt, or to taste
½ teaspoon ground white pepper, or to taste
1 medium onion, coarsely chopped
1 cup water
½ cup white wine
1 tablespoon tomato paste
1 teaspoon Hot Pepper Paste (page 220)
½ teaspoon nutmeg
1 bay leaf

A day ahead

1. Season the rabbit with the garlic, salt, and pepper and place in a shallow dish. In a medium bowl, mix the remaining marinade ingredients and pour over the rabbit. Cover tightly and chill overnight.

The next day

2. Preheat the oven to 350°F. Transfer the rabbit to another dish, reserving the marinade.

3. In large cast-iron skillet or frying pan, heat the oil over medium-high heat and brown the rabbit all over. Place the rabbit in a Dutch oven or prepared clay pot. Add the reserved marinade and the potatoes.

4. Cover and braise in the oven for 1 hour, until the potatoes are easily pierced with a fork and the rabbit is very tender.

When I was a child, our multicultural neighborhood contained French, Polish, Portuguese, Irish, and Mexican families. There was much visiting back and forth, and so there were many opportunities to sample distinctive dishes from other countries. One neighbor, however, who visited our house often, was not enthusiastic about cooking. Having just finished preparing supper as she arrived one evening, my father asked her whether she had ever eaten Spanish chicken. When she answered that she had not, he gave her a dish of his chicken to take home. The next day our neighbor returned the empty plate with compliments to the cook, only to learn that the "chicken" was really rabbit!

It is best to use fresh rabbit whenever possible, and one weighing not more than 3 to 4 pounds.

Serves 4 to 6

OVEN-BRAISED SHORT RIBS

Costelas no Forno

It would be an understatement to say my father was a rib man. Savoring every bite, he would pick the bones clean.

2 garlic cloves, coarsely chopped

2 medium onions, thinly sliced

1 tablespoon paprika

2 tablespoons Sweet Red Pepper Paste (page 219)

Olive oil

½ cup red wine

5 lb meaty beef short ribs or pork spare ribs

1. Preheat the oven to 300°F.

2. In a bowl, combine the garlic, onions, paprika, red pepper paste, and 2 tablespoons of olive oil, blending well. Stir in the wine and ½ cup water.

3. Place the ribs in a roasting pan and pour the seasoned braising liquid over them. Cover and place in the preheated oven. Cook for 2 to 2½ hours, or until the meat is nearly falling from the bone. Remove the ribs from the pan, slice between the bones, and set aside.

4. Heat about ¼ cup olive oil in a large frying pan over medium-high heat until hot, but not smoking. Add the ribs and cook to just brown the meat a bit, caramelizing the juices on the meat. Alternatively, place the ribs under a broiler to brown and crisp the skin. Arrange the ribs on a platter and serve with boiled potatoes and pan juices. Serve hot sauce on the side for extra zing.

Serves 6

PORTUGUESE-STYLE BEEF

Carne Guisada

This is a stovetop braise my father often served on Sundays. He didn't marinate the meat overnight, but feel free to do so, after adding the wine. It is an easy one-pot meal.

3 garlic cloves, finely chopped

1 tablespoon Sweet Red Pepper Paste
  (page 219)

2 teaspoons paprika

2 bay leaves, crumbled

2 tablespoons finely chopped parsley,
  plus extra to garnish

2 tablespoons olive oil

One 3½ lb bone-in chuck roast
  or bottom round roast

2 medium onions, thinly sliced

¼ teaspoon crushed red
  pepper flakes (optional)

1 cup red wine, plus more if needed

2 large very ripe tomatoes, peeled,
  seeded, and coarsely chopped
  (about 2 cups)

2 tablespoons finely chopped parsley

3 lb waxy potatoes, such as Red Bliss
  or large new potatoes, peeled
  and quartered

3 large carrots, peeled and cut into
  large chunks

1. Using a large mortar and pestle, mash the garlic. Add the pepper paste, paprika, bay leaves, and 1 tablespooon of the parsley, mashing well after each addition. While mixing, drizzle in the olive oil. Rub this mixture over the meat and place the meat in a Dutch oven or heavy-based pot, along with the onions and the crushed red pepper, if using.

2. Mix the wine with 1 cup water and pour it into the pot, adding more wine and water in equal amounts, if needed, until the liquid comes one-third of the way up the side of the roast. (At this point, you can marinate the meat, if you wish: cover the pot and refrigerate for several hours or overnight, occasionally turning the meat in the marinade.)

3. Place the tomatoes and 1 tablespoon of the parsley around the meat in the pot. Cover tightly and place over medium-high heat. When the liquid starts to boil, reduce the heat and simmer until almost tender, about 1½ hours.

4. Add the potatoes and carrots. Continue to simmer, covered, for about 30 minutes more, or until the beef is tender and vegetables are done.

5. Transfer the beef and vegetables to a serving platter and cover to keep warm. Return the pot to the heat and boil until the braising liquid has thickened and reduced by half, 5 to 10 minutes. Pour the sauce over the beef and vegetables, garnish with chopped parsley, and serve.

Serves 6 to 8

RATIONS

Rancho

This soul-warming stew comes from northern Portugal. It's ideal for chilly winter days. Definitely a meal in itself, this dish lies somewhere between a soup and a stew. It most likely received its name during times when it was doled out to soldiers as their food ration. My friend Isaura Nogueira, who is originally from the region of Beira Alta in northern Portugal, shared this recipe with me. She suggests using tomato paste rather than fresh tomatoes for a more intense flavor. This dish takes just over 2 hours to prepare, so plan ahead.

2¼ cups (1 lb) dried chickpeas, soaked overnight in enough water to cover by 2 inches

¼ cup olive oil

1 lb stewing beef, cut into 1½ to 2-inch pieces, wiped dry

½ oz chopped salt pork or 2 strips bacon, coarsely chopped

1 medium onion, thinly sliced

3 garlic cloves, finely chopped

1 teaspoon tomato paste

1 teaspoon hot pepper sauce

1 lb chicken pieces (thighs, legs)

2 lb waxy potatoes, such as Red Bliss or new potatoes, peeled and cut into ½-inch cubes

1 lb *chouriço* or *linguiça* sausage (page 168), cut into chunks

1 lb head Savoy cabbage, cored, cut into wedges

½ cup (2 oz) small pasta, such as elbow macaroni

1 teaspoon coarse kosher salt, or to taste

1. Heat the oil in a 5-quart stockpot over medium-high heat until it is very hot, but not smoking. Working in small batches, brown the beef on all sides. Remove the beef, cover, and reserve.

2. Add the salt pork or bacon to the same pot and brown until crisp, rendering the fat. Then remove and discard the solid pieces and reduce the heat to medium. Add the onion to the rendered fat and sauté until a light golden color, 15 to 20 minutes.

3. Mix in the garlic, tomato paste, and hot pepper sauce and cook until the tomato paste is well blended, 3 to 5 minutes.

4. Return the beef to the cooking pot. Drain and add the chickpeas, along with 8 cups of water. Cover and bring to a boil over high heat. Reduce the heat and simmer for 30 minutes.

5. Add the chicken and up to 2 cups of water, enough to cover, and simmer for another 20 to 30 minutes, or until tender.

6. Remove the meats from the pot. Trim the chicken of any bones, skin, and gristle. Cut the chicken meat into pieces and reserve, covered, with the beef.

7. Add the potatoes to the pot and return the soup to a boil. Reduce the heat and simmer for 15 minutes. Toss in the sausage, cabbage, pasta, and salt, and cook for 12 minutes or until pasta is cooked and cabbage is tender but not mushy.

8. Return the meats to the pot and heat through. Serve in bowls with plenty of crusty bread to dip into the broth.

Variation: *For a lighter broth, replace the salt pork with 2 tablespoons of olive oil. One day before you plan to serve, prepare the soup until just before adding the chicken. Chill the broth overnight. Skim the congealed fat and continue with the recipe.*

Serves 6 to 8

AZOREAN-STYLE POT ROAST

Carne Assada Açorean

This is very similar to my father's stewed beef (Portuguese-Style Beef, page 150), but Noelia Ortins, a friend and wonderful cook, who happens to be my husband's cousin, marinates the meat with an Azorean variation on the seasonings and cooks her roast in the oven. Although this dish is called *carne assada*—which means "roast beef"—technically this dish is oven-braised.

DAY AHEAD

One 4 lb bottom round roast or
   bone-in chuck roast

4 garlic cloves, coarsely chopped

1 tablespoon coarse kosher salt, or to taste

1 tablespoon tomato paste

1 tablespoon Hot Pepper Paste (page 220)

1 teaspoon freshly ground black pepper

1 teaspoon ground nutmeg

1 bay leaf

1 medium onion, thinly sliced

1½ cups rosé wine

NEXT DAY

1 cup water or as needed

8 Red Bliss potatoes, or other
   waxy potatoes, peeled, halved if large

2 tablespoons water

2 tablespoons cornstarch

1 tablespoon sugar

1. Place the meat in an enamel or other nonreactive roasting pan. Using a mortar and pestle, mash the garlic with the salt to form a paste. Transfer the paste to a small bowl and mix in the tomato paste, hot pepper paste, black pepper, nutmeg, bay leaf, and onion. Stir in the wine, and pour the mixture over the roast, then turn the meat to coat all sides. Marinate overnight in the refrigerator, turning the meat occasionally.

2. The next day, preheat the oven to 350°F. Remove the roast from the refrigerator and add enough water to the pan so that the liquid comes one-third of the way up the side of the roast. Cover the roasting pan with foil or a lid, and place in the oven. Cook the roast for 1¾ hours, basting frequently.

3. Add the potatoes to the pan, placing them around the meat. Mix the water, cornstarch, and sugar and add to the roasting pan. Cover and continue to roast for 35 to 45 minutes more, until the meat is tender and the potatoes are cooked. Remove and slice the meat and arrange it on a platter, along with the potatoes. Ladle some of the sauce over the meat and serve any extra sauce on the side.

Serves 8 to 10

TERCEIRA-STYLE BRAISED BEEF

Bife Guisada à Moda da Terceira

Lucia Rebelo, who was born in Terceira, taught me to make this tender braised beef dish. With this method, introduced to the Portuguese by the Arabs centuries ago, there is one unusual step: the roast is browned after it is cooked. In this recipe the braising liquid is puréed into a rich sauce.

DAY AHEAD

One 5 lb bottom round roast

1½ teaspoons coarse kosher salt

3 garlic cloves, left whole

1 lb bacon, 3 slices left whole; the rest
   coarsely chopped

2 tablespoons Sweet Red Pepper Paste (page 219)

NEXT DAY

1 cup (8 oz) butter

4 large onions, sliced

3 cups white wine

¼ cup olive oil

A day ahead

1. Using a sharp knife, make three evenly-spaced cuts on one side of the roast, each about 1-inch deep. Into each cut, place ½ teaspoon salt, 1 garlic clove, and 1 strip of bacon.

2. Rub the roast all over with sweet red pepper paste. Cover and chill overnight.

The next day

3. In a Dutch oven, melt the butter. Add the onions and the remaining bacon and sauté until the onions are translucent.

4. Place the roast on top of the onions and bacon in the pot. Add enough wine so that it comes up about one-third of the way up the side of the roast.

5. Cover the pot and bring to a boil. Reduce the heat to its lowest setting and simmer for about 3 hours, until tender. Transfer the roast to a platter, reserving the liquid in the pot.

6. Heat the olive oil in a large cast-iron skillet over medium-high heat until hot, but not smoking. Add the roast and brown the meat on all sides. Transfer the meat to a warm platter, cover, and set aside.

7. Using an immersion blender, purée the juices from the braising pot. Return to the heat and boil until reduced by half, 5 to 10 minutes. Return the roast to the pot, cover, reduce the heat, and simmer for 2 minutes to heat through. Turn off the heat and let rest for 10 minutes. Just before serving, slice the meat, arrange the slices on a platter, and ladle the sauce over them.

Serves 6 to 8

SLOW-BRAISED BEEF RUMP

Alcatra

The Azorean Portuguese from the island of Terceira are famous for this unique dish. Simply seasoned with allspice, pepper, salt, and bay leaves, *Alcatra* is traditionally served on the Feast of the Holy Ghost, but can be served on other occasions as well. Cooked in red wine, the meat takes on a deep mahogany color (other Azorean islands have versions that use white wine). It is most often served with rice, after the Soup of the Holy Ghost (page 62). Lucia Costa learned to prepare this dish as a young girl in Terceira, and says long slow cooking is key.

Alcatra is made in a traditional unglazed red clay pot called an *alguidar*, which is shaped like an inverted lampshade with flared sides. Similar deep, unglazed clay bakers may be found at specialty shops or online. For this recipe, you will need a 4-quart capacity. New clay pots must be seasoned (see Note), soaked before each use, and placed in a cold oven to prevent cracking. You can also use a Dutch oven for this recipe.

½ cup (4 oz) softened butter

3 large onions, thinly sliced

8 oz slab bacon, cut into 1-inch pieces

6 garlic cloves, mashed

2 bay leaves

5 lb beef rump or chuck roast, bone-in,
    cut into 4-inch pieces

1 lb shin bone (if using rump roast)

½ teaspoon allspice berries (Jamaican is best)

½ teaspoon freshly ground black peppercorns

1 teaspoon coarse kosher salt

4 tablespoons (2 oz) firm butter, cut into pieces

4 to 6 cups medium-bodied red or white wine

Uncooked rice (optional)

Note: *A new unglazed clay pot needs to be seasoned to avoid passing an earthy flavor to food. To season, fill the pot with water and add several cabbage or collard leaves and some onion peelings. Place the pot on a diffuser and bring to a boil. Reduce the heat and simmer for 2 hours; drain. When you want to cook in the pot, pre-soak for about 24 hours. Then grease with butter and proceed with the recipe.*

1. Generously grease the interior of a pre-soaked unglazed clay baker or a Dutch oven with the softened butter.

2. Arrange half of the onions in the bottom of the pot, followed by half of the bacon, half of the garlic, and 1 bay leaf. Add the meat, including the bone, followed by the second bay leaf, and the remaining garlic and bacon. Top with the remaining onions. Scatter with the allspice, peppercorns, and sea salt, and dot the top with the pieces of cold butter.

3. Mix 1 cup of the wine with 1 cup of water. Pour this over the ingredients, followed by enough additional wine to cover everything by 1 inch.

4. Place the pot in the cold oven. Set the temperature to 400°F. When the liquid begins to boil (check after about 45 minutes), reduce the temperature to 300°F. Cover the pot with foil and cook, without turning the ingredients, until tender, 3 to 3½ hours more.

5. Turn off the oven. Uncover the pot and remove some of the broth for cooking rice, if desired. Leave the uncovered pot in the oven just until the oven heat has dissipated. The top will brown a little. Serve the meat with rice cooked in broth.

Serves 6 to 8

PORTUGUESE BOILED DINNER
Cozido á Portuguesa

Since the Portuguese are not wasteful, the traditional boiled dinner can encompass a large variety of ingredients, often including pig's ears, feet, and snouts. Other characteristic ingredients in this dish are beef, a variety of sausages, and vegetables. Here in the United States, the above-named pig parts are not always included, especially in my parents' house, because my brothers and sisters did not relish the idea of eating them, but my father occasionally included only a piece or two for himself. This recipe shows a sampling of a broad range of ingredients; however, it can be pared down to simply the brisket, one or two types of sausages, potatoes, carrots, and cabbage.

It is usually served with rice cooked in some of the broth. Black Portuguese olives, cruets of olive oil and vinegar for drizzling over the vegetables, and dense country-style bread are also typical accompaniments to this dish.

DAY AHEAD
2 lb beef brisket

1 lb pork ribs (optional)

Coarse kosher salt

NEXT DAY
2 tablespoons olive oil

½ teaspoon freshly ground black peppercorns

1 bay leaf

2 garlic cloves, whole

1½ lb bone-in chicken pieces (optional)

1 *salpicão* sausage, about 1 lb (page 168, optional)

8 oz *chouriço* sausage (page 168, optional)

1 *farinheira* sausage, about 5 oz (page 168, optional)

8 oz *morcela* sausage (page 168, optional)

2 large onions, peeled, left whole

2 white turnips, peeled and cut into medium chunks

3 large carrots, peeled and cut into large chunks

3 large waxy potatoes, peeled and quartered

1 lb head Savoy cabbage, cored, cut into quarters

2 cups (14 oz) long-grain rice, rinsed and drained

A day ahead

1. Coat the brisket—and ribs, if using—with coarse salt, place in a bowl or dish, and cover. Place in the refrigerator overnight.

The next day

2. Using paper towels, wipe the excess salt from the ribs and brisket. Place the brisket in a 10-quart stockpot. Add the olive oil, peppercorns, bay leaf, and garlic, along with just enough water to cover the meat completely. Tightly cover the pot and bring to a boil over medium-high heat. Reduce the heat and simmer for 30 minutes, skimming the surface occasionally.

3. Add the ribs and continue to simmer for 1½ hours more.

4. Add the chicken, and sausages, if using, and continue to simmer for an additional 45 minutes, or until all the meats are very tender. The chicken should be falling from the bone. Reserving the broth, transfer all of the meats to a bowl and keep warm. If you use *salpicão*, remove the casing now, since it is easier to remove while still warm. Measure 2¼ cups of the broth and pour it into a medium saucepan. Set aside.

5. Taste the remaining broth, and add salt, if needed. Add the onions, turnips, carrots, and potatoes to the pot. Place the cabbage on top. (The vegetables may not be completely submerged, but they will steam.) Cover tightly and bring to a boil over medium-high heat. Reduce the heat and simmer over medium-low heat until the vegetables are cooked, about 25 minutes. Start checking the pot after about 15 minutes, and remove the more delicate vegetables with a slotted spoon as they become cooked to your liking. Cover and set aside.

6. While the vegetables are cooking, prepare the rice: Taste the reserved broth in the saucepan and add salt, as needed. Bring to a boil, add the rice, stir, and reduce the heat to medium-low. Cover and cook until the rice is done, about 25 minutes.

7. Drain the vegetables, reserving the broth for another use. Slice the meats and arrange them on a serving platter, along with all of the vegetables. Serve hot with rice on the side.

Note: *Leftover broth makes a delicious soup base. Simply strain, chill, and remove any solidified fat.*

Serves 4

BROILED GARLIC STEAK

Bife Grelhadao com Alho

Shared by my friend Fatima, this recipe is simple, fast, and so perfect when you're craving garlic. Azoreans are not inhibited when it comes to using garlic. Make sure the steaks are wiped of moisture so that the seasoning will stick. Serve with rice or potatoes.

24 garlic cloves, coarsely chopped
  (6 cloves per steak, 3 per side)
1 tablespoon coarse kosher salt
¼ teaspoon freshly ground black pepper
Juice of 2 lemons
4 tablespoons (2 oz) butter, softened
4 rib-eye steaks, 1-inch thick, blotted dry
2 tablespoons olive oil, or as needed

1. Using a large mortar and pestle, mash the garlic with the salt and pepper to form a paste. Stir in the lemon juice. Mix in the softened butter, blending thoroughly.

2. Divide the garlic butter in half. Using one half of the garlic butter, coat one side of each steak.

3. Drizzle a baking sheet with one tablespoon of the oil. Arrange the steaks, coated side down, in a single layer on the pan. Evenly coat the top of the steaks with the remaining garlic butter. Drizzle the remaining tablespoon of oil over the top of the steaks.

4. Place the oven rack 3 to 4 inches from the heat source and broil the steaks for 3 to 4 minutes per side for medium-rare, or to desired doneness. Serve.

Serves 4

MARINATED BEEFSTEAKS OR EGGS ON HORSEBACK

Bife em Vinho d'Alhos o Bife a Cavalo

Teresa Mendonça recommends white wine instead of red for her marinated steak. You can also use this flavorful marinade with beef tips: skewer and grill them over a hot charcoal fire. The sauce can be made in a separate pan without the caramelized juices or skipped completely. Serve this with fried potatoes.

4 sirloin or rib-eye steaks, 1-inch thick

8 garlic cloves, coarsely chopped

1 tablespoon coarse kosher salt, or to taste

½ teaspoon freshly ground black pepper

1 tablespoon finely chopped parsley

1 bay leaf, crumbled

1 cup white wine

2 tablespoons (1 oz) butter

2 tablespoons olive oil, plus
   extra for frying

½ cup heavy cream

1 teaspoon Dijon mustard

4 eggs (optional)

1. Trim any excess fat from along the outside edges of the steaks. Using a mortar and pestle, mash the garlic with the salt. Mix in the pepper, then the parsley and bay leaf, forming a paste. Season the steaks on both sides with the paste. Place in a deep-sided dish.

2. Slowly pour the wine over the steaks and marinate for 2 hours in the refrigerator. Reserving the marinade, transfer the steaks to a separate dish.

3. In a large skillet, heat the butter and oil over medium-high heat until it sizzles. Quickly fry the steaks in batches until cooked to your liking, 3 to 4 minutes each side for medium-rare. Transfer to a platter, cover, and set aside.

4. Strain the marinade, add it to the pan, and deglaze the caramelized juices, scraping up any brown bits. Remove the pan the from heat, whisk in the cream and mustard, and place over medium-low heat. Return the steaks to the pan and cook for 2 minutes. The sauce should thicken slightly.

5. While the steak is simmering in the sauce, quickly fry the eggs in a separate pan. Transfer the steaks to individual dishes and top each with an egg. Pool some of the sauce around the steak and serve immediately.

Serves 2 to 4

PORTUGUESE BEEFSTEAK

Bife á Portuguesa

Cream or butter is used to enhance the pan juices of this savory garlic-infused steak. While my brothers enjoy this mouth-watering dish with Buttered Rice (page 190), I love it with Portuguese Potato Fries (page 183). When we were kids, our Aunt Ana would pack up freshly cooked steaks for us to take for picnic lunches at a nearby beach. Thinly sliced rump steak is perfectly suited for this family favorite.

1 lb rump steak cut in ½- to ¾-inch thick slices, trimmed of any visible fat

2 to 3 garlic cloves, thinly sliced

6 tablespoons (3 oz) butter

1 tablespoon finely chopped parsley (optional), plus extra to garnish

½ teaspoon coarse kosher salt, or to taste

¼ teaspoon freshly ground black pepper

1. Place the steaks on your cutting board or work surface. Lay half of the garlic slices onto each steak (about 4 on each). Using a tenderizing mallet, pound the garlic into the meat. Flip the steaks over and repeat with the remaining garlic slices.

2. Melt 2 tablespoons (1 oz) of the butter in a skillet over medium-high heat. In batches, sauté the steaks for 2 to 3 minutes on each side for medium-rare. Transfer to a warm, covered plate.

3. Remove the pan from the heat and stir in the remaining 4 tablespoons (2 oz) of the butter, moving it around the edges to melt slowly into the pan juices. Blend well to emulsify and stir in the parsley, if using

4. Return the steaks to the pan, turn to coat them in the sauce, season with salt and pepper, and heat through. Garnish with additional parsley, if desired, and serve with rice or potatoes.

When we were young, we made frequent Sunday trips to the beach. It was like going on safari—Portuguese-style. First, Titi (Aunt Ana) made her Buttered Rice (page 190) and pan-fried rump steaks, covered in natural juices and enriched with butter. We loaded my uncle's station wagon with the playpen, folding chairs, towels, beach toys, and all kinds of essential gear. Then everyone—grandparents, aunt and uncle, cousins, brothers, and I—piled in. Once there, we would find our favorite spot under a shade tree that bordered the sand. We spread the blanket, opened the playpen, unfolded the chairs for my grandparents, and prepared to eat the wonderful picnic lunch my aunt had made. The rest of the afternoon would be ours to enjoy in the sand and water.

Serves 4 to 6

BRAISED LAMB SHANKS WITH POTATOES

Borrego com Batatas Vermelhos

Both goat and lamb are prepared in this manner in the Azores, and both produce a savory delight, with the succulent meat falling from the bone. This recipe is in the style of the island of Graciosa, and typically made in an unglazed clay pot called a *caçoila* or *alguidar* (page 154). If you have an unglazed pot or roaster, it must be seasoned and soaked before use, and placed in a cold oven, but Cousin Evelina says an enamel or steel roasting pan with a cover works well too. It is important to use a cast-iron frying pan to brown the meat, however, since it imparts flavor to the meat. You may find yourself making this dish again and again.

2 oz salt pork, or 4 tablespoons (2 oz) butter
  or olive oil

5 lb lamb or goat forequarter, cut into pieces
  (ask your butcher to do this)

2 medium onions, thinly sliced

2 teaspoons coarse kosher salt

2 garlic cloves, crushed

1 bay leaf, crumbled

½ teaspoon allspice berries (Jamaican is best)

½ teaspoon dried marjoram or oregano

½ teaspoon paprika

½ teaspoon freshly ground white or black pepper

⅛ teaspoon crushed red pepper flakes

1½ cups white wine

1 tablespoon tomato paste

2 tablespoons cornstarch, mixed with
  4 tablespoons water

4 lb waxy potatoes, such as Red Bliss, peeled

Tip: *If your pan is small and leaves little room for the potatoes, transfer some of the broth to a baking dish. Toss the potatoes in the broth, cover tightly, and cook in the oven with the lamb for 1 hour.*

1. Preheat oven to 350°F. In large cast-iron frying pan, fry the salt pork until the fat has been rendered, melt the butter, or heat the oil. Add the pieces of lamb and brown them fairly evenly on all sides. Transfer the meat to a pre-soaked clay pot or large roasting pan and cover with the onion slices.

2. Using a large mortar and pestle, mash the salt with the garlic to form a paste. Grind in the bay leaf, allspice, marjoram or oregano, paprika, pepper, and red pepper flakes. Pour in the wine, tomato paste, and 1½ cups water (combine in a bowl if the mortar is too small), and whisk to blend. Pour over the lamb.

3. Cover the pan and roast in the oven for 1 hour. Remove the cover and stir in the cornstarch slurry, then add the potatoes, giving them a turn in the sauce, and replace the lid. Continue to roast for 45 minutes more. Give the meat a turn in the sauce, then cook for a final 15 to 20 minutes, until the meat is tender and falling from the bone. Transfer to a deep platter, arranging the potatoes around the meat. Spoon some of the sauce over the top; any extra can be served on the side. Make sure to serve with plenty of crusty bread to mop up the sauce.

Serves 4

LIVER MARINATED IN WINE AND GARLIC

Iscas em Vinho d'Alhos

My father always removed the thin membrane from the outside of liver. "If it isn't removed before cooking," he instructed, "the slices will curl." (See Note below.) The classic onion marinade is a great counterpoint for the rich flavor of liver. When cooked, the liver should be slightly pink in the middle; otherwise it will be dry. Serve this with boiled potatoes and a crisp green salad.

4 garlic cloves, finely chopped

1 bay leaf

1 cup dry white wine

1 tablespoon lemon juice

2 tablespoons finely chopped parsley

1 lb pork or calf's liver, sliced ¼-inch thick, membrane removed (see Note)

6 slices fairly lean bacon

2 medium onions, thinly sliced

½ teaspoon coarse kosher salt, or to taste

⅛ teaspoon freshly ground black pepper, or to taste

1. In a small bowl, whisk the garlic, bay leaf, wine, lemon juice, and half of the parsley. Place the liver in a medium glass bowl and pour the marinade over it. Cover and marinate in the refrigerator for 2 hours.

2. Drain the liver well, reserving the marinade.

3. In a large frying pan, fry the bacon over medium-high heat, until crisp. Using a slotted spoon, transfer the solid pieces to a plate, leaving the rendered fat in the pan.

4. Sauté the onions in the bacon fat until golden, about 10 minutes. Using a slotted spoon, transfer the onions to a serving platter and cover. Quickly pan-fry the liver in the pan drippings, for 1 to 2 minutes on each side. Transfer the liver to the serving platter containing the onions, cover, and set aside.

5. Strain the marinade into the pan drippings, add the salt and pepper, and cook over medium-high heat until the liquid has reduced by half, 1 to 2 minutes. Pour the sauce over the liver and garnish with the remaining parsley and the reserved bacon.

Note: *Slicing the liver and removing the membrane is easier if the liver is partially frozen; if the liver is fresh, freeze it just long enough for it to stiffen slightly. Use a sharp knife to slice the liver, or ask the butcher to slice it for you. While the liver slices are still cold and firm, use the point of a sharp paring knife to separate and remove the membrane.*

Variation: *Red wine vinegar, or a mixture of ½ cup dry white wine and ¼ cup white wine vinegar, may be substituted for the white wine and lemon juice. Some cooks use wine vinegar or water to stretch the use of wine in marinades.*

5

SAUSAGES

Salsichas

5 SAUSAGES
Salsichas

Sausage is a key ingredient throughout Portugal. It is used in soups, stews, and seafood dishes. It is often grilled, or simply sliced, and eaten with a torn piece of bread. Sausage varieties vary regionally, but the most well-known are *linguiça* and *chouriço*.

Pigs were customarily slaughtered just before winter, so sausages were made and preserved then. Even today, many old-timers, though they have refrigerators, are still reluctant to make sausages in the warmer months. Today, it is less common for Portuguese families to raise pigs for slaughter, so the sausages made by Portuguese immigrants and their offspring are usually *linguiças* and *chouriços* made with pork purchased from the supermarket. If a whole, live pig is bought from a farm, it is usually for a big celebration feast. After it is slaughtered, the meat, tripe, blood, and intestinal casings are brought home to be used in main dishes and in many types of sausages, including blood sausages.

A variety of marinades are used in sausage-making. Generally, trimmed, cubed pork meat is marinated in white or red wine, or a mixture of the two. If red wine is used alone, the result is a dark sausage that becomes even darker during the smoking process. The wine is sometimes diluted with water. Additional seasoning comes from garlic, salt, hot sauce, or sweet red pepper paste, and whatever else the cook desires. The meat is marinated for 24 to 48 hours and turned occasionally during that period.

In some areas of Portugal, home cooks still hang sausages high inside the kitchen's 5- to 6-foot fireplace opening to smoke or dry. Hanging inside the wood-fueled fireplace, the sausages very often take as long as a week to cure, relying solely on the smoke from cooking. During one of my visits to a great uncle's home in Portugal, I had the experience of cooking dinner in one of these huge fireplaces, which also heat the home. Homeowners, who had "modern" or wood-fired stoves to cook their meals built concrete rooms on the side of the house in which to smoke their sausages and bake their breads. In the Alentejo region, the fire for smoking the sausages is usually fueled with olive tree branches.

Here in the United States, smokehouses of varying sizes, made of brick, cinder block, poured concrete, or metal, dot the backyards of Portuguese immigrants. These are used to smoke fresh pork marinated in wine, seasoned with spices, and stuffed in natural casings.

Among Portuguese immigrant communities, the methods for preparing sausages depend on the availability of equipment. My father cleverly improvised some of the tools he needed for preparing sausages. His homemade funnel consisted of a muffin cup with a hole punched through the bottom. Another piece of metal was attached to the base of the cup, forming the funnel through which the ground meat was forced into sausage casings. Also needed were a large bowl and many willing hands, whose thumbs and fingers substituted for the short wooden dowels we eventually used to press the meat through the funnel.

The procedure my father used was always the same, whatever type of sausage he was making. On the first day, he mixed all the ingredients and marinated the meat for 24 hours. The next day, he called us all into the kitchen and gave us our assignments. Some would attach the readied casings to the funnel end of the muffin cup. Others would tie off the end of the casing or with needles in hand, stand ready to prick any air bubbles. The rest of us, holding the casing securely to the funnel, stuffed the sausage mixture into it, forcing the meat down with our fingers and gently squeezing the mixture to the end of the casing, packing firmly. The ends were

then tied and the sausages were hung to air-dry. The sausages were then smoked and hung again for the color to darken, called the "bloom."

Old methods die hard. While hand-cranked or electric stuffers speed up the process, many traditionalists still stuff the casings by hand. They maintain that mechanical methods alter the meat texture and flavor and pushes the flavorful marinade from the chilled meat as it is cranked through to the casings.

Many Portuguese cooks continue to smoke their sausages the old way, too, using smokehouses in their backyards. These vented smokehouses usually stand between 5 and 7 feet tall and are 40 to 60 square inches. After a blazing wood fire inside the smokehouse dies to smoldering embers, and the heavy dark smoke is gone, the sausages are hung high inside—no closer than 3 to 4 feet above the embers. The door is left open about two inches until any remaining excess moisture or condensation has evaporated. The door is then closed and the sausages are smoked for about 12 hours. Sausages are sometimes smoked for two shorter time periods. At the end of the smoking the exterior of the casings is somewhat firm. The door of the smoker is opened, and the sausages eventually develop a bloom. The texture becomes even firmer as the sausages cool. Here in North America we store the finished sausages in the refrigerator, but in Portugal it is not unusual to store them covered in lard or oil until needed.

COMMON PORTUGUESE SAUSAGES

Chouriço (shor-EE-soo)
Similar to the Spanish *chorizo,* this pork sausage is seasoned with garlic, paprika, spices, and wine; used in soups and stews. It is thicker and spicier than *linguiça.*

Farinheira (far-ren-YEH-rra)
A flour-and-pork sausage, seasoned with garlic, paprika, and sometimes the juice of oranges, it is commonly pan-fried, grilled, or used in boiled dinners.

Linguiça (leeng-QUEE-sah)
This sausage is similar to *chouriço* but made with different cuts of pork. Milder in taste, *linguiça* is usually seasoned with garlic, wine, paprika, or sweet red pepper paste, depending on the region. It is usually grilled or sautéed.

Morcela (mor-SELL-la)
A spiced pork-blood sausage that is commonly used in boiled dinners. It is a combination of pork, fat, pork blood, and spices.

Salpicão (sal-pee-COWN)
This sausage has a diameter of 2½ to 3 inches and is similar to a rolled ham but more heavily flavored with garlic and paprika. It is used for soups, stews, and braises. The casing is usually removed before serving. *Chouriço* can be used in its place.

A combination of *morcela, farinheira,* and *chouriço* is usually included in Portuguese boiled dinner. *Salpicão* and *chouriço* are used in soups, although those who prefer a less spicy sausage usually use *linguiça* in soups or stews, and also cook it with dry-heat methods.

METHOD FOR MAKING SAUSAGES

EQUIPMENT

A manual or electric meat grinder, prechilled,
  large grind plate (or direct your butcher)

A large stainless-steel bowl,
  thoroughly cleaned
  and prechilled

An extra-large stainless-steel bowl,
  thoroughly cleaned

A large quantity of ice

A wide funnel with a 1- to 2-inch opening, or
  the sausage attachment for your meat grinder

Sterilized needle (a threaded needle doesn't
  get lost as easily)

Butcher's twine

An electric or gas smoker

An accurate meat thermometer

Sawdust for electric smokers, enough to fill
  the smoking pan

½- to 1-inch wooden dowels, for hanging
  (length depends on the width of your smoker)

Wax paper

Preparing the pork butt

1. Three-quarters fill an extra-large bowl with ice and set a large stainless-steel bowl inside it. In small batches, quickly cut the pork into ½- to 1-inch cubes. Remove any sinew or gristle. Remove the gland as well, if possible, because it is bitter. You should have about 20% fat to 80% meat. Alternatively, you can have your butcher precut the meat to your specifications, using the extra-large grind on their machine.

Preparing the casings

2. Soak the casings in cool water for 15 minutes. Then rinse them under cold running water: open one end and allow the water to flow through to the opposite end. Store casings in the refrigerator, covered with cold water, until ready to use.

Stuffing the casings

3. If using, wrap your grinder and sausage attachments in plastic and prechill for several hours.

4. Just before stuffing the casings, remove the meat from your refrigerator and mix in the salt, if specified in your recipe. Remove a small amount of meat and fry it in a frying pan. Taste for seasoning and adjust if necessary.

5. Stuff the casings by hand using a funnel that has a wide exit end or use the sausage attachment on a meat grinder without the cutting blade. Apply the readied casings, wetting the attachment nozzle with water so the casings slide easily onto the attachment.

6. Tie off the bottom end of the casing, leaving an 8-inch length of string.

7. Stuff, feeding the meat through the funnel or grinder. Gently squeeze the meat to the end of the casings, but do not overstuff. If you are using a wine marinade, pour a small amount of the marinade into the attachment from time to time to facilitate moving the meat along the casing.

8. Using a sterilized needle, prick any air bubbles that are created. Give the sausage a very gentle squeeze to close up the space where there was an air pocket. The sausages should feel firm, but have a slight give to allow for shrinkage of the casings during smoking.

9. Using the string at the end of the casing, tie off the opposite end, leaving a 2-inch gap of string, and forming a loop. The gap of string will rest on the hanging rod. Continue with remaining meat.

10. Hang the sausage loops on a wooden dowel to let the casings air-dry in a cool room for 12 to 15 hours. The casings will darken somewhat as they dry.

Smoking the sausages

11. The smoking instructions, adapted from Rytek Kutas' book *Great Sausage Recipes and Meat Curing*, are for use with an electric or gas smoker. (See Resource Guide, page 302, for more information.) Keep in mind that the directions for your smoker may differ.

12. Preheat the smoker to 100°F to 110°F.

13. Add the sausages, leave the damper open and the door slightly ajar, and maintain this temperature for until the casings are dry to the touch, about 1 hour. Close the smoker door, then increase the temperature setting to 130°F, building the temperature slowly. The sausages will not smoke properly if the exterior is still moist, if the heat is too hot too soon, or if the process is rushed; they are more likely to steam. Slow-smoking makes a more tender sausage.

14. When the internal temperature of the sausage reaches 100°F, increase the temperature setting to 150°F, then close the damper halfway.

15. After the casings are brown, add a pan of dampened (not soaking) sawdust; close the damper so it is only one-quarter of the way open.

16. When the amount of smoke from the damper decreases, add another pan of dampened sawdust. Repeat two or three times more, or a total of four or five times. Remove the pan completely when the sausage color is dark.

17. If the sausages have not reached an internal temperature of 125°F at this point, adjust the temperature setting of the smoker to 160°F to 165°F and continue to smoke the sausages until they reach 125°F.

18. Continue to smoke the sausages until an internal temperature of 152°F is reached. To reach the final internal temperature of the sausages, it may be necessary to fill the empty sawdust pan with boiling water and place it in the smoker.

19. Remove the sausages from the smoker. Rinse with cool water, reducing the internal temperature to 100°F. Hang the sausages on wooden dowels to dry for 20 to 25 minutes; the sausages will darken—or bloom—as they dry. When completely cool, cover with wax paper and refrigerate. They will keep for up to 2 weeks, well wrapped. You can also place individually wrapped sausages in freezer bags and freeze until needed.

SAFETY TIPS

When making sausages, be especially careful to practice good sanitation. If there is one thing that was emphasized by my teacher, Ernest Vieira, when I studied culinary sanitation practice, it was the importance of keeping ingredients chilled, and working in small batches. All equipment should be clean and sanitary; pre-chill the equipment *and* the ingredients. This is especially important when using meat that is ground or cut into small pieces. As with any recipe, having everything ready before you begin enables you to make the recipe quickly, efficiently, and without compromising food safety.

• When processing the meat, work in small batches and keep unused meat refrigerated. Have all ingredients ready and work quickly, removing the meat from the refrigerator last. (When I am trimming and cutting the meat, I keep it in a bowl placed in a larger bowl that is filled with ice.)

• Salt should be added last, just before the casings are stuffed, because salt will draw juices from the meat. The exception is if you are using Sweet Red Pepper Paste, *Massa de Pimentão* (page 219), which contains salt, in its place.

• For best results, always follow the instructions of your particular smoker. Before placing the sausages in the smoker, be sure that the casings are dry and free of grease. The exterior should have an almost papery feel to it. The sausages should be nearly room temperature to prevent condensation from forming on them. Do not overpack your smoker. Leave sufficient space between sausages to allow air to circulate properly. Condensation will prevent the proper color and finish to form on the casings. This stage should not be rushed. Patience is important for the entire process.

• Maintaining temperature in the smoker is also important. Generally, modern electric smokers have a probe that is inserted into the sausage. The temperature can then be read on an external dial, without decreasing the temperature inside the smoker by opening it.

• At temperatures between 40°F and 140°F, botulism can develop. In commercial and large-scale home production, safety is ensured by the addition of Prague Powder, a preservative that contains sodium nitrate (if you use this, reduce the salt in your recipe). The following recipes have been tested successfully with an electric smoker without using Prague Powder. Strict sanitation procedures, the quantity of salt and acidic wine, thorough mixing, and proper smoking are the factors that ensure success. Both wine and salt act as preservatives.

Old-fashioned sausage-making was not without its taboos. Mixing the meat with seasoning was most often done with one's hands, and it was, and is still, believed by some Portuguese that women should not be allowed to handle the pork meat during the time of their monthly cycle for fear of spoiling the meat.

Makes about 10 pounds

ALENTEJO-STYLE LINGUIÇA

Linguiça à Alentejana

This recipe is my father's and represents the Alentejo region of his birth. It is different from sausages of other regions in that it doesn't contain any wine. The size of the cut meat must be small enough to fit through your stuffing funnel; I have given instructions to do this by hand (page 170), but you can have your butcher do this for you. Typically, the casing is filled in one long continuous length, which is then wrapped around the hanging rod. I like to cut them in shorter lengths, which makes them easier to handle and I can give some away in tied loops. Read through the method and safety tips on page 170–172 and remember to follow the directions for your smoker.

10 lb boneless pork butt, prepared
   according to the instructions on page 170
20 garlic cloves (about 2 heads), finely chopped
1½ cups (10½ oz) Sweet Red Pepper Paste (page 219)
8 oz salt-packed pork intestines, 34 mm,
   cut into 24-inch lengths, prepared for
   stuffing (see page 170)

A day ahead

1. Once the meat has been processed, mix in the garlic and sweet red pepper paste, blending well. Chill for 24 hours, turning the meat occasionally to remix.

To stuff and smoke

2. Follow the method on page 170.

Makes about 12 pounds

ARTHUR ORTINS' LINGUIÇA

Linguiça de Etur Ortins

This recipe comes from my father-in-law, Arthur Ortins, and is one he guarded carefully. He sold this popular sausage in his grocery store for many years, and I acquired his secret recipe only recently. It is unusual because of the spices he included. Follow the method and food-safety procedures outlined on pages 170–172. Be sure to use an accurate thermometer to check the internal temperature of the meat, and to pre-chill and sanitize your equipment.

12 lb boneless pork butt, prepared according to the instructions on page 170

20 garlic cloves (about 2 heads), finely chopped, or ¾ cup (4 oz) garlic powder

2 tablespoons freshly ground black pepper

2 tablespoons paprika

2½ teaspoons onion powder

1½ teaspoons ground allspice (Jamaican is best)

1½ teaspoons ground nutmeg

3½ cups red wine, plus extra if needed

5 tablespoons coarse kosher salt, plus extra if needed

10 oz (34-mm) pork casings, cut to 18-inch lengths, prepared for stuffing (see page 170)

1¾ cups red table wine, plus extra if needed

1¾ cups water, plus extra if needed

A day ahead

1. Place the pork butt in a large bowl.

2. In a mixing bowl, mix the garlic, pepper, paprika, onion powder, allspice, and nutmeg. Mix in the wine and measured water and blend. Pour this mixture over the processed meat and mix well. If needed, add more wine and water in equal parts so that the meat is wet but not swimming in liquid. Mix thoroughly and marinate for 24 hours in the refrigerator, turning occasionally.

To stuff and smoke

3. Follow the method on page 170.

Makes about 5 pounds

CHOURIÇO

Chouriço

Not to be confused with Spanish chorizo, this sausage is made mild or spicy. It is often used in soups, stews, and boiled dinners. Read through the method and safety tips on page 170–172 before you begin.

5 lb boneless pork butt, prepared according
  to the instructions on page 170
10 garlic cloves (1 head), finely chopped
1 cup (4 oz) ground hot or sweet paprika
1 tablespoon Hot Pepper Paste (page 220)
1¼ cups red table wine, plus extra if needed
1¼ cups white table wine, plus extra if needed
2 tablespoons coarse kosher salt, plus extra if needed
10 oz (34-mm) pork casings, cut to 18-inch lengths,
  prepared for stuffing (see page 170)

A day ahead

1. Place the pork butt in a large bowl.

2. In a mixing bowl, combine the garlic, paprika, and hot pepper paste. Add the wines and 2½ cups water and blend. Pour over the processed meat, and mix well. If needed, add more wine and water in equal parts so that the meat is wet but not swimming in liquid. Mix thoroughly and marinate for 24 hours in the refrigerator, turning occasionally.

To stuff and smoke

3. Follow the method on page 170.

Serves 4

GRILLED LINGUIÇA

Linguiça Grelhada

As a light lunch, with soup, or as an appetizer, grilled *linguiça* is hard to beat. The aroma of sausage grilling is irresistible. This charming story captures the essence of its appeal: A man was eating plain bread, surrounded by enticing gusts of *linguiça* drifting from a neighbor's barbecue. When the man's wife asked him what he was eating, he replied, chewing wistfully on his humble bread, "*Comer pão cheira de linguiça*"—"Eating bread with the smell of *linguiça*!"

1 lb *linguiça* sausage, cut into
  4- or 5-inch lengths

4 *Papo-secos* (page 238), or other
  crusty rolls, to serve

1. Grill the sausage over hot coals or broil until the skin is a rich brown color and blistered. Place in crusty rolls or serve with the bread alongside.

Variations: *Grilled sausage can be sliced into rounds and served with toast points as an appetizer. Tossing caramelized onions and/or roasted peppers in a roll with the sausage makes for an immensely flavorful sandwich.*

Linguiça and chouriço *can be cut into small cubes, lightly sautéed, combined with chopped onion and shredded soft cheese, then used as a stuffing for meats, clams, prebaked tartlet shells, or even mushrooms, which can then be placed under a broiler to melt the cheese and lightly brown the tops. Serve as an appetizer or snack.*

Serves 2 to 4

FIREMAN'S LINGUIÇA

Linguiça à Bombeiro

This aptly named appetizer is commonly served in Portuguese restaurants. It is prepared tableside in a clay vessel that looks like a rowboat. (These vessels may be purchased from Portuguese specialty shops; see Resource Guide, page 302.) Clay slats sit crosswise like seats in the boat and hold sausages above alcohol, which is poured into the base of the vessel and then ignited to sear the meat. *Aguardente*—sometimes called "Bang Bang" in the United States—is a distilled liquor made from the grape skins after they have been removed from the wine press. This liquor is similar to Italian grappa, but any brandy, even cognac, can be substituted. Using an unlit outdoor grill—for safety—and with a little improvising, this dish can be prepared pretty easily at home. Please use care when preparing this dish.

1 lb *linguiça* sausage (see page 168), at room temperature, cut into 5-inch lengths

1 cup *aguardente* (see page 177) or brandy, at room temperature, plus extra if needed

1. Make 3 or 4 diagonal slashes around the sausage link.

2. Position a shallow pan securely on the flat surface of your grill, outdoors. Place a small cooking rack in the pan, and arrange the sausage on top of it.

3. Pour the brandy over the sausage into the pan to a depth of about ½ an inch.

4. Carefully ignite the brandy. Use long-handled barbecue tongs to turn the sausage until it is golden brown and heated through. Remove from the heat. Serve with crusty bread and olives, or with a green salad for a light lunch.

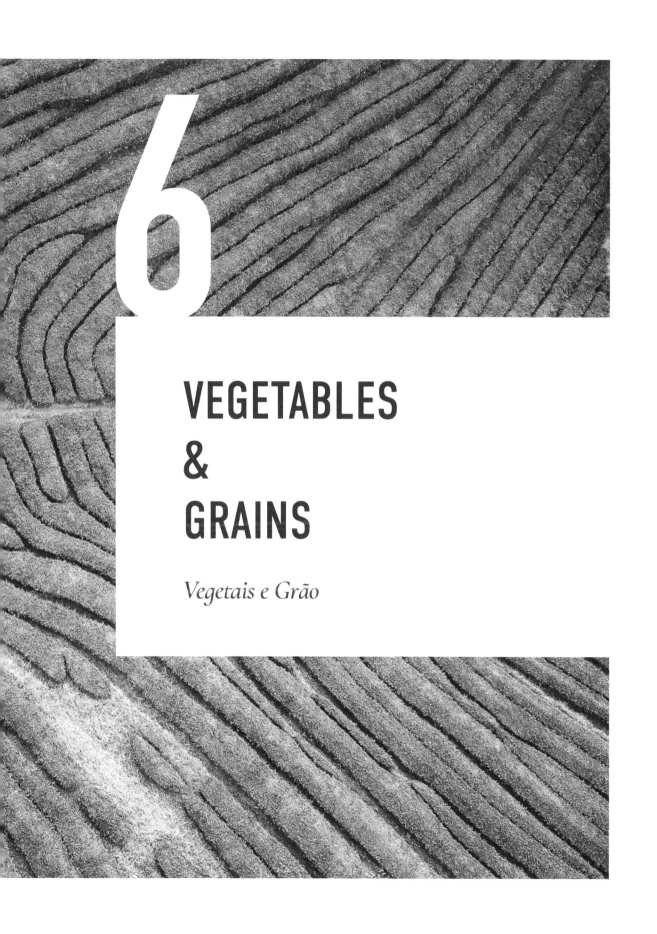

6

VEGETABLES & GRAINS

Vegetais e Grão

6 VEGETABLES & GRAINS
Vegetais e Grão

Typically, a Portuguese family will find a sunny spot in which to plant a vegetable garden, sometimes giving up the entire backyard to the cultivation of fresh produce. Seeds for many familiar favorites are unavailable in the United States, so many immigrants brought seeds with them from the old country, cultivated them, and saved the seeds from their first American harvest to plant the following spring. These seeds were shared among relatives and friends and newcomers from Portugal or the Azores—a practice that continues today. While there is not a large repertoire of vegetable dishes in Portuguese cooking, the benefits of fresh vegetables come primarily from our soups, which more often than not contain the nutritious greens and other treasures harvested from our gardens.

Harvesting freshly ripened vegetables and herbs from the garden is an enjoyable task. Sharing our abundance with friends and neighbors makes it even more so. When I was young, my father planted a huge garden in which he grew parsley, garlic, onions, corn, kale, carrots, peppers, turnips, potatoes, tomatoes, fava beans, strawberries, and of course, cilantro. Planning a meal based on what was ripe in the garden was not uncommon. When all the vegetables had been harvested, we would begin to prepare the garden for the coming winter. One of the important tasks was to collect the plants—cilantro was one of many—that had been allowed to go to seed. We would gather the branches, heavy with seeds, and place them in a large metal box. My father would set this box in a south window in our cellar. The seeds would dry in the warm sunlight and fall from the branches. In the spring the seeds would be re-sown with seed potatoes for the new year's crop.

When the first Portuguese ate a potato, it was the start of a love affair—an affair that recrossed the ocean with the Portuguese immigrants who arrived in America. Punched, roasted, fried, or boiled—potatoes are an irresistible starch, entwined in the fabric of Portuguese cooking.

Rice and legumes, which provide starch and have a long shelf life, are equally favored. Short-grain rice is most commonly used for soup and pudding, while medium- and long-grain rice are used in braises, stews, and individual rice dishes. Parboiled (or converted) rice, because of its non-sticky texture, has become popular with some Portuguese cooks in this country; others continue to use unprocessed long-grain rice. Fiber- and protein-rich legumes are used in soups, stews, and salads (such as Friar's Beans, page 197). They even turn up as beer nuts for snacking—cooked, salted lupini beans, called *tremoços,* are often served with a brew. You eat them by nipping off one end of the shell and squeezing the bean into your mouth. Chickpeas or kidney, roman, lima, and fava beans are all used in hearty proportions.

Serves 4

PORTUGUESE POTATO FRIES

Batatas Fritas à Portuguesa

These fried potatoes are a great favorite in our family. I always make extra because half of the potatoes are eaten before they ever reach the table! They are fried in flavorful olive oil (you can use vegetable oil, but the flavor will be different), and they are terrific with steak, seafood, and especially *Carne de Porco à Alentejana* (page 128), which was traditionally served with boiled potatoes in my father's town. Unlike American fries, these potatoes are tender, rather than crisp. Presoaking and blotting the potatoes removes the excess starch that absorbs oil and prevents them from crisping on the outside.

6 large starchy potatoes, such as russets
Olive oil, for deep frying
Coarse kosher salt

Note: *Frying in small batches allows movement of the potatoes and keeps the temperature of the oil more constant, so the potatoes brown quickly.*

1. Peel the potatoes and slice them into ¼-inch rounds. Soak them in cold water for 30 minutes, then drain and blot them dry with paper towels.

2. In a large pot, pour in olive oil to a depth of 5 inches. Heat the oil over medium-high heat until it quivers (it should be about 350°F). Fry the potatoes in small batches until golden. Using a slotted spoon, transfer the potatoes to a plate lined with paper towels or brown paper to drain. Add salt to your liking.

Serves 4

PUNCHED POTATOES

Batatas à Murro

This popular but simple potato dish can be made on short notice. Waxy potatoes like Red Bliss, Idaho bakers, or new potatoes all work well in this recipe.

8 small or 4 medium waxy potatoes,
  skins intact, scrubbed
Olive oil
1 tablespoon coarse kosher salt, or to taste
8 garlic cloves, finely chopped
Wine vinegar, to drizzle (optional)

1. Preheat the oven to 400°F.
2. Place the potatoes in a bowl and pierce them all over with a fork. Drizzle with a tablespoon or two of olive oil and roll in coarse salt. Arrange the potatoes on a shallow baking dish and bake for 1 hour or until tender.
3. Give each potato a slight punch with the side of your closed fist (hard enough to crack it open a bit, but not hard enough to smash it to smithereens). Scatter the chopped garlic in the opening of each potato. If desired, drizzle with olive oil and vinegar and season with more salt. Serve immediately.

Serves 4

ROASTED POTATOES

Batatas Assadas

You can surround a turkey or roast meat with these potatoes, basting them with savory pan juices. The seasonings create a heady fragrance that stimulates the taste buds.

2 lb waxy potatoes, such as Red Bliss,
  peeled and cut into ¾-inch wedges
4 garlic cloves, finely chopped
1 tablespoon paprika
½ tablespoon coarse kosher salt, or to taste
1 teaspoon freshly ground black pepper
¼ cup olive oil
1½ tablespoons finely chopped parsley

1. Preheat the oven to 350°F.
2. In a large bowl combine the potatoes with the garlic, paprika, salt, and pepper. Gently mix, evenly coating the potatoes. Drizzle with the olive oil and sprinkle with the parsley; mix to coat evenly.
3. Place in a roasting pan (or add to a pan of roasting meat) and roast, turning occasionally, until tender, 45 minutes to 1 hour.

Serves 6

POTATOES WITH WINE AND TOMATO

Batatas com Vinho e Tomate

Wine and tomatoes take roasted potatoes to a new level—one that has more than eye-appeal.

4 tablespoons (2 oz) butter, melted

4 tablespoons olive oil

2 teaspoons paprika

3 garlic cloves, finely chopped

½ tablespoon finely chopped parsley

2 teaspoons coarse kosher salt

1 teaspoon hot pepper sauce

½ teaspoon freshly ground black pepper

6 large waxy potatoes, such as Red Bliss, peeled and quartered

1 medium very ripe tomato, peeled, seeded, and finely chopped; or 1 tablespoon tomato paste

½ cup white wine

1. Preheat oven to 350°F.

2. In a large bowl, combine the butter, olive oil, paprika, and garlic. Stir in the parsley, salt, hot pepper sauce, and ground pepper.

3. Add the potatoes and the tomato, gently mixing. Transfer ingredients to a roasting pan. Slowly pour in the wine. Put the pan in the preheated oven and roast until the potatoes are tender, 50 to 60 minutes.

Serves 4 to 6

RICE WITH SALT COD

Arroz de Bacalhau

It is remarkable how a simple dish can be so satisfying. Accompanied with a salad, bread, olives, and wine, this rice dish makes a tasty meal.

8 oz boneless salt cod, soaked in several changes of cold water for 16 to 24 hours, refrigerated (see page 26)

¼ cup olive oil

1 small onion, finely chopped

1 small ripe tomato, peeled, seeded, and coarsely chopped; or 2 teaspoons tomato paste

1 bay leaf

1 garlic clove, coarsely chopped

¼ teaspoon paprika

⅛ teaspoon freshly ground black pepper

1 cup (7 oz) long-grain rice, rinsed and drained

1 teaspoon coarse kosher salt, or to taste

1 tablespoon finely chopped cilantro or parsley

Note: *Rice dishes, both savory and dessert, are susceptible to Bacillus Cereus intoxication when not handled properly. Hot dishes, fresh or leftover, should be served at temperatures above 140°F. Reheat leftover savory rice dishes to 165°F. Dishes to be served cold should be held at a temperature of 40°F or below and served well chilled.*

1. Remove the fish from the soaking water and rinse. Cut the fish into 2-inch pieces and place in a 2½-quart saucepan. Add 2 cups of fresh water or enough to cover the fish completely. Cover and bring to a boil over medium-high heat. Reduce the heat to medium-low and simmer for 10 minutes. Drain the fish and set aside.

2. Heat the oil in a 4-quart saucepan over medium-high heat. Add the onion and sauté until golden. Add the tomato or tomato paste, bay leaf, garlic, paprika, and black pepper. Cover, reduce the heat, and simmer until the tomato is very soft and partially dissolved, about 15 minutes.

3. Pour in 2 cups of water and re-cover. Bring to a boil, stir in the rice, salt, and half of the parsley or cilantro. Re-cover, reduce the heat, and simmer for 25 minutes, until the rice is done and the liquid is absorbed. Combine with the cooked fish, gently tossing, and transfer to a serving platter. Garnish with the remaining parsley or cilantro.

Serves 6 to 8

SEAFOOD RICE

Arroz de Marísco

Some Portuguese rice dishes are prepared on the stovetop, then finished in the oven to dry any extra moisture. This rice dish with seafood, adapted from Isaura Nogueira's recipe, is a perfect example. For special occasions, pour the rice into a ring mold. After removing it from the oven, invert it onto a serving platter, remove the mold, and place a garnish of cilantro sprigs in the middle. Served with a salad of mixed greens, it makes a perfect lunch, or it can be served as a separate course of a larger meal.

1¼ lb whole boiled lobster

8 oz medium shrimp, peeled and deveined, shells reserved

¼ cup olive oil

1 small onion, finely chopped

1 large very ripe tomato, peeled, seeded, and coarsely chopped

1½ tablespoons tomato paste

1 garlic clove, finely chopped

2 teaspoons coarse kosher salt

1 cup (7 oz) long-grain rice, rinsed and drained

2 tablespoons finely chopped cilantro or parsley, plus extra sprigs to garnish

1 teaspoon hot pepper sauce

¼ teaspoon saffron, crushed and soaked in a tiny bit of water for 15 minutes

½ teaspoon turmeric

½ cup (2 oz) thinly sliced white button mushrooms

8 oz small bay scallops

½ cup (2½ oz) shelled baby peas, fresh or frozen

1 tablespoon butter, softened

1. Preheat the oven to 350ºF. Shell the lobster, collecting as much of the juice as possible. Coarsely chop the meat. Set the meat and juice aside.

2. Place the shrimp shells in a saucepan with 3½ cups water. Cover and bring to a boil over medium-high heat. Reduce the heat to medium-low and simmer for 15 minutes. Strain and reserve the stock, discarding the shells.

3. Heat the oil in a 4-quart pot over medium-high heat. Add and sauté the onion until lightly golden. Add the tomato, tomato paste, and garlic. Cover and simmer until the tomato is very soft and partially dissolved, about 15 minutes.

4. Measure the amount of lobster juice and add enough shrimp broth to make 3½ cups of liquid. Pour this into the onion and tomato. Add the salt and bring to a boil. Stir in the rice, cilantro or parsley, hot sauce, saffron water, and turmeric. Reduce the heat, re-cover, and simmer for 15 minutes.

5. Add the mushrooms to the rice and continue to simmer, covered, until the liquid is almost absorbed and the rice is tender, 5 to 10 more minutes. Mix in the scallops and shrimp. Stir in the peas and the lobster meat. Simmer 1 more minute. Remove from the heat.

6. Butter a 9- by 13-inch glass baking dish or ring mold. Transfer the rice to the baking dish. Bake at 350ºF for 20 minutes to set and absorb any excess liquid. Garnish with cilantro or parsley sprigs before serving.

Serves 4 to 6

RICE WITH CHICKEN

Arroz de Frango

"Use a combination of green, red, and orange bell peppers for a colorful effect," suggests Maria Fernandes Bettencourt. She added that this rice, richly flavored with chicken, can also be served nicely on a buffet table.

3 bone-in chicken thighs

2 tablespoons olive oil

1 medium onion, finely chopped

1 small very ripe tomato, peeled, seeded, and coarsely chopped; or 1 teaspoon tomato paste

1 garlic clove, finely chopped

1 bay leaf

1 teaspoon coarse kosher salt, or to taste

¼ teaspoon white pepper

1 cup (7 oz) long-grain rice, rinsed and drained

1 sweet green, yellow, or red pepper, seeded and cut into ½-inch pieces

1. Put the chicken in a 2½-quart saucepan with 3 cups water and place over medium-high heat. Cover and bring to a boil, reduce the heat to medium-low and simmer until the chicken is tender, about 30 minutes. Remove the chicken, reserving the cooking liquid. Cut the meat into ½-inch chunks, discarding the bones. Set aside.

2. In a separate 2½-quart saucepan, heat the oil over medium-high heat and sauté the onion until soft and lightly colored.

3. Reduce the heat, then add the tomato or tomato paste, garlic, and bay leaf. Cover and simmer until the tomato is very soft and partially dissolved, about 15 minutes. If you are substituting tomato paste, make sure the paste is well blended, about 3 minutes.

4. Pour in 2 cups of the reserved cooking water and the salt and pepper. Stir and cover. Bring to a boil, add the rice, and simmer for 15 minutes, covered. Add the chopped pepper and continue to cook, covered, until the rice is tender and the liquid has been absorbed, about 10 minutes more.

Serves 4

BUTTERED RICE

Arroz de Manteiga

As children, we called this favorite "sticky rice."

3 tablespoons (1½ oz) butter, softened, divided

1 teaspoon coarse kosher salt

⅔ cup (5 oz) short-grain rice, rinsed and drained

1 tablespoon finely chopped cilantro or
   parsley (optional)

1. In a 2½-quart saucepan, place 1 tablespoon of the butter, the salt, and 2 cups water. Cover and bring to a boil. Stir in the rice, cover the pot, and simmer over medium-low heat until the rice is tender and the water is absorbed, 20 to 25 minutes. Add the remaining butter, and the chopped herbs, if using, and mix thoroughly.

Serves 6 to 8

RICE WITH CARROTS AND PEAS

Arroz de Cenoura e Ervilhas

Flavored in a most delicate way with peas and carrots, this rice is elegant enough to serve on special occasions.

1 tablespoon olive oil

1 tablespoon butter

1 small onion, finely chopped

1 teaspoon coarse kosher salt

1 bay leaf

2 cups (14 oz) long-grain rice, rinsed and drained

1 large carrot, peeled and cut into ½-inch cubes

¾ cup (3¾ oz) shelled peas, fresh or frozen

Fresh parsley sprigs, to garnish

1. Heat the oil and butter in a 3-quart pot over medium-high heat. Add and sauté the onion until soft and translucent, about 5 minutes.

2. Add 4 cups water and the salt and bay leaf. Cover and bring to a boil. Stir in the rice. Re-cover, reduce the heat to medium-low, and simmer for 10 minutes.

3. Add the carrots and peas and continue cooking until the carrots are tender and the rice is cooked, 10 to 15 minutes more.

4. For an impressive presentation, butter a ring mold and fill it with the hot rice, packing the mold firmly. Immediately invert onto a serving platter and garnish with sprigs of fresh parsley.

Variation: *Add 8 oz chouriço (page 168), cut into ½-inch cubes, to the onions and lightly brown. Continue with the recipe.*

Serves 4 to 6

RICE WITH CHICKEN LIVERS

Arroz com Figados de Galinha

Unearthing this recipe from family archives was worth the digging. When I was thirteen, a distant cousin in Canada whom I was visiting, made a dish similar to this, using elbow pasta. Although I never got the recipe, I never quite forgot it. Then Elena, a very close friend of my father's, invited me to delve through her family recipes. I couldn't believe my find. This version is made with rice and very much like what I ate when I was young, but it is tasty with pasta or rice.

2 tablespoons olive oil

1 medium onion, finely chopped

2 garlic cloves, finely chopped

1 bay leaf

½ cup (1 oz) finely chopped parsley

1 medium very ripe tomato, peeled, seeded, and finely chopped; or 1 tablespoon tomato paste

8 oz chicken livers, trimmed of any fat and coarsely chopped

1 cup (7 oz) medium- or long-grain rice, rinsed and drained

1 teaspoon coarse kosher salt

1. Heat the oil in a large frying pan over medium-high heat. Add the onion and sauté until translucent, about 5 minutes. Reduce the heat to medium-low.

2. Add the garlic, bay leaf, and parsley, and cook until the garlic becomes aromatic, then stir in the tomato or tomato paste. Cover and simmer until the tomato is soft and partially dissolved, about 15 minutes. If you are substituting tomato paste, make sure the paste is well blended, about 3 minutes.

3. Pour in 2 cups of water and add the chopped livers. Cover and bring to a boil over medium-high heat. Add the rice and salt and re-cover the pot. Reduce the heat and simmer until the rice is tender, about 20 minutes.

Serves 4 to 6

TOMATO RICE

Arroz de Tomate

From the moment I had my first taste of it, as a young girl at Prima Marguerida's (Cousin Margaret's) farm in Portugal, I was hooked. It would be foolhardy not to take advantage of the ripest and most flavorful tomatoes at harvest time to prepare this rice dish, which is a Portuguese favorite. The tomatoes should be as fresh as possible; the best ones, of course, would be vine-ripened, straight from your garden. I like to use the Portuguese variety *coração de boi/toro* (page 31), but any meaty variety like beefsteak is a good substitute. This dish is especially good with seafood. Because the growing season for tomatoes is limited in some parts of North America, in the dead of winter, use good-quality canned tomatoes or tomato paste rather than the pale supermarket tomatoes.

3 tablespoons olive oil, or 2 slices smoked bacon, coarsely chopped

1 medium onion, finely chopped

2 large very ripe tomatoes, peeled, seeded, and chopped (about 2 cups); or 1 tablespoon tomato paste

1 garlic clove, finely chopped

1 teaspoon coarse kosher salt

1 cup (7 oz) long-grain rice, rinsed and drained

1 tablespoon finely chopped parsley

6 small black olives, to garnish

1. Heat the oil or bacon in a 2½-quart saucepan over medium-high heat. (If using bacon, remove the crisp solids after the fat is rendered.) Add and sauté the onion until lightly colored. Reduce the heat to medium-low. Stir in the tomatoes or tomato paste and the garlic, cover, and cook until the tomatoes are soft and partially dissolved, about 15 minutes. If using tomato paste, make sure it is well blended, about 3 minutes.

2. Add 2 cups of water and bring to a boil over medium-high heat. Add the salt, then toss in the rice, stir, and cover the pan. Reduce the heat and simmer for about 20 minutes.

3. Stir in the parsley and continue cooking until the rice is tender and the liquid is absorbed, 5 to 10 minutes more.

4. For an impressive presentation, lightly oil custard cup molds and and fill them with serving-size portions, packing the rice firmly. Immediately invert the molds onto individual serving plates. Remove the molds, center a black olive on top of each portion, and serve.

Serves 4

BEANS WITH RICE

Feijão Guisado com Arroz

This common peasant recipe makes a simple but delicious side dish, or a light vegetarian meal.

½ cup (3½ oz) dried red kidney beans, soaked
  overnight in enough water to cover by 2 inches

3 tablespoons olive oil

1 small onion, finely chopped

1 garlic clove, finely chopped

½ bay leaf

1 teaspoon coarse kosher salt, or to taste

1 cup (7 oz) short- or long-grain rice,
  rinsed and drained

1 tablespoon wine vinegar

½ teaspoon ground white pepper

1. Drain the beans from the soaking water and rinse. Place the beans in a 1-quart saucepan with 2 cups fresh water. Cover and bring to a boil over medium-high heat. Reduce the heat and simmer until very tender (about 45 minutes). Drain and keep warm.

2. Heat the oil in a 2½-quart saucepan over medium-high heat. Add the onion, garlic, and bay leaf and sauté until the onion is translucent, about 5 minutes. Add 2 cups of water. Cover, bring to a boil, and add the salt.

3. Stir in the rice and reduce the heat to medium-low. Simmer the rice until tender, 20 to 25 minutes, and remove from the heat.

4. Add the reserved beans, vinegar, and pepper to the rice and mix well. Remove the bay leaf and serve.

Serves 4

CHICKPEA SALAD WITH SALT COD

Salada de Grão de Bico com Bacalhau

Accompanied with a simple green salad, olives, crusty bread, and *vinho verde*, this dish makes a no-fuss meal. When I am in a hurry or if I get a sudden impulse for this dish, I will use canned chickpeas and canned oil-packed tuna. I pile it on a bed of lettuce and lunch is ready.

1 cup (8 oz) dried chickpeas, soaked for at least 15 hours in 3½ cups water

8 oz salt cod with skin, soaked in several changes of cold water for 24 to 36 hours, refrigerated (see page 26)

1 small sweet onion, finely chopped

1 large garlic clove, finely chopped

3 tablespoons olive oil

1 tablespoon cider vinegar

1½ tablespoons finely chopped parsley or cilantro

1 teaspoon coarse kosher salt, or to taste

2 hard-boiled eggs, chopped or cut in wedges

½ teaspoon paprika

1. Drain and rinse the chickpeas, and place them in a 3-quart saucepan with enough water to cover them by 2 inches (about 4 cups). Cover and bring to a boil over medium-high heat. Reduce the heat and simmer until very tender, but not mushy, up to 1½ hours. Drain and set aside.

2. Remove the fish from the soaking water and rinse. In a medium pot, bring 4 cups of water to a boil. Turn off the heat and add the cod. Cover and leave for 15 to 20 minutes, then drain. Set aside until it is cool enough to handle.

3. Hand-shred the cod, discarding any skin or bones, and place the flesh in a serving bowl, along with the chickpeas, onion, and garlic.

4. In a small bowl, whisk the oil with the vinegar. Stir in the parsley and salt, if needed. Pour the dressing over the chickpea mixture and toss gently.

5. Garnish with the eggs and a sprinkling of paprika. This dish can be served hot, cold, or at room temperature, as a light meal or as a side dish for fish.

Serve 4 to 6

BEAN AND SAUSAGE STEW

Feijoada

Feijoada, a traditional dish in Brazil as well as in Portugal, contains beans, the ears and feet of a pig, and a combination of sausages, stewed meat, and dried beef. The northeast region of Portugal, Trás-os-Montes, is well known for its *feijoada*, which includes cabbage. My dear friendMarguerite (whose recipes also appear elsewhere in this book) shared her simple version of *feijoada* with me many years ago. A favorite in my family, it is easy to prepare and very satisfying on a cold night. I do not include the pig's ears and feet. If you wish to use the ears, belly, and hocks of a pig, be sure to scrape the ears well of any hairs, then cook the meat in plain water until quite tender before adding to the pot of beans. Azoreans often use kidney beans for this dish, while Continentals use white lima beans, and Brazilian Portuguese use black beans. I encourage you to try different beans—lima, fava, or kidney beans—and substitute or combine other Portuguese sausages for variety. Serve with plenty of crusty bread to dip in the broth.

1¼ cups (8 oz) dried red or white kidney beans, soaked overnight in enough water to cover by 2 inches

4 tablespoons olive oil

1 medium onion, finely chopped

1 very ripe tomato, peeled, seeded, and coarsely chopped

1 tablespoon paprika

1 garlic clove, finely chopped

1 bay leaf

1½ lb *linguiça* sausage (see page 168), cut into ¼-inch rounds

¼ cup red wine

2 medium starchy potatoes, such as Yukon Gold or russets, peeled and cut into 1-inch cubes

1. Drain and rinse the beans, and place them in a 2-quart saucepan with 3 cups of water, or enough to cover the beans by 1 inch. Cover and bring to a boil over medium-high heat. Reduce the heat to medium-low and simmer for 45 minutes, or until tender. Set aside.

2. Heat the oil in a 4-quart pot until quite hot. Add and sauté the onion until a light golden color. Toss in the tomato, paprika, garlic, and bay leaf and stir. Reduce the heat. Cover and simmer until the tomato is soft and almost dissolved, about 15 minutes. Add the *linguiça* sausage and continue to cook for 2 minutes.

3. Pour in the wine, if using, and simmer for 2 minutes. Add the potatoes, along with just enough cold water to cover them. Cover the pot and bring to a boil over medium-high heat. Reduce the heat and simmer until the potatoes are almost tender, about 15 minutes.

4. Stir in the beans with enough of their cooking broth to barely cover them (about ½ cup). Simmer, uncovered, for an additional 15 minutes. Turn off the heat. Allow the stew to stand for about 15 minutes before serving.

Serves 6

FRIAR'S BEANS

Feijão Frade

Black-eyed peas give this vegetarian bean salad a healthy and interesting appeal. Serve it with fish or alone as a light meal.

1¼ cups (8 oz) black-eyed peas, soaked for at least 6 hours in enough water to cover by 2 inches

1 small red onion, finely chopped

3 tablespoons olive oil

1 tablespoon wine or cider vinegar

1 tablespoon parsley, finely chopped

1 teaspoon coarse kosher salt, or to taste

2 hard-boiled eggs, peeled and chopped or cut into wedges

1. Drain and rinse the beans. Place in a 2-quart saucepan with enough fresh water to cover, about 4 cups. Cover and bring to a boil over medium-high heat. Reduce the heat and simmer until very tender but not mushy, about 40 minutes. Drain well. Place the cooked beans in a medium bowl with the onion.

2. In a separate bowl or measuring cup, whisk the oil with the vinegar and parsley. Season with salt. Pour this over the beans and toss gently. Transfer the beans to a serving dish and garnish with the eggs. Serve hot or at room temperature.

Variation: *Add flakes of cooked fresh tuna or well-drained, oil-packed canned tuna.*

Serves 2 to 4

SAUTÉED GREENS

Esparregado

Usually, young tender greens (*grelos*) like spinach, mustard greens, and broccoli rabe are simply sautéed in garlic oil and seasoned with salt and pepper, but this traditional preparation of tender spinach is very popular in our home, especially when served with pork (though it also goes well with beef). Baby mustard greens and spinach are most often used in this recipe, each one possessing a unique flavor. Frozen spinach can be used; just be sure to cook it and then drain it well.

1 lb spinach, thick ribs removed

3 tablespoons olive oil

1 garlic clove, mashed or halved

1 bay leaf

2 tablespoons all-purpose flour

1 tablespoon cider vinegar

1 teaspoon coarse kosher salt, or to taste

⅛ teaspoon freshly ground black pepper, or to taste

1. Place the spinach in a pot large enough to accommodate it. Add enough water to just cover it (about 1 cup), and bring to a boil. Reduce the heat and simmer over medium-low until the spinach is barely wilted, about 5 minutes. Drain well, coarsely chop, and set aside.

2. Heat the oil in a small frying pan (preferably nonstick) until hot, but not smoking. Lightly brown the garlic and bay leaf in the oil until the garlic is light golden color, then remove the garlic and bay leaf from the pan.

3. Reduce the heat to medium-low and add the spinach, turning it in the oil to coat thoroughly. Sprinkle the flour over the spinach and mix.

4. Drizzle the vinegar over the spinach and season with the salt and pepper. Turn the greens, almost mashing them onto themselves, until well mixed. Cook until any excess moisture evaporates and the greens start to hold together and pull away from the pan surface, almost like a mousse. Pull the pan back and forth over the burner so that the greens roll into a log shape. Roll out onto a serving plate as you would an omelet.

Serves 4

LITTLE FISH OF THE GARDEN

Peixinhos da Horta

As a child, I made this special dish with my father called *peixinhos da horta*, or "little garden fish." Going into the garden with him was always an adventure. Together we discovered what was ripe, harvested our crop, and decided what we would make with our ingredients. Without doubt, eating the rewards of our labor was the best part of having a garden! I did not particularly like green beans, but when they were prepared this way, I couldn't eat enough. Today, I serve them as an appetizer, and I find they do not last much longer than when I was a child.

1 lb flat green beans, trimmed

1½ teaspoons coarse kosher salt, or to taste

4 eggs, lightly beaten

½ cup (2¼ oz) all-purpose flour

¼ teaspoon white pepper, or to taste

1 cup olive oil

Variation: *For an egg-free version, substitute ¾ cups water or wine for the eggs.*

1. Place the beans in a medium saucepan with 1 teaspoon of the salt and enough water to cover by 1 inch. Cover and bring to a boil over medium-high heat. Reduce the heat and simmer until almost tender, about 3 minutes. Drain well and blot to remove excess water.

2. In a small mixing bowl, beat the eggs and whisk in the flour, pepper, and remaining ½ teaspoon of salt to make a batter.

3. Heat the olive oil in a small frying pan until hot, but not smoking. Working with three beans at a time, dip the beans in the batter, forming a group of three.

4. Immediately place the grouped beans in the pan and shallow-fry until golden, 1 to 2 minutes per side. The beans should stick together as they fry, although sometimes you may get one or two that separate. Using a slotted spoon, transfer to paper towels to drain. Serve hot or at room temperature.

Serves 6

STEWED GREEN BEANS

Feijão Verde Guisado

Fresh green beans never had it so good! The vinegar, tomato, and cilantro combine to make ordinary green beans zesty and flavorful. A little touch of cumin—Cousin Evelyn's Azorean influence—goes a long way.

1 tablespoon olive oil, or 2 oz salt pork, coarsely chopped

4 oz *linguiça* sausage (see page 168), cut into ¼-inch slices

1 medium onion, coarsely chopped

1 medium very ripe tomato, peeled and finely chopped; or 1 tablespoon tomato paste

4 garlic cloves, finely chopped

1 bay leaf

4 tablespoons finely chopped cilantro

1 teaspoon coarse kosher salt, or to taste

Pinch ground cumin

¼ teaspoon white pepper

¼ teaspoon crushed red pepper flakes (optional)

¼ cup wine vinegar

1 lb green beans, trimmed and cut into 2-inch lengths

Toasted pine nuts or sliced almonds, to garnish (optional)

1. In a large frying pan, heat the oil or render the fat from the salt pork over medium-high heat. Remove and discard any solid pieces of salt pork. Lightly brown the sausage slices in the oil or rendered fat, then transfer to a dish.

2. Toss in the onion and sauté until a light golden color. Add the tomato, garlic, and bay leaf. Reduce the heat to medium-low and cover. Simmer until the tomato is very soft and partially dissolved, about 15 minutes.

3. Add ½ cup water and 2 tablespoons of the cilantro, along with the salt, cumin, pepper, and crushed red pepper. Pour in the wine vinegar and stir.

4. Add the beans to the pot, re-cover, and simmer until the beans are just tender with a little bite left, 10 to 12 minutes. Return the sausage to the pan. Garnish with a sprinkling of the remaining cilantro and pine nuts or almonds.

LEMON CARROTS

Cenoura com Limão

In Portuguese kitchens vegetables usually appear in soups instead of as side dishes. This dish is a delicious exception, especially if carrots are your passion. This recipe is simple enough to make at short notice. The lemon juice is a perfect counterpoint to the sweetness of carrots.

1 lb carrots, peeled and cut into
   ¼-inch rounds

2 tablespoons olive oil

3 tablespoons (1½ oz) butter

1 garlic clove finely chopped

¼ cup lemon juice

1 tablespoon finely chopped cilantro,
   plus extra to garnish, if desired

1 teaspoon coarse kosher salt, or to taste

1. In a 2-quart saucepan, place the carrots and 1 cup water or enough to cover them. Cover the pan and bring to a boil over medium-high heat, then reduce the heat and simmer for about 5 minutes or until the carrots are nearly tender. Drain the water.

2. Heat the oil and butter in a frying pan until quite hot. Add the garlic and sauté until it becomes aromatic. Add the lemon juice, cilantro, and salt and simmer for 1 minute.

3. Toss in the carrots, turning them in the pan to coat thoroughly. Cover tightly and simmer for 4 minutes or until desired doneness. Transfer to a serving dish and garnish with extra cilantro, if desired.

Makes 3 to 4 cups

ROASTED SWEET PEPPERS

Pimentas Assadas

This is a great accompaniment to fish dishes and grilled sausages. It can be served alone as an appetizer, accompanied with fresh cheese, or even popped into a sandwich. Allow the peppers to marinate in the dressing for several hours, or even overnight. When I was young, we would roast these peppers over the open flame of our gas stove, turning them as they charred. It was fun peeling them, especially knowing that eating them was the final step.

6 medium sweet bell peppers, red, green, yellow, or a combination

¼ cup Portuguese olive oil or good-quality extra-virgin olive oil

1 tablespoon red wine vinegar or cider vinegar, or to taste

3 garlic cloves, finely chopped

1 teaspoon coarse kosher salt, or to taste

1 teaspoon ground marjoram or dried oregano

¼ teaspoon freshly ground black pepper

1. Rinse the peppers and dry them well. Place them on a baking sheet and broil about 4 inches from the heat source, turning often, until the skin blisters and blackens, 25 to 30 minutes. When all sides are done, remove the peppers and set aside briefly until cool enough to handle. Slip off the skins and core, scraping off the seeds, then slice or leave whole.

2. Place in a bowl and drizzle with oil, vinegar, garlic, salt, marjoram or oregano, and pepper. Toss gently and chill for several hours. Bring to room temperature to serve.

Serves 2

EGGS WITH LINGUIÇA

Ovos com Linguiça

Enjoy this Portuguese-style omelet for a weekend breakfast. Aromatic and flavorful, it is a wonderful way to start the day.

2 tablespoons olive oil

1 tablespoon finely chopped onion

2 oz *linguiça* sausage (see page 168), sliced into ¼-inch rounds

3 eggs, lightly beaten

2 teaspoons finely chopped parsley

1. Heat the oil in a frying pan over medium-high heat. Add and sauté the onion until a light golden color, about 10 minutes. Toss in the sausage and cook for 1 to 2 minutes, until lightly browned. Reduce the heat to medium-low.

2. Mix the eggs with the parsley and pour over the sausage and onion.

3. Cook the eggs without stirring, making a flat omelet. Invert onto a plate and slide back into the pan to cook the other side for 1 more minute. Slide onto a serving dish.

Variation: *Add ½ cup coarsely chopped cooked asparagus with the eggs.*

Serves 8

GRACIOSA-STYLE TORTAS

Tortas da Graciosa

The Azoreans speak fondly of tortas. The name, which means "tart," is misleading; these are more like miniature omelets. This traditional version is definitely for cumin lovers. Traditionally, they would be made using any leftover meat or fish, and seasoned with a scallions and spice. They make tasty snacks, and also work well as an appetizer or sandwich filling.

7 large eggs, lightly beaten

1 cup leftover cooked meat or fish, coarsely chopped

3 cups (3½ oz) finely chopped scallions (3 bunches)

1 cup (2 oz) finely chopped parsley

4 garlic cloves, finely chopped

2 teaspoons coarse kosher salt

3 tablespoons white or yellow corn flour
   (all-purpose flour can be used in a pinch)

½ teaspoon ground cumin

½ teaspoon freshly ground black pepper
   or hot pepper sauce

¼ teaspoon ground nutmeg

Olive or corn oil, for frying

1. In a mixing bowl, combine all of the ingredients, except for the oil, and stir to blend. The mixture should be somewhat thick.

2. Pour enough oil into a large frying pan to cover the base in a shallow layer (about ¼ cup), and place over medium-high heat. Once hot, use a soup spoon to scoop up some of the egg mixture and place in the pan, spreading it out evenly with the back of the spoon until it is just under ½-inch thick. You can probably fit two or three in the pan at once. Pan-fry until golden, 1 to 2 minutes on each side, making sure they are cooked in the middle. Remove and drain on paper towels. Transfer the *tortas* to a serving dish and serve hot or at room temperature.

Serves 4 to 6

MARY'S TORTAS

Tortas à Maria

You don't have to wait for leftover meat to make tortas. This version is from my sister-in-law Laraine Ortins, whose mother, Mary Jodrie, used canned tuna. It is less spicy but just as tasty as the traditional recipe. I like it as a late-night bite with a salad.

3 eggs, lightly beaten

3 or 4 slices day-old bread, slightly moistened with
  water and shredded

6 oz oil-packed canned tuna, drained and flaked
  (or any leftover meat or fish)

1 small onion, finely chopped

1 tablespoon finely chopped parsley

1 teaspoon coarse kosher salt, or to taste

⅛ teaspoon freshly ground black pepper,
  or to taste

Olive oil, for shallow frying

1. In a mixing bowl, combine all of the ingredients except for the olive oil, and stir to blend. The mixture should be somewhat thick.

2. In a frying pan, heat 2 tablespoons of oil over medium-high heat. Using a soup spoon, place one scoop of the mixture into the hot pan and, using the back of the spoon, spread it out evenly to about ¼-inch thick, like a small pancake.

3. Cook for 2 minutes. When the *torta* is golden underneath, turn and cook an additional minute or two, making sure the egg is cooked, especially in the middle. Repeat, frying 2 or 3 at a time, and topping up with oil, as needed. Transfer to a serving dish and serve warm or at room temperature.

Serves 4

SWEET PEPPER SALAD

Salada de Pimenta Doce

This "salad" is really just the accompaniment that we usually serve alongside boiled potatoes and grilled sardines. Consider the quantities merely as a guide; you can adjust the ingredients' quantities to your preference.

1 large sweet green pepper, cored, seeded, and thinly sliced

1 large tomato, sliced (optional)

1 medium onion, thinly sliced in rounds

¼ cup (½ oz) unpitted black olives

½ cup olive oil, or to taste

¼ cup red wine vinegar or cider vinegar, or to taste

1 teaspoon coarse kosher salt, or to taste

⅛ teaspoon freshly ground black pepper, or to taste

1 tablespoon finely chopped parsley

1. Arrange the pepper, tomato, and onion slices on a serving platter or on individual salad dishes, and top with the olives. Drizzle oil and vinegar over the salad, season with salt and pepper, and garnish with parsley.

PORTUGUESE-STYLE SALADS

Portuguese salads, especially in the early part of the growing season, are a simple combination of tender spring garden lettuce, a bit of onion, perhaps watercress, and cilantro. With our year-round availability of tomatoes, occasionally Portuguese families adopt the American custom of adding tomatoes and cucumbers to salads. Before supermarkets, what was being harvested from the garden dictated the contents of a salad. Prepared salad dressings were unheard of; one simply drizzled a salad with olive oil and vinegar to taste, a habit that is still popular.

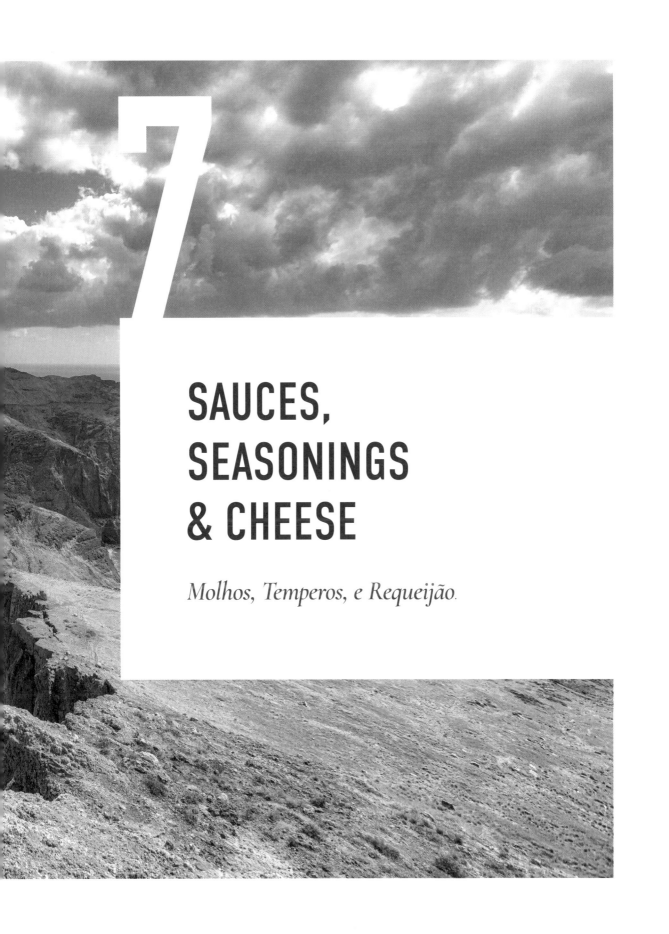

7

SAUCES,
SEASONINGS
& CHEESE

Molhos, Temperos, e Requeijão.

7 SAUCES, SEASONINGS & CHEESE
Molhos, Temperos, e Requeijão

Essential to Portuguese cooking are the wine-and-garlic marinades, *vinhos d'alhos,* that flavor beef, pork, chicken, game, seafood dishes, and the famous sausages. Variations on the basic components of wine and garlic may be as subtle as using red wine in place of white. Although red wine is most often used with beef and sausages, it is also used on occasion with rabbit and chicken, turning the meat a darker color. It is also not uncommon for white wine to be used for marinating beef. White wine is frequently used for pork, poultry, seafood, and sausages. Alternatively, some cooks use equal amounts of both in a single marinade, especially in sausage-making (see Chapter 5). A rule of thumb I like to follow is white, light-bodied wines for delicate-flavored meats and fish, and red wine for full-flavored meats.

Optional ingredients in marinades include hot chili peppers, onions, bay leaves, cilantro or parsley, paprika, lemon juice, wine vinegar, and olive oil. Choices and quantities are dictated by the ingredient being marinated and, as always, personal taste.

VINEGAR SAUCES

In Portuguese cooking, fish—especially fried fish—is often served with a tangy vinegar sauce. In the Azores the sauce is called *molhanga* or *molho cru* (raw sauce) and on the mainland it is called *escabeche.* Raw vinegar sauce is similar to vinaigrette, but with more zest. It makes for one of the most extraordinary ways to enjoy fried or grilled fish. The olive oil used in preparing the sauce can be the same oil that was used to fry the fish; just be sure that the oil is not too brown with excess flour, in which case I suggest using fresh olive oil.

There are many variations for this tangy sauce, each one having its own special flavor. If the garlic is lightly browned in a bit of olive oil before the remaining ingredients are combined, the sauce is considered cooked. These sauces, which are typically prepared without cooking, can be served on the side as a dipping sauce or poured over fried fish before serving. The sauce is even poured over boiled potatoes if they are served with the fish. Sometimes the cooked fish is left to marinate in the vinegar sauce for 2 or 3 days in the refrigerator, then brought to room temperature and served.

Left: Hot Pepper Paste (page 220)

Makes about 5½ cups

AUNT CUSTODIA'S TOMATO SAUCE

Tomatada à Tia Custodia

My Uncle Ilidio nods his head in praise of his aunt Custodia's tasty sauce. Aunt Custodia often spooned it over boiled potatoes. Made from his recollections and her instructions, the sauce pleases us as well. Vegetarians might agree.

4 oz salt pork; or 4 slices of bacon, coarsely chopped; or ¼ cup olive oil

1 medium onion, finely chopped

1 to 2 garlic cloves, coarsely chopped

6 large (2½ lb) very ripe tomatoes, peeled, seeded, and coarsely chopped (about 6 cups)

2 teaspoons coarse kosher salt, or to taste

⅛ teaspoon freshly ground black pepper

1. Heat the salt pork, bacon, or olive oil in a 2-quart saucepan over medium-high heat. Sauté the salt pork or bacon until the fat has been rendered. Discard the solid pieces.

2. Add the onion to the pan and sauté until translucent, about 5 minutes. Toss in the garlic and cook until it is aromatic, about 1 minute. Mix in the tomatoes, cover, and bring to a boil. Reduce the heat to medium-low and gently simmer, partially covered, for 1 hour. Even after the tomatoes have cooked down, the sauce should still have some texture and not be too thick. Season with salt and pepper. Use immediately or refrigerate or freeze for future use.

Variations: *Give the sauce some zing by adding 1 teaspoon or more of Hot Pepper Paste (page 220). If you prefer a smoother texture, simply purée it using a handheld blender. This sauce can be used to flavor stews and other dishes.*

Makes about 1 cup

SPICY VINEGAR SAUCE

Molhanga

Our cousin Evelina Ortins Cunha shares her wonderful recipe for *molhanga*, which packs extra tang and stands out among the best. If you use the oil left over from frying fish, make sure it is not too dark. If it is, use fresh olive oil.

1 teaspoon cumin seeds, or ¼ teaspoon ground cumin
6 garlic cloves, finely chopped
½ teaspoon coarse kosher salt, or to taste
¾ teaspoon safflower (see page 29) or paprika,
  or ½ teaspoon saffron threads
¼ teaspoon freshly ground black pepper
¼ teaspoon sugar
1 teaspoon Hot Pepper Paste (page 220)
3 tablespoons finely chopped parsley
¾ cup wine vinegar
1 tablespoon olive oil (fresh or leftover from frying the fish)

1. Using a mortar and pestle, blend the cumin, garlic, salt, safflower, paprika, or saffron, pepper, and sugar well. Add the pepper paste and parsley.
2. Transfer to a bowl. Whisk in the vinegar, ¼ cup water, and the olive oil. To use, pour over the cooked fish or serve on the side.

Variation: *Our other cousin, Noelia, makes her* molhanga *very much like Evelyn's. While the amounts are different, the ingredients and method are the same, though Noelia's variation includes a dash or two of freshly ground nutmeg, which adds another dimension to the sauce.*

Makes about 1¼ cups

VINEGAR SAUCE WITH TOMATO

Molhanga com Tomate

This is another variation of vinegar sauce from Graciosa in the Azores, where my husband Philip's family comes from. Today's convenience of tomato paste gives a deeper dimension of tomato flavor to this sauce. Before the availability of tomato paste, a peeled, seeded, and chopped tomato was used. This recipe works well as a "cooked" sauce for soft-shell crab (see Variation).

1 head of garlic, peeled and finely chopped
1 teaspoon coarse kosher salt
1 teaspoon ground safflower (see page 29) or paprika
¼ cup (½ oz) finely chopped parsley
1 tablespoon tomato paste
½ cup wine vinegar
½ cup olive oil

1. Using a mortar and pestle, mash the garlic with the salt and safflower to form a paste. Blend the parsley and tomato paste into the garlic mixture. Mix in the vinegar and transfer to a medium bowl.
2. Gradually whisk in the olive oil. Serve alongside or poured over fish.

Variation: *For a cooked sauce, just sauté the garlic, salt, safflower, and tomato paste in the olive oil over medium-low heat until the tomato paste is blended in. Remove from the heat and whisk in the vinegar. Serve alongside, or drizzled over boiled and cracked soft-shell crabs.*

Makes about 2 cups

SWEET RED PEPPER PASTE

Massa de Pimentão

Massa de pimentão is a very important and frequently used ingredient in Portuguese dishes. Because of its salt content, a little bit goes a long way, and additional salt is not usually necessary. I remember my father leading me through the simple steps of its preparation. Together we washed, quartered, and seeded the peppers. He would pour a thick layer of coarse salt into a wooden vegetable crate, and place a single layer of pepper slices, skin side up, on the salt, flattening any curves in the peppers. He would then cover the peppers with another layer of salt. A second and sometimes a third layer was made, ending with a covering of salt. He would weigh them down, pressing with dinner plates, and the box was tipped slightly so that the juices would drain away. It would remain like this for a few days or until the peppers stopped draining. He would remove them from the box, shake off the excess salt, and process them through a hand-cranked grinder. We packed the peppers into sterilized baby-food jars, poured olive oil over the top, and stored away our treasure to enjoy in future dishes.

You will need a freestanding stainless-steel sieve or footed colander with mesh or small holes, or cheesecloth can be used to line a colander that has large holes. This makes enough to fill two half-pint (8 oz) preserving jars, which should be sterilized. They should have tight-fitting lids.

5 lb coarse salt (not pickling salt; it is too fine)
4 large sweet red peppers, cored, seeded, and quartered
½ cup good-quality imported olive oil

Notes: *I do not recommend adding garlic to this paste. Instead, use fresh garlic in recipes calling for pepper paste instead.*

You can sometimes still find wooden produce crates. Check your local market.

I like to use fresh cayenne peppers in this recipe.

1. Set the colander inside a large noncorrosive pan or dish with sides. Pour a 1-inch layer of salt into the colander to form the base. (Some salt will seep out.)

2. Place a layer of peppers, skin side up, on the salt, pressing them into the salt. Be sure to uncurl even the smallest part of the pepper, otherwise mold will form.

3. Cover completely with a ½-inch layer of salt, and repeat with the remaining peppers, ending with another ½-inch covering of salt. Place a heavy dish on top to weigh it down. Let stand for up to 5 days to allow the peppers to drain. After the fourth day, the the peppers will be about ¼-inch thick. The salt will be damp and the draining liquid will be barely a trickle.

4. Shake off the excess salt and coarsely process the peppers using either a hand-cranked grinder, food processor, or blender. The texture should not be smooth—more like coarsely ground tomatoes.

5. Fill the jars, leaving about 1 inch at the top. Pour olive oil over the top to a depth of ½ inch. Close the jar tightly and refrigerate.

6. To use *massa de pimentão*, simply push aside the congealed olive oil with a spoon and remove what you need, replacing the oil and adding more, if necessary. Use sparingly, since it is salty. It will keep for several months in the refrigerator if stored as directed. The salt acts as a preservative.

Makes about 2 cups

HOT PEPPER PASTE

Massa de Malagueta

Making this paste is so easy, and it keeps for at least six months in the refrigerator. It is traditionally made with the meatiest available *malagueta/piri piri* peppers (page 20), but you can easily substitute your favorite chili pepper variety. The method is different from sweet pepper paste because water is not drained off and the seeds are retained to strengthen the fire of the chili peppers. Some recipes add a touch of lemon juice or vinegar and garlic, but I prefer to keep the paste simple and add flavorings to the dish separately. When adding *massa de malagueta* to recipes, keep in mind that it is quite salty; you will need to taste the dish before adding any additional salt. You will need a sterilized jar, about 1 pint (16 oz) in capacity.

1 lb Thai bird's eye chili peppers, or your
   favorite chili peppers, rinsed and patted dry
½ cup (4 oz) coarse kosher salt
⅓ cup olive oil

Note: *Any time you cut hot chili peppers, be sure to wear food-safe gloves to protect your skin. Do not touch your eyes or face. Should you accidentally do so, rinse the affected area with milk; it will stop the burning almost immediately.*

1. Rinse and pat-dry the chili peppers. Using food-safe gloves to protect your skin (see Note), cut off and discard the green caps and stems, but do not discard the seeds. Finely chop the peppers by hand, or using a grinder or food processor. Transfer the peppers to a medium bowl. Stir in the salt, mixing thoroughly. Loosely cover the bowl with plastic wrap and refrigerate for 8 days, giving the mixture a few turns every day.
2. On the eighth day, pack the mixture into a sterilized jar, top it off with ½-inch of olive oil, and refrigerate.
3. Massa de malagueta will keep for several months in the refrigerator when stored as directed. The salt acts as a preservative.

Makes about 2 quarts

PICKLED CHILI PEPPERS

Malagueta na Vinagre

Every culture has rituals involving food. Like drinking tequila with salt and lime, the Azoreans have a method for eating pickled chili peppers: First you take a bite of the chili pepper. Then as quickly as you can, you chase it down with a spoonful of soup to quiet the fire.

These fiery vinegar pickles are traditionally made with the smallest *malagueta/piri piri* chili peppers (page 20). You can use your favorite chili peppers, from large to tiny, for this preparation. Whatever variety you use, this colorful pickle can be given as gifts to friends. This recipe fills two 1-quart (32 oz) jars. You can recycle any mayonnaise or pickle jars that have tight-sealing lids—just adjust the amounts of ingredients depending on the size of your jars. Sterilize or wash the jars and lids thoroughly before using.

1 lb Thai bird's eye chili peppers, or your favorite chili peppers (or enough to fill your jars)

Apple cider or wine vinegar

Boiling water

3 garlic cloves (optional)

1 tablespoon coarse kosher salt

1 tablespoon dried marjoram or oregano (optional)

5 whole allspice berries or black peppercorns

1 tablespoon olive oil

1. Rinse the peppers. Cut off and discard the green caps and stems.

2. Pack the peppers into the jars, and cover with equal amounts of boiling water and vinegar. Add your chosen seasonings and top the jars with 1 to 2 tablespoons of olive oil.

3. Allow to cool completely, then cover tightly and refrigerate for 2 to 3 weeks before using. During that time, occasionally turn the jars upside down, giving the peppers an occasional shake.

Makes 2 cups

WHITE WINE AND GARLIC MARINADE

Vinho d'Alhos

This marinade uses the sweet red pepper paste of the Alentejo. We use it for pork and beef.

4 peppercorns
6 garlic cloves, coarsely chopped
2 bay leaves, crumbled
1 tablespoon Sweet Red Pepper Paste (page 219)
Pinch crushed red pepper flakes (optional)
2 cups red or white wine, as needed

1. Using a mortar and pestle, finely grind the peppercorns. Add and mash in the garlic, blending well. Incorporate the bay leaf, sweet red pepper paste, and red pepper flakes, mixing until well blended.
2. Coat the meat in the paste and place in a nonreactive dish. Pour the wine over the meat. Marinate overnight in the refrigerator.

Makes about 2 cups

MARINADE FOR SEAFOOD

Vinho d'Alhos para Frutos do Mar

This marinade is especially good with swordfish or tuna steaks, but also works with fish fillets, or even shrimp (see Note).

1 to 2 garlic cloves, finely chopped
1 teaspoon coarse kosher salt
¼ cup (½ oz) finely chopped cilantro
1 tablespoon lemon juice
½ bay leaf
⅛ teaspoon crushed red pepper flakes
3 white peppercorns, or ⅛ teaspoon ground white pepper
½ cup olive oil
1 cup light white wine, such as *vinho verde* or light chablis

Note: *For shrimp, whisk the wine and oil together with the garlic and lemon mixture and pour over the shellfish. Marinate for 1 hour. Be sure to use a nonreactive bowl.*

1. In a mortar, combine the garlic, salt, and cilantro and mash well. Add the lemon juice, bay leaf, crushed red pepper flakes, and white pepper, continuing to blend. Drizzle in 1 tablespoon of the olive oil and mix to incorporate thoroughly.
2. Coat the fish with the marinade and place in a nonreactive dish. Combine the wine and remaining oil. Pour over the fish and marinate for 1 hour in the refrigerator.

WINE AND GARLIC MARINADE

Vinho d'Alhos

This marinade can be used for chicken, pork, or beef.

3 or 4 garlic cloves
1 tablespoon paprika
1 teaspoon coarse kosher salt, or to taste
6 black peppercorns
1 tablespoon olive oil
1 cup red or white wine or a mixture

1. Using a mortar and pestle, mash the garlic and add the dry ingredients one at a time, blending well. Drizzle in the olive oil.
2. Rub the meat with the spice mixture and place in a nonreactive dish. Pour the wine over the meat to partially or entirely cover it, depending on the recipe.
3. Marinate the meat in the refrigerator, turning occasionally, for several hours or overnight.

WHITE WINE MARINADE

Vinho d'Alhos

This is best for fish, chicken, or pork.

1 or 2 garlic cloves
3 green or black peppercorns
1 bay leaf
1 cup white wine, or as needed
1 medium onion, thinly sliced
1 tablespoon finely chopped parsley

1. Using a mortar and pestle, mash the garlic and grind in the peppercorns and the bay leaf. Stir in the wine. Transfer to a bowl or shallow dish, add the remaining ingredients, along with the fish, poultry, or meat. Marinate overnight in the refrigerator.

VINEGAR SAUCE WITH GARLIC AND HERBS

Molho Escabeche

This Portuguese mainland version of vinegar sauce can be used to marinate fish that has been fried or grilled. Refrigerate the cooked fish for two to three days in the sauce, then serve.

½ cup olive oil (fresh or leftover from frying fish)

1 small onion, finely chopped

6 garlic cloves, finely chopped

1 bay leaf

¼ cup (½ oz) finely chopped parsley

1 tablespoon paprika

½ cup cider vinegar or red wine vinegar

½ teaspoon coarse kosher salt, or to taste

¼ teaspoon white or black pepper

1. In a frying pan, heat the oil over medium-high heat and fry the onion until translucent. Reduce the heat, add the garlic, and cook until it becomes aromatic, about 2 minutes. Add the bay leaf, parsley, and paprika. Heat through and remove from the heat.

2. Add the vinegar, salt, and pepper. Mix well and pour over cooked fish or serve on the side.

Makes two 1 lb cheeses or four 8 oz cheeses

FRESH CHEESE

Requeijão/Queijo Fresco

This cheese has the flavor of cottage cheese, but with a firmer texture that allows it to be sliced. In my family, we always made our own molds for cheesemaking. These molds must be perforated to allow the liquid whey to drain. Now I use small-mesh plastic baskets (pint or half-pint size), but when I was young, we used cleaned shallow, perforated tin cans—the ones that held tuna or pineapple rings.

You can fashion molds easily and inexpensively from deli, margarine, cream cheese, or other plastic food containers. Using a sharp utility knife, make slashes in the bottom and sides of the container for drainage. Or use a hole punch to make small holes instead of slashes. Wash well and your molds are ready. Place filled cheese molds in a shallow pan. In the refrigerator, place the pan at a slight tilt so that the whey drains away from the molds.

Some brands of whole milk don't work as well as others. Milk with a minimum of 3% fat, straight from a local farm, and without additives is best. You may need to experiment with different brands. Some people use less rennet, but bear in mind that less rennet means longer processing.

EQUIPMENT

A 4-quart pot

An instant-read thermometer

A stainless-steel fine-mesh strainer

Two one-pint (16 oz) or 4 half-pint (8 oz) cheese molds

4 to 5 rennet tablets, 2 teaspoons powdered rennet, or 20 to 25 drops of liquid rennet

1 gallon whole milk, minimum 3% fat (do not use ultra-pasteurized milk)

⅓ cup coarse kosher salt, or to taste (omit if making cheese for *Queijadas*, page 277)

1. If using rennet tablets, place them in a small dish or a mortar and grind them into tiny pieces.

2. Pour the milk into a 4-quart pot and place over low heat. Heat the milk until it is lukewarm (78°F). Be careful not to overheat it. Remove ½ cup of the warm milk from the pot and transfer to a cup. Dissolve the rennet in the ½ cup of milk. Quickly return the rennet mixture to the pot of milk. Add the salt and stir well with a wooden spoon.

3. Cover the pot with a lid and place a towel over it. After 20 minutes, give the milk a turn with the wooden spoon and re-cover. Let stand for 1 to 1½ hours, or until the milk mixture springs back when pressed. The curds should have the texture of semi-firm custard, the whey should be visibly separate, and the edge of the curds defined.

4. Suspend a large fine-meshed strainer or sieve over a deep bowl or pot. Use a small-mesh hand strainer or slotted spoon to carefully transfer the curds into the large strainer or sieve, allowing the whey to drain away. You may lose some bits of curd if you use a slotted spoon. Let the curd stand in the

Continued overleaf

strainer for 15 minutes, or until the draining slows to a mere trickle. Tilt and roll the strainer back and forth to assist the draining. The cheese will reduce in size and thicken as the whey is drained.

5. Place the molds in a shallow pan. Spoon the curds into the molds, pressing lightly to push out more whey. Repeat until they are completely filled. The whey will continue to drain for several hours.

6. Refrigerate for at least 24 hours, occasionally draining the whey from the pan as needed. The cheese is ready when no more whey drains out and the cheese is fairly firm. It will keep for 4 to 5 days in the refrigerator. Season with additional salt, if needed, and serve with crusty bread.

Serving Suggestion: *The following is adapted from a dish served at the Atasca Restaurant in Cambridge, Massachusetts. Cut the cheese into ½-inch slices and arrange on a plate with chopped tomato and red onion. Add fine slices of* presunto *ham and drizzle with olive oil and wine vinegar.*

OLD-FASHIONED CHEESEMAKING

In Portugal the age-old method of making fresh cheese used unpasteurized milk straight from the sheep and goats. My great-grandfather Luis Elvas, who was a shepherd in the Alentejo region, would milk the animals. Together, he and my great-grandmother Ana Maria would make cheese to sell. They would gather *alcachofra* (*cynara scolymus*), the artichoke-like flower of a thistle plant called *cardo* (field eryngo), which grows wild in Portugal. The tips of the flowers were cut by hand and dried. For cheesemaking, the dried flowers were tied into little bundles and soaked in water. The liquid squeezed from the plants went into the warm milk to curdle and ferment it. The curds were placed in molds made from leaves and cloth. When the cheese was ready, my great-grandmother would make her rounds to sell them. The process of cheesemaking may seem daunting but do not be intimidated by the instructions. The steps are detailed and easy to follow. The process is certainly easier today than it was for my great-grandparents! Although the centuries-old tradition of using wild thistle to curdle milk for cheese may continue in areas of Portugal, here in the United States, rennet has gained popularity as a curdling agent. Keeping sheep and goats in our backyards is no longer a common practice, so pasteurized cow milk is used.

8

BREAD

Pão

8 BREAD
Pão

Some of the first breads in Portugal and the Azores were made of cornmeal, which had to be softened with hot water before baking. Once the method of leavening was learned, new types of breads were created. While most Portuguese bread is made with wheat flour alone, some varieties, especially from northern mainland Portugal, contain wheat flour combined with rye and corn flours. These rustic, peasant-style breads are still made in the homes of Portuguese immigrants and their descendants in America, though they can taste a little different from those made in Portugal, due to the differences in the flour and cornmeal available here, and adapted methods. The most common types of bread found in Portuguese homes in the United States are the crusty rolls called *papo-secos,* cornmeal breads (called *broa* or *pão de milho,* depending on their region of origin), and homestyle bread, *pão caseiro.*

Traditional Portuguese methods use small batches of dough starter, made days in advance, or sponge fermentations (*fermente*) that do not incorporate sugar with the yeast. Traditionally, no fat is added to the dough for *papo-secos* or *pão caseiro.*

Some cooks have adopted the use of sugar and fat to assist fermentation, give color, and prolong shelf life while making the bread more tender. Before you embark on making the bread recipes in this chapter, here are some points to remember:

• Have your ingredients at room temperature.
• Yeast comes in different forms—fresh cake, active dry, rapid rise, and active instant. One block of fresh cake yeast weighing 0.6 oz is equivalent to one ¼ oz envelope (2¼ teaspoons) active-dry yeast, rapid-rise yeast, or instant yeast. Do not use rapid-rise yeast for the breads in the following recipes.
• Water that is too hot will kill the yeast before you have begun, so pay attention the temperature specified in the recipe.
• Do not add salt during the proofing stage (the first mixing of the yeast with a warm liquid).
• Store freshly baked breads wrapped in clean kitchen towels made of broadcloth or in cloth bags. Plastic bags ruin a crisp crust and also promote spoilage in breads that have a moist interior.
• Once your baked breads have cooled completely, they can be wrapped tightly in plastic to seal out air, followed by a layer of aluminum foil, then frozen. Allow to thaw at room temperature, then warm in a moderate oven for a few minutes.

Left: Homsestyle Bread (page 236)

Makes 3 or 4 loaves

CORNBREAD

Broa/Pão de Milho

Reflecting the type of corn grown in each region, the cornmeal bread of mainland Portugal, called *broa*, calls for yellow cornmeal, while the Azorean version, *pão de milho*, uses a finely ground white cornmeal. Portuguese home cooks and bakeries in North America typically use fine white or yellow corn flour (which is a finer grind than fine cornmeal). The ratio of corn flour to wheat flour can vary. This Azorean-style recipe uses white corn flour and requires only one rising. Originally, it was baked in a stone oven. The finished product should be a medium heavy bread, with a fine, somewhat moist interior (for a drier interior, bake at 500°F for 15 minutes, then lower the heat to 375°F for the remaining 35 to 40 minutes).

SPONGE

Two ¼ oz envelopes (4½ teaspoons) active-
   dry yeast
½ cup warm water (between 90 and 112°F)
1 tablespoon all-purpose flour

DOUGH

7 cups (2 lb) white corn flour
1 tablespoons table salt
5 cups boiling water
7¼ cups (2 lb) unbleached all-purpose flour,
   plus extra for dusting
Tepid water, as needed

1. To make the sponge, dissolve the yeast in the water and set aside for 10 minutes. Mix in the flour, cover, and set aside for 30 minutes.
2. Place the corn flour in a large bowl.
3. Dissolve the salt in the boiling water. Pour the salted water over the corn flour and, stirring quickly with a wooden spoon, mix thoroughly for 5 minutes, making sure all the flour has been moistened. It should look like lumpy mashed potatoes. Set aside until it is cool enough to handle, about 15 minutes.
4. Then gradually mix in the all-purpose flour, the yeast sponge, and ½ cup of tepid water, until the dough comes together. If it seems dry, mix in ½ cup more water, but only if absolutely necessary. Knead in the bowl for about 10 minutes. The dough should be wet enough to stick to your hands a little. Dust the dough with flour and cover with a clean towel. Set aside in a in a warm, draft-free spot to rise until doubled in size, 2½ hours.

5. When this time is up, preheat the oven to 500°F and flour 3 or 4 aluminum pie dishes or 8-inch round cake pans (depending on how many loaves you wish to make).
6. Do not punch down the dough. Rather, cut the dough into 3 or 4 equal portions, and briefly set aside on a floured work surface without shaping. You don't want to deflate the risen dough.
7. Swirl some water in a 1-quart bowl, empty it, and immediately dust the bowl with about 1 tablespoon of flour.
8. Place one portion of dough into the bowl, taking care not to compress it. Holding the bowl with both hands, swirl the dough once or twice to shape it. Quickly invert the bowl into one of your prepared pans. Repeat with the remaining portions of dough.
9. Place the pans on the middle rack of the oven and bake for 35 to 45 minutes, depending on the size of your loaves. When done, the bottoms should sound hollow when tapped. Wrap with a clean tea towel until needed.

FRIED FLATBREAD

Pão de Sertã

Long before knowledge of leavenings, breads were flat. Today, Portuguese Americans from the Azores continue to make these unleavened breads. My friend Marguerite remembers her mother cooking this particular flatbread in a long-handled cast-iron frying pan. It is made from corn flour and wheat flour fried in corn oil, and should be served hot, accompanying a hearty meal. You will need a 10-inch cast-iron frying pan, tongs, and a spatula.

2 cups (8½ oz) white or yellow corn flour

2 teaspoons table salt

1¾ cups boiling water

1 cup (4½ oz) all-purpose flour

⅓ cup tepid water

Corn oil, for frying

1. In a large bowl, combine the corn flour and salt and mix until the salt is evenly distributed.

2. Pour about half of the boiling water over the corn flour. Using a wooden spoon, quickly stir, blending well. Add the remaining boiling water and mix well. It should look like lumpy mashed potatoes. Set aside for 20 to 30 minutes or until cool enough to handle.

3. Gently cut the all-purpose flour into the corn flour mixture, alternating with the measured tepid water. Knead lightly without working the dough too much, for 5 to 10 minutes, making sure all the flour is incorporated. The dough should be a little lumpy, soft, and not very elastic. Let the dough rest for 10 minutes.

4. Divide the dough into two equal portions. Gather and gently shape each portion into a ball. Dust one ball with flour and, holding it in the palm of one hand, pat it with your other hand, gently flattening to a maximum thickness of ½ inch, about the same diameter as your pan or a little smaller. It is important to press the dough gently.

5. Pour corn oil into a 10-inch cast-iron or other heavy skillet to a depth of ¼-inch (about ½ cup). Place over medium-high heat until the oil is hot, but not smoking. Place the flattened dough carefully into the hot pan. The oil should not rise over the top of the bread.

6. Fry for about 5 minutes or until the bottom is evenly golden. Using tongs, or a fork and wide spatula, lift the dough to check the bottom. As soon as it is evenly golden, turn to cook the other side. When the other side is golden, about 5 minutes more, transfer the fried bread to paper towels to drain. Repeat with the second portion of dough. Serve while still warm. The texture will be slightly crisp, with a very moist interior. This is usually served with stews, as an accompaniment to fried marinated pork, or enjoyed on its own.

Makes two 8-inch loaves

BAKED FLATBREAD

Pão Estendido

This version of Portuguese flatbread from the island of Pico is one of my favorites. The difference lies in the ratio of the ingredients and the fact that it is baked. Not only does it have a crunchy texture and drier interior, but it contains no oil. It is best to bake this bread on a preheated oven stone and use a wooden peel (though you can also use a cornmeal-coated baking sheet with good results). It can easily be reheated in an oven the next day. This bread is perfect to serve with most anything.

$1\frac{2}{3}$ cups (6 oz) white or yellow corn flour, plus extra for dusting

$1\frac{1}{2}$ teaspoons table salt

$2\frac{1}{4}$ cups boiling water

$1\frac{1}{2}$ cups ($6\frac{3}{4}$ oz) all-purpose flour

Cornmeal, for dusting (if using a peel)

1. Set an oven stone or baking sheet in the cold oven and preheat to 450°F. Combine the corn flour and salt in a medium-sized bowl and mix thoroughly.

2. Pour 1 cup of the boiling water over the corn flour and, using a wooden spoon, mix thoroughly, making sure that all of the corn flour is moistened. Stir in the remaining $1\frac{1}{4}$ cups of now hot water and mix well. It will look like lumpy mashed potatoes. Set aside for 20 to 30 minutes or until it is cool enough to handle.

3. Mix in the all-purpose flour and, without overworking the dough, knead gently for about 5 minutes. Divide into two equal portions and gently shape into balls.

4. Take one portion of dough and dust it liberally with corn flour. Holding the dough in the palm of one hand, use the other hand to gently flatten the dough, rotating to shape it until it is about ½-inch thick. It doesn't need to be perfectly round; when it bakes, any uneven peaks or ridges add extra crunch and character to the bread.

5. Liberally dust your peel with cornmeal and place the dough on the peel. Stretch the loaf a little, but not so that it is thinner than ½-inch. Place the tip of the peel at the far edge of the stone. Pull back with slight jerks until the dough slides off the peel. It won't slide if there is insufficient cornmeal on the peel.

6. Bake until the bread is a rich brown, about 45 minutes. Using tongs or the peel, remove the bread. If it seems too soft, return it to the oven to bake for up to 5 minutes longer. Repeat with the second ball of dough. (If your stone is large enough, the two loaves can be baked simultaneously.) The long baking time is needed to ensure that the interior is done. Allow to cool slightly, then cut into wedges and serve immediately. The crust should be very crunchy with a slightly moist, chewy interior.

Makes 2 large or 4 small loaves

HOMESTYLE BREAD

Pão Caseiro

Patience and gentle handling go a long way in creating this rustic home-baked staple. Traditionally, a small part of the dough from a previous bread-making would be used as a starter, but this recipe has been adjusted to use a yeast sponge, or *fermente*, left to rise overnight. If you are in a hurry, more yeast can be used, and the *fermente* can be ready in 5 to 6 hours. For the best results, I highly recommend using an oven stone and peel, like those used to make pizza (or a cornmeal-coated baking sheet). I also recommend using a stand mixer, if you have one. It is a sticky dough, so dipping your hands or spatulas in water will make handling and shaping it easier. Here in the United States some Portuguese bakers—like Alex Couto, owner of Central Bakery, in Peabody, Massachusetts— produce this bread with some modification of ingredients and modernization of methods. The recipe that follows is adapted from an old one, but includes beaten egg white, as suggested by Alex, for added protein as well as to open the grain. Read the recipe through before beginning and pay attention to the water temperatures.

EQUIPMENT

Free-standing electric mixer (optional)

Two baking sheets or an oven stone and peel

Pastry brush

Heavy deep baking pan

Instant-read thermometer

SPONGE

½ teaspoon active-dry yeast

1 cup warm water (90 to 100°F)

1 cup (4½ oz) unbleached all-purpose flour

1 teaspoon sugar (optional)

DOUGH

7¼ cups (2 lb) white bread flour (12% protein) or unbleached all-purpose flour, plus extra for dusting

1 tablespoon table salt

¼ cup egg whites, at room temperature

1¾ teaspoons active-dry yeast or ⅔ teaspoon fresh yeast

2 cups room-temperature water (70°F), or as needed

Coarse cornmeal, for dusting

A day ahead, make the sponge

1. In a large bowl, dissolve the yeast in ¼ cup of the measured water, and set aside for 10 minutes. Mix in the flour, sugar (if using), and the remaining room-temperature water, stirring until well blended. Cover with plastic and let rise in the refrigerator for 7 to 8 hours or overnight (or for about 2 hours at room temperature, then in the refrigerator overnight). Remove from the refrigerator 2 hours before using to bring the sponge to room temperature. Don't be alarmed if the sponge has collapsed during its stay in the refrigerator; it will foam up again as it warms.

The next day

2. In a mixing bowl, or the bowl of a free-standing electric mixer, combine the flour and salt. Using the dough paddle or a whisk, mix on low speed for 1 minute to evenly distribute the salt.

3. In a small bowl, lightly beat the egg white with a fork until very frothy. Change the attachment on your mixer to the dough hook. Make a well in the middle of the flour and pour in the yeast, beaten egg white, sponge, and room-temperature water. Mix on low speed for 2 minutes until the ingredients are fully incorporated, or a little longer if mixing by hand. Let the dough rest for 10 to 15 minutes to give the flour time to take in the water. Increase the speed of your mixer to the maximum. Continue to mix until the dough has pulled away from the sides of the bowl, about 10 minutes. The dough will be a slightly sticky consistency.

4. If using a mixer, use a spatula to reach deep into the bowl and scrape the bottom and sides. If mixing by hand, moisten your hands, transfer the dough to a moistened work surface (not wood), and then mix or knead for another 3 to 5 minutes until smooth. Remove the dough hook from the bowl of your mixer, or place the dough into a clean bowl. Cover the bowl tightly with plastic wrap.

5. Moisten a kitchen towel with warm water and set it under the bowl. Cover the bowl with a dry kitchen towel, followed by a sheet of plastic. Place another larger towel over the bowl. (I always double-cover rising dough to ensure a consistent temperature and protect against drafts.) Set aside to rise until it has doubled in size, 2 to 2½ hours. After rising, the dough temperature should be 75 to 84°F.

6. When the time is up, use a moistened hand to reach down to the bottom of the bowl and lift the dough, folding it onto itself. Cover and let rise again until doubled in size, about 1 hour more.

7. Do not punch down. Turn the dough out onto a well-floured work surface. Lightly dust the top of the dough with flour. Using a wet dough scraper or kitchen knife, divide the dough into 2, 3, or 4 equal portions. Using wet hands, gently stretch each portion of dough, folding it over onto itself to shape them into rounds or logs. Let the dough rest again until it has risen to about a ¾ rise (almost double), about 1 hour.

8. If you are using a baking stone, place it on the middle rack of your oven. Place an additional rack in the bottom of your oven. Preheat the oven to 450°F.

9. Dust your baking sheets or a wooden peel with coarse cornmeal and place the readied pan or peel close to the shaped dough. Carefully lift the loaves onto the prepared baking sheets or peel. You might need a dough scraper to lift and support the unbaked breads. Lightly dust the tops with flour. Using a dough razor or very sharp knife, make a couple of slashes across the top of the breads.

10. Place a pan of boiling water on the bottom oven rack. Slide the breads onto the preheated oven stone or place the baking sheets in the oven and quickly close the oven door to trap the steam. Bake for 35 to 45 minutes (add an additional 5 minutes for larger loaves), until the bottoms of the breads sound hollow when tapped. The breads should feel fairly light. Cool slightly before cutting.

Makes about 2½ dozen

CRUSTY ROLLS

Papo-secos

When my father made these rolls at his bakery, they practically flew out of the place. These traditional rolls are delicious simply slathered with butter or eaten with grilled sausages or sardines. The old method of making these rolls takes a long time—three days or more. Bakers made sponges and dough starters before mixing the final dough, and the slower fermentation created a fuller flavor. John M. Silva, owner of Danversport Bakery, in Danvers, Massachusetts, explains that bakeries, especially in the last twenty years, have adopted dough accelerators and conditioners to hasten production while attempting to maintain the flavor of the traditional recipes.

A former baker, Manuel Galopim helped me convert the type of recipe used in my father's bakery—and in his own—to one more suited to home baking. Like the old method, this recipe requires patience to allow the flavor to develop, and you will need to start a day ahead. The amount of yeast, salt, and sugar for these rolls is based on the amount of flour used, not the amount of water. The addition of a fat (lard or shortening), which can improve shelf life and flavor, is optional. Try it with and without. Water hardness can affect the dough. The best flour to use is hard spring-wheat flour with high protein, which absorbs more water, will hold the shape of the dough, and yield a better crumb. Some flours are cured or dried longer than others, reducing moisture and flavor in the product. Check with your local bakeries; sometimes they will sell bread-baking flour in small quantities. Specialty baking and health-food stores sometimes carry high-protein flour, and 12% protein bread flours will also work well. Using other flours can still yield good results, but you will miss out on the uniquely delicious texture and flavor that comes from high-protein flour. A second package of yeast is added during the mixing of the dough, giving a boost to the strong flour. Find detailed photos showing how to shape and roll the dough on page 241.

EQUIPMENT

Stand mixer (optional, but recommended)
4 kitchen towels
Pastry brush
Instant-read thermometer
Baking sheet or oven (pizza) stone and peel
Shallow pan to hold water

SPONGE

¼ oz envelope (2½ teaspoons) active-dry yeast
1 cup room-temperature water (65 to 70°F)
1 cup (4½ oz) high-protein bread flour

continued overleaf

Make the sponge at least 6 hours ahead

1. In a medium bowl, dissolve the yeast in the measured water. Mix in the flour until blended. Cover with plastic and set aside at room temperature for a minimum of 6 hours, or up to 8 hours. If you plan to start the dough in the morning, mix the sponge just before you retire the night before, cover, and chill overnight. Bring the sponge completely to room temperature (it will take about 2 hours), before using.

To make the dough, shape, and bake

2. Place the flour in a large bowl. Use your fingers to rub the lard or shortening into the flour to distribute evenly. If using a free-standing mixer, transfer the mixture to the bowl of the machine; if mixing by hand, continue in the same large bowl.

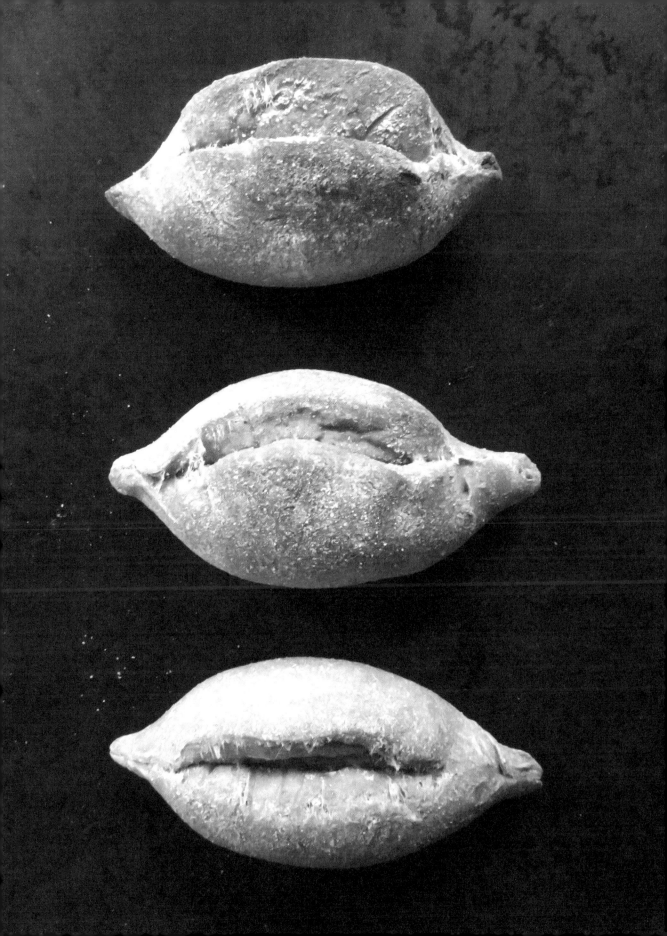

DOUGH

6¼ cups (1¾ lb) unbleached bread flour
  (12% protein), plus extra for dusting

2 scant tablespoons lard or shortening

2 tablespoons (1 oz) sugar

¼ oz envelope (2½ teaspoons) active-dry yeast

1½ to 2 cups room-temperature water (65 to 70°F)

scant 1 tablespoon (½ oz) table salt

Rice flour (optional, see Note)

Fine cornmeal, for dusting

Note: *Although my father and I never used rice flour, Alex Couto suggests using it to help maintain the center crease of the rolls; it prevents them from ballooning out, which is an effect of the humidity in the oven.*

Add the sugar and yeast, and whisk until evenly distributed. Make a well in the flour mixture and add the sponge, along with 1½ cups of the room-temperature water.

3. ***If you are using a mixer:*** Attach the dough hook and mix on low speed until the dough starts to come together, about 5 minutes. If the dough seems stiff, add some of the remaining room-temperature water, a little at a time, and mix at medium speed until you see the dough ease up. Gradually increase the speed to high, and continue to mix for about 10 minutes, adding in the salt as soon as you start to see the dough pull away from the sides of the bowl.

If you are mixing by hand: Use your fingers in a claw-like formation to incorporate the water and sponge into the flour. Mix well until it comes together into a ball and starts to leave the sides of the bowl. Add the salt and continue to mix, turning the dough onto itself, until the sides of the bowl appear clean. If the dough seems stiff, add some of the remaining room-temperature water, a little at a time, and continue to mix until you see the dough ease up. Turn the dough out onto a lightly floured surface and mix by hand for 10 to 15 minutes.

The dough is ready when smooth and elastic, springs back when pressed with a finger, and has a slight sheen. To test, pull off a small piece of dough and stretch it until it is so thin you can almost see through it. If it tears, mix for a few more minutes and test again.

4. Place the dough in bowl (or keep in the bowl of your mixer), and cover with a kitchen towel, followed by plastic wrap. Set in a warm, draft-free place until doubled in size, about 2 hours. When the dough is ready, an indentation will remain when it is pressed lightly with your finger. Punch down to redistribute the yeast and let the dough rise for 1 more hour.

5. Punch down the dough again, then turn it out onto a lightly floured work surface. Divide the dough into 24 to 36 equal-sized pieces, 2 to 3 oz each, or the size you prefer.

6. On an almost flour-free area of your work surface, use the palm of your hand, with slightly curled fingers and medium pressure, to rotate the pieces of dough against the work surface until each piece is a smooth, fairly tight ball. Set 2 inches apart on a floured surface, cover with a towel, and let rest for about 30 minutes.

7. On the floured work surface, flatten each ball into a disk about ½ inch thick and 3 inches in diameter. Dust the surface of the dough facing you with some all-purpose or rice flour (see Note). Using the outside edge of your hand, press a crease into the dough, as if you're going to cut it in half, but don't go completely through.

8. Fold the disks in half along the crease and pinch the ends firmly, giving the dough a slight lengthwise stretch while twisting or rolling the ends to a point.

9. Arrange the rolls, smooth side up, and the crease opening down, on lightly floured towels, 2 inches apart, in rows. Pull the towels up slightly between rows, so the rolls won't touch. Cover with another towel, top with plastic wrap, and let rise until nearly doubled, 45 minutes to 1 hour. Meanwhile, place an oven stone on the middle shelf of the cold oven and a shallow pan on the bottom shelf. Preheat the oven to 400°F.

10. Lightly dust the wooden peel or a baking sheet with fine cornmeal. Remove 6 rolls from under the towels and place them on the peel, facing up, with the smooth side down, forming two rows toward the edge farthest away from the handle. Or place the rolls on a baking sheet and place this on the middle rack of the oven. Pour hot water into the pan on the lower shelf, then quickly place the tip of the wood peel at the far edge of the hot stone. Using smooth, small jerking motions, pull back the peel while sliding the rolls gently onto the stone. They should stay upright. Bake for 15 to 20 minutes, until they are a rich golden color and sound hollow when tapped on the bottom. Remove, shoveling them up with the peel. Repeat, baking the remaining rolls 6 at a time.

SHAPING AND ROLLING CRUSTY ROLLS

Rotate each piece of dough into a smooth, fairly tight ball

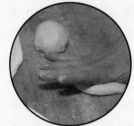

Flatten each ball into a disk about 3 inches in diameter

Using the outside edge of your palm, press a crease into the dough

Fold the disks in half along the crease

Pinch the ends firmly, stretching slightly

Roll the ends to points

Place the rolls, smooth side up, crease opening down on lightly floured towels

Place rolls facing up on a lightly cornmeal-dusted wooden peel or baking sheet

SWEETS

Doces

9 SWEETS
Doces

Portuguese desserts, usually quite sweet and high in egg content, have never been a nightly habit. The more common ending to a typical family meal is a serving of cheese and fresh fruit. Despite, or perhaps because of this, the Portuguese hold their desserts, homespun as they may be, in very high regard. I can remember as a young girl looking forward the vast array of sweets that graced the Portuguese dessert table. Today, dessert habits have not changed much. Weekends, holidays, and special occasions still bring out a wide variety of sweets that we are very happy to indulge in. With so many to choose from, I have had to relegate certain desserts to particular holidays. In our home, Thanksgiving has a more American theme, but when it comes to Christmas or Easter, the richer Portuguese desserts come forth. Although I always like to include something new, the traditional ones are expected. Delectable lemon- or orange-infused cookies, creamy rice puddings, lusciously smooth caramel-custard flans, egg-rich sweet bread, tasty cakes, and, especially, brandy-flavored fried squash fritters, are sure to grace the table. At Easter time, in addition to the sweet breads and rice puddings, sweetened egg-white meringue puddings and pastry tarts are included in the array.

The majority of the desserts, as you will notice, are flavored with lemon or orange peel (interchangeable, as you wish), and occasionally vanilla. Feel free to use extracts, but keep in mind the depth of flavor will suffer. Cinnamon, caramelized sugar, and occasionally brandy and port wine are also used for flavoring.

The common method for cakes is to separate the eggs and fold the stiffly beaten egg whites into the batter. To get the best volume of your egg whites, make sure the bowl and beaters are clean and free of any traces of fat. It is also not unusual to combine the sugar and butter with milk and heat until the butter is melted and the sugar is dissolved before incorporating them with dry ingredients.

Cookies are usually just brushed with egg wash before baking, but they can be decorated with nonpareils. Recipes made with American flour have a somewhat different texture from those made in Portugal. While heirloom recipes of cakes and cookies that relied on a large quantity of eggs for leavening are made here in the same way, there are some that now include baking powder. The recipes that follow are representative of the traditional desserts that have continued to satisfy the Portuguese sweet tooth. More than one version has been given for some recipes to show the possibilities of texture and flavor. My favorite—it's so very hard to choose!— would probably be *farofias* (Meringue Puffs, page 265), but then again, it could be . . . .

These recipes can easily be modified to be less sweet. I suggest that you follow a recipe as directed the first time, and then adjust the amount of sugar to your preference thereafter.

Left: Traditional Sweet Bread (page 270)

Makes 4½ to 5 dozen

WASHBOARDS

Lavadores

When I was in Portugal, I washed clothes outdoors, without hot water, in a soapstone washtub that had a washboard attached at one end. How we scrubbed those clothes on the washboard to get them clean! These cookies, marked horizontally with the tines of a fork to resemble the lines of washboards, are appropriately named. With their delicate lemon flavor, these are especially delicious with tea.

½ cup (4 oz) butter, softened,
  plus extra for greasing
1½ cups (10½ oz) sugar
4 eggs
Grated zest of 1 lemon
4 cups (1 lb 2 oz) all-purpose flour
1 tablespoon baking powder

1. Preheat the oven to 350°F. Lightly grease or line baking sheets with parchment paper.

2. In a large mixing bowl, beat the butter with 1 cup (7 oz) of the sugar at medium-high speed on an electric mixer or by hand, for about 1 minute. Beat in the eggs, one at a time, blending well after each addition, until the mixture is fluffy and pale yellow, 2 to 3 minutes. Stir in the lemon zest.

3. In a medium bowl, whisk together the flour and the baking powder, stirring to distribute the ingredients evenly. Using a wooden spoon or spatula, fold the flour into the butter and egg batter. Mix the ingredients together well, gently kneading the dough in the bowl for about 5 minutes.

4. Place the remaining sugar in a shallow dish. Shape the dough into 1½-inch balls. Roll each ball in the sugar and place on the prepared pans, 2 inches apart. Flatten gently with the tines of a fork to make horizontal lines, like those of a washboard.

5. Bake, in batches, until a light golden color, 20 to 25 minutes.

Makes about 5 dozen

ORANGE COOKIES

Biscoitos de Laranja

Children big and small love *biscoitos de laranja*. Festively colored with nonpareils for special occasions, these keep well for 3 to 4 weeks stored in plastic containers. They are especially popular at Christmas time.

6 cups (1 lb 10 oz) all-purpose flour

2 teaspoons baking powder

½ teaspoon baking soda

¼ teaspoon salt

1½ cups (10½ oz) sugar

1 cup (8 oz) butter, softened, plus extra for greasing

3 whole eggs, at room temperature,
   plus 1 egg, lightly beaten

½ cup orange juice

Colorful nonpareils (optional)

1. Preheat the oven to 350°F. Lightly grease or line 2 to 3 baking sheets with parchment paper.

2. In a medium bowl, sift together the flour, baking powder, baking soda, and salt. Set aside.

3. In a large bowl, beat the sugar and butter until smooth, using the high speed of an electric mixer or by hand. Crack in the whole eggs, one at a time, alternating with the orange juice and blending well after each egg. The texture will look muddled, not smooth and emulsified.

4. Fold in the flour mixture, then knead briefly in the bowl, about 3 minutes.

5. Lightly grease your hands with some butter. Pull off a 1-inch piece of dough and roll it into a ½-inch diameter rope about 5 inches long. Shape into a coil. (These can also be made into twists by folding the length of rolled dough in half, then twisting a few times. This shape produces a crisper cookie.) Repeat with the remaining dough.

6. Place on the prepared pans, 1½ inches apart, and brush with the beaten egg. Sprinkle with nonpareils, if using. Bake, in batches, until the bottom is lightly browned and the top is a light golden color, 15 minutes (for crisper cookies, bake for 5 minutes longer until a rich gold color).

Makes about 3 dozen

DRY RINGS

Rosquilhas Secas

These popular Azorean cookies have very little sugar in them; in fact, they are more of a dry biscuit and are frequently dunked into coffee, hot chocolate, or even wine. They are made from a yeast dough and, while they are very simple to make, they require extra oven time to dry after baking. For a sweeter version, you can make a simple sugar glaze (see Variation below).

Two ¼ oz envelopes (5 teaspoons) active-dry yeast
½ cup warm water (110°F)
1 cup milk
1 cup (8 oz) butter or margarine, softened
3 rounded tablespoons sugar
2 large eggs, at room temperature
5 to 5½ cups (1 lb 6 oz to 1 lb 8 oz) all-purpose flour

1. In a small cup, dissolve the yeast in the water and set aside for 10 minutes.

2. Meanwhile, in a 1-quart saucepan, combine the milk with the butter or margarine and sugar. Place over medium-low heat until the butter has melted and the sugar has dissolved.

3. In a large mixing bowl, beat the eggs. Gradually whisk in the hot milk. Then mix in 2 cups (9 oz) of the flour. Add the dissolved yeast and the remaining 3 cups (13 oz) flour, to form a medium-textured dough—if the dough is too soft, add up to ½ cup (2 oz) more flour. Knead in the bowl until smooth and elastic, 10 minutes. Cover and set aside in a warm place to rise until it has doubled in size, 2 hours.

4. Punch down and let the dough rise once more until it has nearly doubled, 1 hour. When the dough is ready, an indentation should remain in the dough after lightly pressing with your finger.

5. Preheat the oven to 350°F. Lightly grease or line baking sheets with parchment paper.

6. Pinch off walnut-sized pieces of dough. Using a gentle hand, roll the pieces into balls, then into ropes, ½-inch thick and 6 inches long. Press the ends firmly together, forming a ring. Stretch the rings slightly to open the center hole. Place on the prepared baking sheets, 1½ inches apart.

7. Bake for 15 minutes, then reduce the oven temperature to 300°F and continue to bake just until the rings start to color, about 5 minutes. Reduce the oven temperature to 250°F and continue to bake for 1 more hour. Turn off the oven and let the cookies remain in the oven until they are dry. Depending on the dough and the weather, it may take as long as it takes for the oven to cool down, but do not let the cookies get deep brown. They should be crisp and dry, not hard and overbaked.

Variation: *You can dress these up with a sugar glaze. Combine 3 cups (12 oz) confectioner's sugar and ½ cup of water until smooth. Add a teaspoon of vanilla extract for flavoring. Drizzle over the rings and allow the glaze to dry completely before storing or serving.*

Makes about 4 dozen

LIZARDS

Lagartos

These cookies are named for the impressions made in the dough, which are supposed to represent the ridges on a lizard's back. Make sure your egg whites are at room temperature to obtain the best volume.

1¼ cups (9 oz) sugar

1 cup (8 oz) butter, softened

4 eggs, separated, at room temperature

Grated zest of 1 lemon

1 teaspoon baking soda

4 cups (1 lb 2 oz) all-purpose flour

1. Preheat the oven to 350°F. Lightly grease or line baking sheets with parchment paper.

2. Using the high speed of an electric mixer or mixing by hand, beat the sugar with the butter in a large bowl for about 1 minute, until smooth. Beat in the egg yolks and lemon zest and mix until fluffy and pale yellow, 2 to 3 minutes.

3. In a separate bowl and using clean beaters, beat the egg whites at high speed until stiff peaks form, 4 to 5 minutes. Then fold into the butter-and-sugar mixture.

4. Blend the baking soda with the flour, distributing it throughout. Mix the flour into the batter and blend well. Gently knead in the bowl for about 5 minutes, thoroughly incorporating the flour to form a medium-textured dough.

5. Pinch off walnut-sized pieces of dough, roll into balls, then into ropes, ½-inch thick, 4 to 5 inches long, and tapered at one end. With the edge of a fork, make 3 vertical lines down the length of dough.

6. Place on the prepared baking sheets, 2 inches apart, giving them a slight S shape. Bake until golden, about 20 minutes.

Makes about 4 dozen

BAKING-SODA COOKIES

Bolachas de Bica Bernato

These tasty cookies from the Azores can be decorated with colored sugar or other decorative sprinkles. Like most Portuguese cookies, they are very simple to make and fun for children to shape.

1 cup (7 oz) sugar

½ cup (4 oz) butter, softened

1 egg

6 tablespoons milk

1 teaspoon vanilla (optional)

1 teaspoon baking soda

⅛ teaspoon salt

4 cups (1 lb 2 oz) all-purpose flour, plus extra for dusting

2 egg yolks, lightly beaten

Decorative sugar (optional)

1. Preheat the oven to 350°F. Lightly grease or line baking sheets with parchment paper.

2. In a large bowl, beat the sugar and butter using an electric mixer at high speed or by hand for about 1 minute. Add the whole egg, milk, vanilla (if using), baking soda, and salt, and mix at medium speed until well blended, 2 to 3 minutes.

3. Using your hands, mix in the flour. Then knead in the bowl for about 5 minutes to form a medium-textured dough.

4. Divide the dough into four equal parts. Using a lightly floured rolling pin and on a lightly floured work surface, roll out one part until it is ¼-inch thick. Cut into triangles or circles, 2½ to 3 inches in size. Repeat with the remaining dough.

5. Place on the prepared baking sheets, about 2 inches apart. Brush the tops with beaten egg yolk and sprinkle with white or colored sugar. Bake until golden, 15 to 20 minutes.

Makes about 5 dozen (depending on size and shape)

CORN SILK TASSELS

Espigas de Milho

Azoreans shape these cookies using an ingenious method. Using a die plate like a six-pointed star inserted into an old-fashioned meat grinder, they extrude the dough into a ridged rope. The rope is cut into 5- or 6-inch lengths, placed on baking sheets, and curved into S shapes. A pastry bag with a 6-pointed star tip or a cookie press can create the same effect, but you can also drop the dough by spoonfuls onto greased baking sheets.

4 sticks (1 lb) butter

1 tablespoon lard or shortening

7 cups (2 lb) fine white corn flour

12 large eggs

3 cups (1 lb 5 oz) sugar

7 cups (2 lb) all-purpose flour

1 tablespoon baking powder

Grated zest of 1 lemon

1 teaspoon table salt

1 tablespoon cinnamon

1. Preheat the oven to 350°F. Lightly grease and flour baking sheets, or line them with parchment paper.

2. Place the butter and lard in a 1-quart saucepan over medium-high heat until melted. Put the corn flour in a medium bowl and pour the hot melted butter over it. Mix until thoroughly blended. It will look like lumpy mashed potatoes. Set aside to cool to room temperature.

3. Put the eggs in a separate medium bowl and, using the high speed of an electric mixer or mixing by hand, beat the eggs until frothy. Gradually mix in the sugar, beating for about 3 minutes.

4. In a large bowl, combine the all-purpose flour, baking powder, lemon zest, salt, and cinnamon. Stir with whisk or fork to blend thoroughly.

5. When the corn flour has cooled, incorporate it into the egg and sugar mixture. Blend well, then add to the large bowl of dry ingredients. Using your hands, gently turn the ingredients completely, incorporating all the flour and forming a fairly soft dough.

6. Use a cookie press or pastry bag with a star tip to form the dough into a rope. Cut the rope into 5- or 6-inch lengths, then place on the prepared baking sheets, shaping them into S shapes. (Alternatively, you can simply pipe the cookies directly onto the prepared baking sheets or make simple drop cookies.) Bake in batches until just lightly golden, 15 to 20 minutes.

BEER CAKE

Bolo de Cereveja

This recipe comes from the archives of Senhorina Bettencourt as it was given to her by Senhora Aurora of Carapacho, Graciosa, in the Azores. Light or regular beer works equally well in this cake.

2 cups (14 oz) sugar

1 cup (8 oz) butter, softened

4 large eggs, separated, at room temperature

1 cup beer

3 cups (13 oz) all-purpose flour

1 teaspoon baking powder

1. Preheat the oven to 350°F. Lightly grease and flour a 10-inch tube pan.

2. In a large bowl, using the high speed of an electric mixer or mixing by hand, beat the sugar with the butter until smooth, about 1 minute. Beat in the egg yolks, at medium speed, until the ingredients are fluffy and pale yellow, 2 to 3 minutes.

3. Pour in the beer, mixing to blend. Add the flour and the baking powder and mix thoroughly, about 1 minute.

4. In a separate clean bowl and using clean beaters, beat the egg whites until stiff. Gently fold into the batter. Pour into the prepared pan and bake in the preheated oven until a wooden skewer comes out clean and the cake springs back when lightly pressed with your finger, about 50 minutes. Cool for about 5 minutes before removing from pan.

Serves 10 to 12

FLUFFY BREAD

Pão de Ló

Before the time of baking powder and other leavening agents, eggs and sugar were beaten to incorporate air, enabling the cake to rise, and producing this light and airy sponge cake. According to oral history, this well-known dessert made its debut in Portugal some 4 centuries ago, during the Renaissance period, and most likely originated in Spain. Across Europe, it is known as the "bread of Spain," though my friend Antonio knows it as *pão de Ló*, "bread of the Lord." Many names and variations exist, not only between countries, but I can think of 5 versions in Portugal alone. One version contains as many as 12 eggs. Another version, called *alfeizerão*, is only partially baked in a very hot oven, resulting in a pudding-like cake, eaten the day after baking.

Sometimes flavored with lemon or orange, this version is typically served plain, though in some parts of Portugal it is eaten with a soft and mild cheese called *queijo da serra* (page 19). You can dress it up with a custard or fruit sauce, but I think you will enjoy it just the way it comes out of the oven. You will need a 10-inch tube pan.

8 large egg yolks, at room temperature
1½ cups (10½ oz) sugar, preferably superfine
Grated zest of 1 lemon or orange (optional)
1¼ cups (5½ oz) all-purpose flour
6 large egg whites, at room temperature

1. Preheat the oven to 325°F. Grease a 10-inch tube pan.
2. Using the high speed of an electric mixer or mixing by hand, beat the egg yolks in a large bowl until frothy, then gradually beat in the sugar. Continue beating until the eggs are thick and pale yellow, at least 5 minutes. Stir in the grated zest.
3. Add the flour to the egg batter and mix on medium speed until thoroughly incorporated.
4. In a separate bowl, free of any grease or yolk, beat the egg whites, using clean beaters and the mixer's high speed, until quite stiff, 4 to 5 minutes. Gently fold the whites into the yolk batter, turning the ingredients carefully so volume is not lost, until the egg whites are thoroughly incorporated.
5. Pour immediately into the prepared tube pan. (If the batter is allowed to sit, it will begin to deflate and will not reach its maximum height.) Bake at 325°F for about 1 hour or until the cake is golden brown and the top springs back when lightly pressed.
6. Remove from the oven and allow to cool for 5 to 10 minutes. Loosen all around the sides of the cake with a thin spatula. Invert onto a flat plate, then invert again onto a serving dish so that the cake is upright. Use a serrated knife for slicing.

Serves 10 to 12

COIMBRA CAKE

Bolo de Coimbra

This recipe comes from northern Portugal, named after the city of Coimbra. Excavated from the recipe archives of Senhorina Bettencourt, it proves to have been a worthy find.

1 cup (8 oz) butter, softened
2 cups (14 oz) sugar
8 eggs, separated, at room temperature
2½ cups (12 oz) cake flour
2 teaspoons baking powder
1 teaspoon cinnamon
Grated zest of 1 lemon

1. Preheat the oven to 325°F. Lightly grease and flour a 10-inch tube pan.

2. Place the butter in a large bowl and, using the high speed of a mixer or mixing by hand, gradually pour in the sugar, beating until fairly smooth. Add the egg yolks, one at a time, beating well after each addition. Set aside.

3. Put the egg whites in a clean medium-sized bowl and beat them with clean beaters on high speed until stiff peaks form, 4 to 5 minutes. Set aside.

4. In another large bowl, combine the flour, baking powder, cinnamon, and lemon zest. Blend well to distribute the ingredients evenly. Fold the dry ingredients into the bowl containing the egg yolks, making sure all the flour is well blended.

5. Using a rubber spatula, gently and completely fold the stiff egg whites into the batter. Pour the batter into the prepared tube pan. Bake at 325°F for 45 to 50 minutes; the cake will spring back when lightly pressed with your finger. Cool about 5 minutes before removing from pan.

Makes about 1½ dozen

ORANGE SQUARES

Quadradas de Laranja

This is one of the few Portuguese cakes that are baked and cut into squares and then glazed with syrup—a technique more common in eastern Mediterranean countries. The flavor of oranges adds another dimension.

1 cup (7 oz) sugar

1 cup (8 oz) butter, softened

6 large eggs, separated

Grated zest of 2 oranges

1 cup milk

2 cups (9 oz) all-purpose flour

2 teaspoons baking powder

¼ teaspoon salt

GLAZE

1 cup (7 oz) sugar

Juice of 4 oranges (about 2 cups)

1. Preheat the oven to 350°F. Lightly grease and flour a 9- by 13-inch baking dish.

2. In a large bowl, using the high speed of an electric mixer or mixing by hand, beat the sugar with the butter until it is fairly smooth, about 1 minute. Add the egg yolks, one at a time, beating well after each one. Stir in the grated orange zest and the milk.

3. In a separate clean bowl, using the high speed of the mixer and clean beaters, beat the egg whites until stiff peaks form, 4 to 5 minutes. Fold the egg whites into the batter.

4. In a separate bowl, combine the flour with the baking powder and salt, mixing well. Fold the flour into the batter, gently mixing to incorporate all of the flour. Transfer to the prepared pan and spread evenly. Bake for 35 to 40 minutes, until a toothpick inserted into the center comes out clean.

5. While the cake is baking, make the glaze: In a small saucepan, combine the sugar and orange juice and place over medium-high heat. Bring to a boil and reduce the heat to medium-low. Simmer for 20 to 30 minutes, until the sugar has dissolved and a medium-thick syrup thickly coats a wooden spoon.

6. When the cake is done, remove it from the oven. Using a toothpick or skewer, prick holes all over the cake. Spread the warm syrup evenly over the cake. For a slightly caramelized glaze, you can return the pan to the oven and heat it briefly under the broiler just until the glaze starts to bubble. Cut into squares and serve.

Serves 4 to 6

SWEET RICE PUDDING

Arroz Doce

This age-old pudding goes hand in hand with *Massa Sovada*, a traditional sweet bread (see pages 270-272). We would eat the sweet bread topped with the rice pudding. One of my earliest memories is of my grandmother sprinkling cinnamon in the pattern of a cross onto platters of *arroz doce* for Easter. There are many variations, since this dish is on the table at every Portuguese event, but the version that follows is the one I knew growing up. Covering the chilling pudding with plastic wrap keeps the surface from drying. Bring almost to room temperature before serving. I usually use Italian arborio rice.

2 cups whole milk

1 cup (7 oz) short-grain rice, such as arborio

¼ teaspoon table salt

Peel of 1 lemon, without pith, in large pieces

1 cup (7 oz) sugar

Ground cinnamon, for dusting

1. In a small saucepan, scald the milk (heat it to just below boiling point), stirring frequently. Remove from the heat and set aside to cool until warm.

2. Pour 2 cups water into a separate 2½ quart saucepan, cover, and bring to a boil over medium-high heat. Stir in the rice and salt and reduce the heat to medium-low. Cover and simmer until the liquid is nearly evaporated, and the rice is barely tender, 20 to 25 minutes.

3. Stir in the warm milk and add the pieces of lemon peel. Stirring constantly, continue to simmer until the mixture starts to thicken slightly, 20 to 25 minutes.

4. When the rice is well cooked, stir in the sugar and continue to cook until the sugar has dissolved and the pudding has thickened to the consistency of oatmeal, 5 to 10 minutes more. The rice should be very tender. Remove from the heat. It will continue to thicken as it cools.

5. Remove the pieces of lemon peel. Pour the pudding onto a large flat serving platter or individual flat plates to a thickness of not more than ¾ inch.

6. Taking a pinch of ground cinnamon between thumb and forefinger, gently rub your thumb and finger together close to the surface of the rice. (If your fingers are held too high, the cinnamon will scatter over a wider area.) Dust the surface of the rice in a design of your choice, perhaps forming the initials of a guest. Cool and serve or chill the rice to serve later. (See the Note on page 187 about safely storing cooked rice dishes.)

Variation: *Beat 3 or 4 egg yolks in a small bowl. When the pudding is done but still hot, remove ¼ cup of pudding and gradually mix it into the egg yolks. (This will temper the egg yolks and prevent curdling.) Add the yolk mixture to the pudding and quickly blend it in, stirring constantly for 1 minute to cook the eggs. Pour onto platters as above. This version will be thicker and tinted yellow, with a custardy texture and flavor. Some versions from the Azores are so thick they can be cut into wedges and eaten like slices of pizza.*

Serves 4 to 6

MRS. NOGUEIRA'S SWEET RICE

Arroz Doce à Senhora Nogueira

Note that in all recipes for Portuguese rice pudding, the amounts of sugar and rice are equal. Despite the similarity of ingredients, the preparation method and quantity can vary. In this recipe from Isaura Nogueira, the rice is cooked almost entirely in milk. For an extra-large batch, just triple the quantities.

5 cups whole milk

1 cup (7 oz) short-grain rice, rinsed and drained

½ teaspoon salt

Peel of 1 orange, without pith, in large pieces

1 cup (7 oz) sugar

Ground cinnamon, for dusting

Tip: *Use a vegetable peeler and light pressure to remove peel from lemons and oranges without removing the pith.*

1. Pour the milk into a 2½-quart saucepan and heat over medium-high until little bubbles form around the edges and the milk starts to steam (this is called scalding). Remove from the heat.

2. Put the rice and salt into a separate 2½-quart saucepan. Add enough water to just cover the rice (about 1 cup). Place over medium-high heat, cover, and bring to a boil. Reduce the heat to medium-low and, stirring constantly, cook the rice just until the water evaporates, being careful not to burn it.

3. Stir in the scalded milk (now warm) and the orange peel. Cover and continue to simmer the rice until tender, another 20 to 25 minutes. Remove the orange peel and add the sugar. Continue to simmer for 5 more minutes, stirring constantly, until the sugar has dissolved. The pudding should be somewhat thick, like oatmeal. It will continue to thicken as it cools.

4. Pour the pudding onto a flat platter or individual serving dishes and garnish with cinnamon in the Portuguese style: pinch some cinnamon between your index finger and thumb, drop it close to the surface of the rice, and make a design or the initials of a guest of honor. Chill.

5. Serve chilled or bring to room temperature before serving. (See the note on page 141 to safely store cooked rice dishes.)

Serves 10 to 12

MOLOTOFF PUDDING

Molotoff

Airy meringue desserts are very popular with the Portuguese. This recipe comes from Maria Fidalgo, whose version is the best I have ever had. It calls for caramelized sugar syrup, which sounds more difficult than it is, so don't let that stop you from making this heavenly treat. An electric mixer is highly recommended. You will need an 8-cup capacity angel food cake pan or bundt pan, and a larger pan for the water bath (*banho maria*).

MERINGUE

16 large egg whites, at room temperature
  (save 6 yolks for the sauce)
1 cup (7 oz) sugar, plus 3 tablespoons extra

SAUCE

2 cups whole milk
5 tablespoons sugar
Grated zest of 1 lemon
6 egg yolks

Butter, for greasing

For the meringue

1. Preheat the oven to 350°F and butter an angel food cake pan or bundt pan with an 8-cup capacity.

2. In a large bowl, beat the egg whites until frothy using the high speed of an electric mixer. Continue beating, gradually adding the 1 cup (7 oz) of sugar. Beat until stiff peaks form, then set aside.

3. In a 1-quart saucepan placed over medium heat, melt the remaining 3 tablespoons of sugar without stirring, until lightly caramelized, 10 to 15 minutes. While it is still hot, quickly whisk half of the caramelized sugar syrup into the egg whites (reserve the rest of the syrup).

4. Carefully transfer the egg-white mixture to the buttered pan. Set this in a larger deep pan. Pour enough water into the larger pan to come halfway up the side of the meringue pan, forming a water bath. Set the pans in the oven and bake for 10 minutes without opening the door. Turn off the oven and leave the meringue in the oven for another 20 minutes. Carefully remove the pans from the oven. Remove the meringue pan from the larger pan and set aside to cool.

For the sauce

5. In the saucepan containing the reserved caramelized sugar (which may be hard), combine the milk, sugar, and lemon zest. Warm over medium-high heat, stirring until the sugar has dissolved and the milk is scalded (heated to just under boiling). When you see tiny bubbles around the edges and steam rising from the milk, turn off the heat and allow to cool slightly.

6. In a medium bowl, beat the egg yolks, then quickly whisk a small amount of the warm milk mixture into the yolks to temper them. Add the yolk mixture to the pan of milk. Stirring constantly, slowly reheat the milk mixture over medium-low heat, until it thickens to the consistency of heavy cream. Chill the sauce until ready to serve.

7. Unmold the meringue by dipping the bottom briefly in a bowl of hot water. Invert onto a rimmed serving platter and chill. Drizzle some of the sauce over the meringue. Slice into wedges as you would a cake, and drizzle additional sauce over each serving or pass the sauce around.

Serves 6

CREAMY FLAN PUDDING

Pudim Flan

Flan makes an elegant dessert and yet it is simple to prepare. This version is particularly rich and creamy. It is rare that this luscious treat fails to make an appearance, especially for holidays. Condensed milk gives it a creamy texture. Extra flavoring is not needed, although you can add touch of lemon. It is not unusual for a Portuguese cook to make the caramel sauce without adding any water at all, but it only takes a momentary distraction for the beautiful golden color to darken and burn. Even with the addition of water, care must be taken to obtain the right color. You must also take care when handling the very hot sugar syrup. You will need a shallow 9-inch bundt or tube pan (6-cup capacity), or a 9-inch round cake pan 2 inches deep, as well as a larger pan that can hold the water bath (*banho maria* in Portuguese).

CARAMEL

1 cup (7 oz) sugar

CUSTARD

14 oz can (1¼ cups) sweetened
   condensed milk

1¾ cups whole milk

4 large eggs, lightly beaten

Curls of lemon peel or mint sprigs,
   to decorate (optional)

For the caramel

1. In a 2-quart saucepan, combine the sugar with $\frac{1}{3}$ cup water, stir, and bring to a boil over medium-high heat.

2. When the sugar has dissolved, reduce the heat and simmer without stirring until the syrup turns golden, about 15 minutes.

3. Remove the syrup from the heat once the desired color is reached. Use a pot holder to hold the mold, especially if it is made of metal. Carefully pour the hot caramel into the bottom of a shallow 1½-quart bundt or tube pan, turning the pan to coat the bottom, then the sides with caramel. Don't worry if the sides do not get completely coated. Set the pan aside to cool thoroughly.

For the custard

4. Preheat the oven to 350°F.

5. In a large bowl, combine the condensed milk, whole milk, and eggs. Mix well, strain if you wish, and pour into the cooled mold.

6. Set the flan pan into a larger pan and place in the oven. Carefully pour hot water into the larger pan so that it comes halfway up the side of the flan pan.

7. Bake until a knife inserted into the middle of the custard comes out clean, about 30 minutes.

8. Carefully remove the flan pan from the larger pan and chill for several hours. Before serving, loosen the edges of the flan with a spatula. To serve, look for a serving plate that has a rim around the edges to catch the sauce. Place the plate over the pan, invert the pan and plate, and shake gently. Remove the pan; the caramel will flow over the custard. Garnish with lemon curls or sprigs of mint.

Serves 10

CUSTARD FLAN PUDDING

Pudim Flan

The version of flan that I grew up with is not as rich as some. It is made the old-fashioned way, with whole milk and lots of eggs. I often serve this on Christmas day or Easter. Pick one of the flavor options to suit your taste. You will need a shallow 10-inch bundt or tube pan (8-cup capacity), or a 10-inch round cake pan, 2 inches deep, as well as a larger pan that can hold the water bath (*banho maria* in Portuguese). Flans can also be made in individual serving molds, but it's traditional to make this in a single mold and serve it—like most Portuguese food—family style.

CARAMEL
1 cup (7 oz) sugar

CUSTARD
8 large eggs
2 large egg yolks
½ teaspoon cinnamon
1¼ cups (8¾ oz) sugar
4 cups whole milk

FLAVORINGS (CHOOSE ONE)
1 tablespoon port wine or Beirão brandy
Peel, without pith, of 1 whole lemon or
   orange, in large pieces

For the caramel
1. In a 2-quart saucepan, combine the sugar with ⅓ cup water, stir, and place over medium-high heat.
2. When the sugar has dissolved, lower the heat and simmer without stirring until the sugar syrup turns a golden color, about 15 minutes.
3. Using a pot holder to hold your 10-inch (2-quart) bundt pan or cake pan, carefully pour the hot caramel into it, quickly rotating to coat the bottom, then the sides. Don't worry if the sides do not get completely coated. Set the pan aside to cool thoroughly. The caramel will crackle as it cools.

For the custard
4. Set a rack in the middle of your oven and preheat to 350°F.
5. Using the high speed of an electric mixer or mixing by hand, beat the eggs, egg yolks, and cinnamon in a large bowl until frothy.

6. In a 2½-quart saucepan, combine the sugar, milk and your choice of flavoring. Place over medium-high heat and warm until the sugar has dissolved.

7. While stirring with a whisk, gradually pour the warm sweetened milk into the eggs and cinnamon.

8. Remove the zest, if used, and strain the custard. Then pour the custard mixture into the prepared pan. Place the custard pan into a larger pan and place in the oven. Add enough hot water to the larger pan so that it comes about halfway up the side of the custard pan. Bake for 35 minutes, or until a knife inserted into the middle of the custard comes out clean.

9. Chill thoroughly before serving. To unmold, run a knife around the edges of the custard. Look for a serving plate that has raised sides to catch the caramel. Place the plate over the pan, invert the pan and plate, and unmold, letting the caramel sauce cascade over the top and sides. Cut into wedges to serve.

Serves 4 to 6

MERINGUE PUFFS

Faròfias

I first tasted this cloudlike dessert while visiting my cousin Marguerida at Quinta Vale dos Moinhos, her family's farm near the village of Almoster in the Alentejo region. When I was thirteen, Aunt Ana taught me how to make it, and I've made it ever since. It is quite easy and fun to make! Meringue is poached in milk, then set afloat in a lemony custard. It is perfect even after a heavy meal. You can make the meringues a day ahead.

MERINGUES

4 egg whites, at room temperature
¾ cup (5¼ oz) sugar
1¾ cups whole milk

CUSTARD

Fresh whole milk, as needed
2 teaspoons cornstarch
4 large egg yolks
Peel of 1 lemon, without pith

Cinnamon, for dusting

Notes: *If the milk has boiled during poaching, add ½ cup of cold fresh milk when you make the sauce, or discard the reserved milk and use 1½ cups of fresh milk instead. If you plan to make the meringues a day ahead, make the sauce using fresh milk.*

For the meringues

1. In a mixing bowl, beat the egg whites, by hand or using the high speed of an electric mixer, until soft peaks form, 2 to 3 minutes. Gradually add ¼ cup (1¾ oz) of the sugar and continue to beat until the whites are stiff. Set aside.

2. In a 2½-quart saucepan, heat the milk with the remaining ½ cup (3½ oz) sugar, over medium-high heat. When the milk is about to boil, reduce the heat to maintain a simmer.

3. Using a slotted spoon, place 1 or 2 large spoonfuls of meringue mixture into the simmering milk. Poach for about 1½ minutes in the steaming milk. The meringues may rise, but do not let the milk boil or it will curdle (see Notes if this happens). Turn the puffs over to cook the other side for 1½ minutes until slightly firm. Using a slotted spoon, transfer the cooked meringues to a colander set in a bowl to capture the milk that drains off. Drain well. Repeat with the remaining mixture. Reserve the drained milk, and any milk left over in the pan (unless you are making ahead, see Notes). Transfer the puffs to a serving platter or plates (or cover in plastic and refrigerate overnight).

For the custard

4. Gradually mix the milk into the cornstarch. In a small bowl, combine the yolks and lemon peel and stir in the cornstarch mixture. Set aside.

5. Measure the reserved milk. You should have 1½ cups (top up with fresh milk if necessary). Alternatively, use 1½ cups fresh milk (see Notes). Place in a clean 1-quart saucepan.

6. Stir the egg yolk mixture, then quickly add it to the milk in the pan. Cook, stirring constantly, over medium-low heat, until the custard sauce thickens to the consistency of heavy cream, 4 to 5 minutes. Do not allow it to boil. Remove the lemon peel. Drizzle the sauce over the puffs or pool it around them. Sprinkle with cinnamon and serve at room temperature, or chill for 20 minutes before serving.

Serves 6

PASTA PUDDING

Aletria

This pudding, which is similar to rice pudding, makes use of angel-hair pasta, but vermicelli can also be used. I find the best way to make this pudding come together is to cook the pasta in the milk, not separately in water.

6 cups whole milk

2 tablespoons (1 oz) butter

2 cinnamon sticks

Peel of 1 lemon, without pith

¼ teaspoon table salt

2 cups (6 oz) broken angel-hair or
   vermicelli pasta (1- to 2-inch pieces)

1 cup (7 oz) sugar

6 large egg yolks

Ground cinnamon, for sprinkling

1. In a 4-quart saucepan, combine the milk, butter, cinnamon sticks, lemon peel, and salt and bring to a high simmer over medium-high heat. Do not boil.

2. Add the pasta, stir, and reduce the heat to medium-low. Simmer until the pasta is just tender, but not mushy, 3 to 5 minutes, depending on the type of pasta. You want the integrity of the strands to be maintained.

3. Stir in the sugar, then continue to simmer until the pasta has softened, the sugar has dissolved, and the pudding starts to thicken, 10 to 15 minutes. Remove from the heat.

4. In a small bowl, beat the egg yolks. To temper them, quickly whisk ¼ cup of the hot pudding into the yolks. Whisk in more pudding in small quantities until the eggs are quite warm.

5. Quickly whisk the egg mixture into the pan containing the remaining pudding, stirring thoroughly to cook the eggs. Remove the cinnamon sticks and the lemon peel and discard. Then pour the pudding onto a platter or individual dishes. Sprinkle with ground cinnamon.

IDEAL DESSERT

Sobremesa Ideal

The people from the island of São Miguel have their own special meringue dessert. This lemon-flavored pudding, which floats in a caramel sauce and is topped with airy meringue, is a specialty brought from her homeland by Maria Coimbra, who made sweet bread in my father's bakery.

CARAMEL

½ cup (3½ oz) sugar

PUDDING

4 large egg yolks, at room temperature
  (save the whites for the topping)

3 tablespoons sugar

Peel of 1 lemon, without the pith, in large pieces

14 oz can sweetened condensed milk

4 tablespoons cornstarch

4 cups whole milk

TOPPING

4 large egg whites, at room temperature

7 tablespoons sugar

For the caramel

1. In a 1½-quart saucepan, combine the sugar and ¼ cup water and mix well. Without stirring, warm over medium-low heat until the sugar dissolves and becomes a rich golden color, 10 to 15 minutes. Quickly pour the caramel into a 9- by 13-inch ovenproof serving dish, tilting it back and forth to coat as much of the bottom as you can. Don't worry if it doesn't cover it completely.

For the pudding

2. Preheat the oven to 300°F. In a heavy-bottomed 2½-quart saucepan, combine the egg yolks, sugar, and the lemon peel. Using a wooden spoon, stir in the condensed milk and cornstarch, mixing thoroughly. While stirring, gradually pour in the milk.

3. Heat the ingredients, stirring constantly, over medium-low heat until the pudding starts to bubble, 20 to 25 minutes. The pudding will have thickened enough for a spoon to leave a swirl when it is drawn through it. (Don't leave this pudding to simmer without constantly stirring and don't rush it by raising the heat because it can easily burn.) Remove the lemon peel and pour the pudding into the serving dish over the cooled caramel, spreading it evenly.

For the topping

4. Beat the egg whites in a small bowl and gradually add the sugar until very stiff peaks are formed. Spread evenly over the pudding layer, pulling up little peaks with the tines of a fork. Bake in the preheated oven until the peaks start to turn golden, about 15 to 20 minutes. Cool gradually at room temperature before chilling well. Serve this treat with a glass of port wine.

Makes about 3 dozen

CREAM-FILLED BAKED FRITTERS

Filhos do Forno

There is much music and dancing—and eating—during Carnival time, which occurs three days prior to Ash Wednesday. These fritters, similar to cream puffs, and *Malassadas* (page 274), are popular pastries enjoyed by all.

1 cup (8 oz) butter

2 cups (9 oz) all-purpose flour

8 large eggs

¾ cup (5¼ oz) sugar

5 tablespoons cornstarch

4 cups whole milk

6 egg yolks

1 teaspoon vanilla or
  whole peel of 1 lemon,
  without the pith

1. Preheat the oven to 425°F. Grease and flour three muffin pans, or line them with paper baking cups.

2. In a 3-quart saucepan, combine the butter and 2 cups water and bring to a boil over medium-high heat. The butter will melt in the boiling water.

3. Place the flour in a large bowl. Pour the hot water and butter over the flour, stirring thoroughly until the mixture pulls away from the sides of the bowl and forms a medium-textured dough.

4. Add one egg at a time, mixing well after each addition.

5. Spoon the thick batter into the prepared muffin pans—each cup should be three-quarters full. Bake for 40 to 45 minutes, without opening the oven door, until the fritters are golden and cooked through. Remove from the oven and allow to cool fully.

6. Meanwhile make the filling: In the top of a double boiler (or a heatproof bowl suspended over a pot of water), combine the sugar and cornstarch. Gradually stir in the milk. Mix in the yolks and the lemon peel, if using. Place the double boiler or pan over medium-high heat and, stirring constantly, bring the ingredients to the edge of a boil. Reduce the heat and continue to simmer without boiling until thickened, 10 to 15 minutes. Remove from the heat and transfer the filling to a clean bowl. Stir in the vanilla, if using, and allow to cool fully. If you added lemon peel, remove it at this time.

7. When the pastries are fully cooled and shortly before you are ready to serve, slice off the top third of each pastry and add some cream filling. Replace the tops and serve immediately, so they don't become soggy. Store unfilled pastries in a tin or covered with aluminum foil. If filled, it is best to store in the refrigerator, well covered.

Makes about 5 dozen

WINTER SQUASH FRITTERS

Bêilhoses

Christmas Eve dinner would not be complete without these tasty fried puffs. In fact, I cannot remember a single Christmas without them. This dessert, and its name *bêilhoses* is unique to the Alentejo region. The delectable fritters are also known as *filhos de Natal* (Christmas fried dough).

If you have time, cook the squash early in the day or the night before to give it enough time to drain well. The nutrients in the cooking water are not wasted because the liquid is used in the dough. The squash is puréed by hand or with the help of a food mill. I like to use Blue Hubbard squash in this recipe.

1 lb winter squash or pumpkin, peeled, seeded, and cut into chunks (about 2 cups)

¼ oz envelope (2½ teaspoons) active-dry yeast

¾ cup squash cooking water

4 large eggs, at room temperature

¼ cup orange juice

2 tablespoons brandy (optional)

½ teaspoon cinnamon

½ teaspoon table salt

About 4½ cups (1 lb 4 oz) unbleached all-purpose flour, plus extra for dusting

1 cup (7 oz) sugar

½ to 1 teaspoon ground cinnamon

Corn oil, for deep-frying

1. Place the squash in a 3-quart saucepan with just enough water to cover, about 1½ cups. Cover tightly and bring to a boil over medium-high heat. Reduce and simmer until the squash is fork-tender, about 20 minutes. Reserving ¾ cup of the cooking liquid, transfer the squash to a colander to drain very well for a few hours, or even overnight. When the squash is well drained, purée using a food mill, handheld immersion blender, or by hand, until quite smooth. You should have 2 cups. Set aside.

2. Make sure your reserved cooking liquid has cooled to between 90 and 110°F. Dissolve the yeast in ¼ cup of the warm cooking liquid and set aside for 10 minutes to proof.

3. In a large bowl, beat the eggs at high speed with an electric mixer or by hand, until light and frothy. Mix in the dissolved yeast and the 2 cups of puréed squash, blending thoroughly. Stir in the juice, brandy, cinnamon, and salt.

4. Mixing thoroughly, gradually add enough of the flour to form loose dough, like a very thick batter. Add about ½ cup of the reserved cooking liquid, if needed. Be careful not to add too much flour or liquid, or the dough will be too heavy, and cook unevenly. Dust the top of the dough liberally with flour, cover with a towel, and set aside in a warm, draft-free spot to rise until double in size, about 2 hours. Punch down and let it rise for 1 more hour (make sure it rises sufficiently).

5. On a shallow dish, mix the sugar and cinnamon and set aside. Pour corn oil into a deep 3- or 4-quart saucepan to a depth of 5 or 6 inches. Heat over medium-high until it seems to quiver (350°F). Dip two teaspoons into the hot oil, and then use one oiled spoon to scoop up small walnut-sized balls of dough (1½ inches in diameter), and the other spoon to carefully drop them into the oil. Oiling the spoons first helps the dough slide into the oil. Fry just a few puffs at a time until they are golden brown, 3 to 5 minutes per batch. Using a slotted spoon, transfer immediately to the dish of cinnamon and sugar, and roll to coat completely. Serve warm.

Makes 4 rings or rounds, or 5 loaves

TRADITIONAL SWEET BREAD

Massa Sovada Antigamente

Nothing can take the place of Portuguese sweet bread! It perfectly complements Sweet Rice Pudding (page 258), but toasted sweet bread, served simply with a little butter and a cup of strong coffee, is an indescribable pleasure. This traditional recipe, provided by Delta Ortins, who is known for her sweet bread, takes several days to make, so Portuguese families typically make it in big batches to share. For a quicker version in a smaller quantity, see page 272.

Massa sovada literally means "beaten dough," in reference to the method used to knead the dough. Many years ago, when I first learned to make it, I learned the old way: With both hands suspended over a mixing bowl containing a large quantity of eggs, I spread my fingers wide. Plunging them into the bowl, I beat the eggs, whipping my fingers through them in a rotating motion. Another person stood ready to add the next ingredient, and when the flour was added, I used my palms and fists (the "beating") to incorporate the flour and form a dough. It was hard work! If large batches of dough were needed, women took turns mixing and kneading the dough.

Traditionally, after setting the dough to rise, we would bless it so that it rises well. This recipe requires patience and a very slow rising time—you will need to allow 4 days—but that is the secret to the bread's flavor. You can shape the bread into rings, rounds, or loaves (instructions given for each), and I have included a variation typically baked for Easter. I suggest using a scale to measure ingredients, and make sure to read through the recipe before you start.

SPONGE (*FERMENTE*)

¼ oz envelope (2½ teaspoons) active-dry yeast

¾ cup warm water (110°F)

5 tablespoons all-purpose flour

3 large eggs, lightly beaten, at room temperature

3 tablespoons sugar

DOUGH

3½ cups (1 lb 8 oz) sugar

2 cups whole milk

1 tablespoon table salt

5 sticks (1¼ lb) butter, plus extra for greasing

24 large eggs, at room temperature

2 tablespoons lard, melted

6 lb (22 cups) unbleached bread flour
    (12% protein)

2 teaspoons ground cinnamon

2 eggs, lightly beaten, for egg wash

Day 1, make the sponge

1. In a medium bowl, combine the yeast with the warm water in a medium bowl and stir well. Set aside for 10 minutes. Mix in 2 tablespoons of the flour and allow to rise for 3 hours. To complete the sponge, add the eggs, sugar, and the remaining 3 tablespoons of flour. Mix thoroughly. Cover and set aside in a cool, not cold, place for 2 days. The sponge will appear to have settled, with some froth on top.

Day 3, make the dough

2. In a 2-quart pot, combine the sugar, milk, salt, and 4 sticks (1 lb) of the butter, and bring just to the edge of a boil. Set aside.

3. In an extra-large mixing bowl, combine all 24 eggs and the melted lard and whisk until quite frothy. While quickly stirring, slowly pour in the warm milk.

4. Stir the sponge and add it to the eggs. Fold in the bread flour and cinnamon, mixing well. Knead well in the bowl until smooth, elastic, and semi-firm, without being stiff. It takes some effort! Melt the last stick (4 oz) of butter and pour it over and around the dough. Give the dough a few more turns to incorporate the butter completely. Cover well and set to rise in a draft-free place for about 12 hours.

Day 4, shape and bake

5. Start early in the day, if possible. Butter your hands and punch down the dough. The punching will remove excess gases and redistribute the yeast.

6. *To shape into rings:* Lightly grease and flour four 10-inch pie dishes, pizza pans, or cake pans and line them with parchment paper. On a lightly buttered work surface, divide the dough into four equal portions. Take one portion of dough and stretch it into a log about 24 inches long and 5 inches in diameter. Pat the dough lightly with your hands until it is of even thickness. Starting in the middle of the log of dough, lift and lightly twist one half, as if you're wringing a towel. Put that half down. Return to the middle and lightly lift and twist the other half, twisting in the opposite direction. Bring the ends together to form a circle, pinching together or tucking them under one another. Place the ring of dough on a prepared baking sheet, stretching the hole in the center until it is about 3 inches in diameter. Repeat with the rest of the dough.

    Or, to shape into rounds or loaves: Lightly grease and flour four 10-inch pie dishes, pizza pans, or cake pans (for rounds), or five 9- by 5-inch loaf pans (for loaves) and line with parchment paper. On a lightly buttered work surface, divide the dough into four equal portions for rounds, or five equal portions for loaves. Shape each portion into a ball, rotating and pulling the dough across the work surface until it is fairly tight and smooth. Set the dough into the greased pans.

7. When the dough has been shaped, cover the pans and set aside in a draft-free place to rise a second time until nearly double (¾-proofed), about 4 hours. The dough will finish springing in the oven.

8. Arrange the rack on the lower-middle shelf of your oven and preheat the oven to 325°F. Just before baking, use clean kitchen shears to make four evenly spaced snips, about 2 inches long, in the surface of your rings or loaves. If you make rounds, cut a cross in the center of the top. Brush the surface with egg wash.

9. Bake on the lower-middle rack of your oven until a long wooden skewer inserted into the thickest part comes out clean, and just a touch sticky, 35 to 40 minutes for rings, and 40 minutes for rounds or loaves. Remove the bread from the oven and brush with melted butter.

Variation: *When we make sweet bread for Easter, we reserve a small amount of dough before shaping the loaves. After the dough has been shaped and risen for the second time, make small indentations in the soft dough and gently press whole raw eggs (unshelled and at room temperature) into each one. Roll the reserved dough into strips and crisscross these over the raw eggs. Brush the strips with egg wash and bake as above. For safety, store leftovers in the refrigerator, and discard any eggs that have been at room temperature for more than two hours.*

Make 2 loaves

SÃO MIGUEL–STYLE SWEET BREAD

Massa Sovada à Moda de São Miguel

For this quicker version of Portugal's most popular bread (see page 270), I have scaled the recipe for smaller families. It is delicious flavored simply, but I have included an unusual version, influenced by my friend and a lovely lady, Emma Silva, whose family came from São Miguel in the Azores. In this version, fennel tea is used to give the bread a light anise flavor.

FENNEL TEA

Peel of 2 whole lemons

2 teaspoons whole fennel seeds, crushed

Two 2-inch cinnamon sticks

1 cup water

DOUGH

2¼ cups (15 oz) sugar

2 sticks (8 oz) butter, plus extra for greasing

1 cup whole milk

Grated zest of 1 lemon

½ teaspoon ground cinnamon

¼ teaspoon table salt

1 cup warm fennel tea (100°F)

Two ¼ oz envelopes (4½ teaspoons) active-
   dry yeast

½ cup warm water (110°F)

6 extra-large eggs, at room temperature

9 cups (2½ lb) unbleached bread flour
   (12% protein), or as needed

1 large egg, beaten with 1 tablespoon water,
   for egg wash

Note: *You can make 3 smaller loaves or rounds, if desired.*

1. First make the tea: Combine the lemon peel, fennel seeds, cinnamon sticks, and water in a small pot. Cover and bring to a boil. Reduce the heat and simmer for 10 minutes. Remove from heat, strain, and discard the solids. Set the tea aside until needed.

2. In a 3-quart pot, combine 1 stick (4 oz) of the butter, the milk, sugar, lemon zest, cinnamon, salt, and ½ cup of the tea. Heat over medium heat just until the sugar is dissolved and the butter is melted. Remove from the heat and set aside until it is warm, about 100°F.

3. In a small bowl, combine the yeast and the warm water, stir, and let the mixture stand for 10 minutes, until frothy.

4. In a medium bowl, beat the eggs at medium-high speed using a hand-held electric mixer until very frothy. Set aside.

5. Sift the flour into a large bowl and make a well in the center. Pour the eggs and yeast mixture into the well. Bend the fingers of your dominant hand like a claw, and scramble the liquid into the flour. Using your other hand, slowly and gradually pour in the remaining ½ cup warm tea. Mix until the ingredients come together in a ball of dough, leaving the bowl almost clean.

6. Melt the remaining 1 stick (4 oz) of butter and pour it, warm, around the dough in the bowl, mixing it in and kneading well until the dough springs back slightly when pressed with your finger, 10 minutes. Cover the bowl tightly

with plastic wrap and then a heavy towel, and set aside to rise in a warm, draft-free spot, until doubled in size, about 2 hours. The dough will be somewhat sticky.

7. Line one large baking sheet or two pie pans (if making rounds), or 2 loaf pans (if making loaves), with parchment paper. With buttered hands, divide the dough into 2 equal portions, and shape into rounds or loaves. Place on the baking sheet or pie pans, or into the loaf pans. Re-cover and set aside to rise again for 45 minutes.

8. Arrange a rack on the lower-middle shelf of your oven and preheat the oven to 325°F. Brush the dough with the egg wash. If making rounds, use a sharp knife to make a 1-inch cross in the center of each one. Bake for 35 to 40 minutes, until a long wooden skewer inserted into the middle comes out clean, but a touch sticky.

9. Sweet bread is best fresh, but if you would like to freeze it, allow it to cool completely, double-wrap it in plastic, and freeze for up to 4 months.

Makes about 2 dozen

FRIED DOUGH

Malassadas/Filhoses

This Azorean recipe for fried dough, *malassadas*, does not include squash or pumpkin. It is more like sugared, raised donuts or the fried dough sold at country fairs. They are very popular at Carnival festivals and Christmas time. In some regions of continental Portugal, these would be called *filhoses*—except the *filhoses* of the Alentejo are crisper and more delicate.

SPONGE

¼ oz envelope (2½ teaspoons) active-dry yeast

¼ cup warm water (110°F)

1 tablespoon all-purpose flour

1 tablespoon sugar

DOUGH

4 eggs, at room temperature

Generous ¾ cup (6 oz) sugar

½ cup milk

4 tablespoons (2 oz) butter, softened

4¼ cups (1 lb 3 oz) bread flour (12% protein)

¼ teaspoon salt

1 cup (7 oz) sugar

1 teaspoon ground cinnamon

Corn oil, for deep-frying

For the sponge

1. In a small bowl, dissolve the yeast in the warm water and set aside for 10 minutes. Mix in the flour and sugar, stirring to blend. Cover and set aside.

For the dough

2. Crack the eggs into a large bowl. Using an electric mixer or by hand, beat until frothy and, continuing to beat, gradually incorporate the sugar. Beat the eggs and sugar at medium-high speed, until they are light and pale yellow, about 3 minutes.

3. In a 1-quart saucepan, heat the milk and butter over medium-low heat until the butter has melted.

4. Alternating with the milk, add the flour and salt to the eggs. Add the yeast mixture and mix thoroughly, forming a medium-textured dough. Knead in the bowl for 10 to 15 minutes. Cover and set aside in a warm, draft-free spot to rise until it has doubled in size, about 1 hour. Punch down to redistribute the yeast and cover. Let rise again for 1 more hour.

5. On a shallow dish, mix the sugar and cinnamon and set aside. Pour corn oil into a deep 3- or 4-quart saucepan to a depth of 5 or 6 inches. Heat over medium-high until it seems to quiver (350°F). With oiled hands, pinch off a 3-inch piece of dough and flatten it slightly with your hands. You can shape it in the style of Graciosa by using your thumb to poke a hole in the middle, then stretch and pull it into a doughnut shape, 4 to 5 inches in diameter. Or shape it São-Miguel style by stretching the piece of dough into a ½-inch thick circle, 4 to 5 inches in diameter, leaving a rim around it like a pizza base. Deep-fry until golden, 2 to 3 minutes per side.

6. Drain on brown paper or paper towels, then toss the warm pastries in the cinnamon sugar to coat. Serve.

Makes about 3½ dozen

DREAMS

Sonhos

After you eat one of these delightful puffs, you may think you are dreaming. These always put a smile on my father's face. They are essentially a choux pastry dough, which is deep fried and then drizzled with a syrup flavored with orange and brandy, or you can simply roll them in cinnamon and sugar. For extra flavor, you can use Grand Marnier instead of plain brandy.

SYRUP

½ cup (3½ oz) sugar
2 tablespoons brandy
Peel of 1 orange

DOUGH

½ cup (4 oz) butter
¼ teaspoon table salt
1 cup (4½ oz) unbleached all-purpose flour
4 large eggs

Corn oil, for deep-frying

For the syrup

1. In a saucepan, combine all of the syrup ingredients with 1 cup water and simmer for 15 minutes. Discard the orange peel and set the syrup aside.

For the dough

2. In a 2-quart saucepan, combine the butter, salt, and 1 cup water and bring to a boil. When the butter has melted, reduce the heat and add the flour. Using a wooden spoon, beat thoroughly until a dough forms. Keep stirring until the dough comes away from the sides of the pan.

3. Remove the pan from the heat and cool for one minute. Add the eggs one at a time, beating well after each addition and incorporating as much air as possible.

4. Pour corn oil into a deep 3- or 4-quart saucepan to a depth of 5 or 6 inches. Heat over medium-high until it seems to quiver (350°F). Use oiled teaspoons to scoop up small walnut-sized balls of dough (1½ inches in diameter), and carefully drop them into the oil. Deep-fry until golden, 2 to 3 minutes. Drain on paper towels, then arrange in a mound on a serving dish. Allow to cool completely. Just before serving, drizzle with syrup. These are best eaten on the day they are made.

Variation: *You can omit the syrup and coat the balls in cinnamon and sugar instead. Mix 1 cup (7 oz) of sugar and 1 teaspoon of cinnamon in a shallow dish. Do not drain the hot puffs on paper towels. Roll them in the sugar mixture and serve. Do not cover them while they are hot or they will get soggy. These are best eaten fresh.*

Makes about four dozen 2½-inch tartlets

PASTRY TARTLETS

Pastéis/Queijadas

Dilia Luz, who is constantly asked to make these dainty tarts, shares her wonderful recipes for the pastry and three fillings. She uses an Italian pasta machine to shorten the labor-intensive rolling of the dough. The term *queijadas* is sometimes used loosely to include tarts that have fillings without cheese, even though the name implies cheese. The pastry dough can be used for any of the filling recipes that follow, all of which can be made a day ahead or early on the day of baking. Just make sure the fillings have cooled completely before using. Make your fillings first (each filling recipe fills half of the pastry quantity here, so select two).

EQUIPMENT

Hand-cranked pasta machine

48 2½-inch diameter fluted tart tins

Pastry brush

PASTRY DOUGH

3⅔ cups (1 lb) all-purpose flour,
   plus extra for flouring

¼ teaspoon table salt

4 tablespoons (2 oz) butter, softened,
   plus extra for greasing

3 tablespoons sugar

Note: *You can use different size tart tins but keep in mind that the shape and size of the tart tins you use will determine the number of pastries you get.*

1. Select and make your choice of fillings first.

2. Make the pastry dough: Combine the flour and salt in a large bowl, mixing to evenly distribute the salt. In a small bowl, mix the butter, sugar, and 1 cup water together, then pour into the middle of the flour. Using one hand, draw the flour into the water and mix until the dough leaves the sides of the bowl. Knead in the bowl about 5 minutes, until a smooth soft dough is formed. (If the weather is warm or the flour very dry, you might need ¼ cup more water.) Cover and set aside to rest for about 20 minutes. Preheat the oven to 350°F.

3. While the dough is resting, use the pastry brush to butter the tins. Remove a lump of dough, about 4 inches in diameter, place it in a small bowl of flour, and set aside. You will use this as a press to form the pastries. Line up about 6 tins in a single row, end to end.

4. Pinch off a lemon-sized piece of dough from the main batch. Set the dial on your pasta machine to #3 and roll out the dough. Turn the dial to #5 and roll the sheet of dough through again. It should be almost as thin as filo dough. (Not all pasta machines use the same numbering system. You may need to experiment to achieve a dough that is slightly thicker than filo pastry.) Alternatively, roll by hand. Let the sheet of dough rest for 10 minutes.

5. Drape the sheet of dough over the lined-up, buttered tins. Take the reserved floured ball of dough and press it gently but firmly into each tin. Pull away the excess dough. Place the tins on a baking sheet and repeat with the remaining dough until all the tins have been lined (scraps of dough can be re-rolled to line more tins). Fill each tin a scant three-quarters full with the filling (about 2 full tablespoons). Place the baking sheet the preheated oven and bake the tartlets for 15 to 25 minutes, until golden. (The cheese filling will cook more quickly than the other fillings.) Remove the tartlets from the tins while they are still warm or they may stick.

Makes 3½ cups, to fill 2 dozen tartlets

CHEESE FILLING

Queijadas

Queijadas, or cheese pastries, are extremely popular in Portugal, especially those from the town of Sintra. The recipe in Sintra is very secret, so we must make do with this tasty substitute.

2 eggs

5 egg yolks

12 oz Fresh Cheese (page 225), or use
   farmer's or ricotta cheese

1 cup (7 oz) sugar

½ teaspoon cinnamon

½ teaspoon vanilla or lemon extract

2 tablespoons (1 oz) butter, softened

1. Place the cheese in a sieve set in a bowl, and refrigerate overnight to drain.

2. The next day, whisk together the whole eggs and yolks in a mixing bowl. Using a whisk, beat in the cheese, sugar, cinnamon, extract, and butter.

3. Strain the filling through a fine mesh strainer to break down any large lumps. Cool completely before using.

Makes 3½ cups, to fill 2 dozen tartlets

MUDDLED FILLING

Atrapaladas

Not quite cheese, the milk is "muddled" with vinegar and has a surprising and delightful taste. Since this filling takes time, make it before the dough, even a day ahead.

4 cups whole milk

2 cups (14 oz) sugar

1 tablespoon vinegar (cider, wine, or white)

1 tablespoon butter

10 large egg yolks, lightly beaten

¼ teaspoon lemon extract

1. In a 5-quart pot, combine the milk and sugar. Bring to a boil over medium-high heat. Drizzle the vinegar over the milk and reduce the heat. Simmer on medium-low heat for about 2 hours, until the milk has reduced and somewhat thickened, and 90% of the clear liquid has evaporated. The milk will be curdled. Break up any large curds with a spoon and mix in the butter.

2. While quickly whisking, gradually pour a little of the hot milk into the yolks to temper them. Vigorously whisk the tempered yolks to the pot, and return the filling to a simmer. Cook until it has thickened and is just about to boil, about 10 minutes. Remove from the heat. Stir in the lemon extract. Allow to cool completely before using.

Makes 3½ cups, to fill 2 dozen tartlets

BEAN FILLING

Feijão

Some versions of this filling include finely ground almonds.

1 cup milk

4 cups (1 lb 12 oz) sugar

2 cups (13 oz) cooked and drained white or red kidney
  beans or chickpeas, puréed (canned ok)

16 egg yolks

Grated zest of 1 lemon, or ½ teaspoon lemon extract

1. In a 4-quart pot, combine the milk, sugar, and puréed beans. Place over medium-high heat and bring to a boil. Reduce the heat and simmer, stirring frequently, for 30 minutes.

2. In a medium bowl, mix the yolks with the lemon zest or extract. Whisking vigorously, slowly pour some of the hot bean filling into the yolks to temper them. Gradually add more of the filling to the yolks until they are quite warm. Transfer the yolk mixture to the pan. Return the filling to a simmer, stirring constantly, just to the point of boiling. Remove from the heat and cool completely before using.

Makes about thirty 2½-inch tarts

CUSTARD CREAM TARTS

Pastéis de Nata

As the story goes, over 300 years ago, in Belém, a district of Lisbon, the nuns of the Jerónimos monastery used egg whites to starch their habits, resulting in an abundance of egg yolks. These yolks were used to make pastries to sell to the public, including the delicious custard tarts now famed around the world. Eventually, the monastery closed and the recipe was passed to the owners of what is now Belem Pastries, a short walk away, which is frequented by locals and tourists alike. The recipe is said to be so secret that it is known only to a few, but that hasn't stopped pastry chefs from trying to recreate these delicious tarts. Some make the filling with eggs and cream and others make a white sauce egg-yolk filling, as in this recipe, which I learned from Chef Albert F. Cunha.

They are known as *pastéis de nata* (cream pastries). The official label of *Pastéis de Belém* (Belém pastries) belongs to those made in the Belém factory, and for those, you will need to travel to Portugal. I guarantee you won't be able to resist them long enough to bring any home.

The pastry dough requires patience; it must be chilled between each of six rollings, and must be made a day in advance, though as a shortcut, you can substitute ready-made puff pastry (the pastry will not puff up as much, but they will still be delicious). The tarts must bake quickly at a very high temperature—as high as your oven will go. Commercial bakeries bake them at 600°F, which is not attainable with a home oven, so do not be disappointed if your tarts don't caramelize in quite the same way.

EQUIPMENT

Thin rolling pin without handles or a long 1-inch dowel
Pastry brush
30 to 32 pastry tins, 2½ inches in diameter by
  1 inch deep (not fluted)
Large baking sheet
Candy thermometer

DOUGH

Makes about 2½ lb puff pastry, enough for 30 pastries

2½ cups (11½ oz) unbleached all-purpose flour,
  plus extra for dusting
1¼ cups (5½ oz) cake flour (see Note)

Continued

Day 1, make the dough

1. Sift the flours together into a large bowl or in a mound on your work surface. Make a well in the center of the flour. In a cup, combine the cold water, salt, and lemon juice together. Gradually pour the liquid into the well in the flour, using the outstretched fingers of one hand to draw the flour into the liquid, turning the ingredients gently to mix. Continue mixing until you have a rough dough; it should not be smooth at this point. (Be careful not to overwork the dough, which can toughen it.) Shape the dough into a ball and place in a bowl. Cover and set in the refrigerator to rest for 15 minutes.

2. Meanwhile, prepare the butter: Make sure the butter is chilled and firm, but still pliable. Unwrap the butter and lightly dust with flour. Place the sticks side by side on a sheet of waxed paper or plastic wrap on a pastry board. Using a long 1-inch dowel or thin rolling pin, gently flatten the butter,

1¼ cups ice-cold water, or as needed

½ teaspoon salt

2 teaspoons lemon juice (added to relax the gluten)

4 sticks (1 lb) unsalted butter, chilled,
    firm but not hard

1 cup (8 oz) soft margarine

FILLING AND ASSEMBLY

½ cup (2¼ oz) all-purpose flour

1½ teaspoons table salt

1 cup plus 6 tablespoons whole milk

2 cups (14 oz) sugar

1 cup plus 1½ tablespoons water

5 large egg yolks, room temperature

1 whole egg, room temperature

1 teaspoon vanilla or lemon extract

Ground cinnamon and/or Beirão brandy,
    to serve (optional)

Note: *Because American flour is different from the flours used in Portugal, various formulas attempt to replicate the old-world flavor and texture of the puff pastry. Bakers commonly use all bread flour (12% protein). You can use half bread flour and half pastry flour or, if you do not have access to pastry flour, use a ratio of three parts all-purpose flour to one-part cake flour.*

shaping it into a neat 6-inch-square block. It should end up being about 1 inch thick. Set aside.

3. On a generously floured surface, roll out the dough into a 10-inch square, about 1-inch thick. The object is to enclose the butter in the dough. Place the block of butter diagonally on top of the dough so the corners of butter fall inside the edges of dough. Fold the corners of the dough over the butter to meet at the center. Pinch the seams together, making sure the butter is completely enclosed by the dough.

4. To roll out the dough: Keep your work surface and rolling pin well-floured. Place the block of dough in front of you. Use a rolling pin without handles. Begin at the end of the block farthest from you and gently press into the dough with the rolling pin. Next, press the rolling pin into the middle of the dough, and then the end closest to you. Continue making horizontal ridges at even intervals (like speed bumps). This spreads out the butter and dough evenly. Using small strokes, roll out the dough, extending it in one direction (away from you) to about three times the length of the original block of dough, to a thickness of ½ inch. Using a pastry brush, dust off any excess flour. Fold the dough into thirds: first fold one-third over. Brush off any excess flour. Fold the other end over, aligning the sides to make a neat rectangle. (If the dough seems to be getting too soft, chill for about 20 minutes before continuing.)

5. Roll out the dough in this manner four more times, for a total of five times, chilling in between. Begin each rolling with the rectangle of dough extending lengthwise away from you. After each roll out, make light impressions in the dough with the tip of your finger to remind you how many times you have rolled out the dough.

6. On the sixth roll-out, roll out the dough to a ¼-inch thick rectangle, about 22 inches long. This time, do not fold. Instead, turn the dough so that the long edge is closest to you. Spread a thin layer of margarine over the surface of the dough, covering it. Starting from the long edge farthest from you, roll the dough towards you, creating a long jellyroll shape. Keep the rolling even and firm. (If it is difficult to manage, cut the roll in half and roll each half separately.) The diameter of the final roll should be about 2½ inches, to match the bottom diameter of the tart tins. Wrap the rolled dough tightly in plastic wrap and refrigerate for 24 hours.

Day 2, fill and bake

7. Unwrap the pastry dough and, using a very sharp knife, slice the dough into scant ¾-inch-thick slices (about a thumbnail's width). Place one slice over the top of each ungreased pastry tin and let rest for 20 to 30 minutes.

For the filling

8. In a 2-quart saucepan, combine the flour and salt. While stirring, slowly pour in 6 tablespoons of the milk, whisking to blend thoroughly, creating a thick slurry.

9. Heat the remaining 1 cup milk in a 1-quart saucepan until it is quite hot, but not scalding. Slowly, while stirring quickly and constantly to avoid burning, pour the hot milk into the slurry. Place the saucepan over medium heat and simmer the white sauce for 2 to 3 minutes to cook the starch. Remove from the heat and set aside, keeping it hot.

10. Next, make a sugar syrup: In a separate 1-quart saucepan, combine the sugar and water over medium-high heat. When bubbles start to form, reduce the heat to medium-low. Do not allow the mixture to color, but heat until the sugar dissolves and the syrup reaches the pearl stage (230°F), dripping slowly from the spoon like honey. Remove from the heat. Pouring slowly, fiercely whisk the hot syrup into the hot white filling. Simmer for 2 to 3 minutes over medium-low heat. Remove from the heat, set aside, and allow the filling to cool for 30 minutes..

Complete the filling and assembly

11. Return to the pastry cups. Moistening your thumb with water, press the center of each slice of dough straight down into the middle of the pastry tin, making sure the bottom is very thin (⅛ inch) without bumps, otherwise it won't bake completely. Keeping your thumb slightly moistened, pull the dough against and up the sides of the tin to the top edge, forming a lip just above the edge (it will shrink slightly during baking). Repeat, working your way around the tin, each time pulling from the center outward, until the tin is evenly lined with the pastry dough. The pastry should look as though even rings line the tin. Place the lined tins on a large baking sheet, leaving an inch between them. Cover with plastic and let them rest, chilled, for another 30 minutes.

12. In a medium bowl, lightly beat the egg yolks and whole egg. Just before filling the lined tart tins, make sure the reserved white sauce is quite warm. Quickly whisk enough of the warm sauce, a little at a time, to temper the eggs. Once the yolks have become quite warm, immediately whisk them fiercely into the remaining sauce, stirring constantly to blend thoroughly. Stir in the vanilla or lemon extract. You should have about 4 cups of filling. Cover with plastic wrap, pressed onto the surface of the filling, and refrigerate until completely cool.

When you are ready to bake

13. Arrange a rack in the middle of your oven and preheat to your oven's highest temperature (500°F to 525°F). Using a small ladle, fill the shells so they are just over three-quarters full. Take care not to over-fill them, or to spill any of the filling on the edges of the pastry, which will prevent the pastry from puffing.

14. Place the pastries immediately onto the middle shelf of the preheated oven. Bake until the pastry is a rich golden color and the custard is semi-firm, 18 to 20 minutes. (The filling will puff up during baking and deflate as it cools.)

15. Cool for about one minute then remove the tarts from the pastry tins—if they are allowed to cool too long, they will stick to the tins. These tarts are best served warm or at room temperature. The most luscious way to serve them is slightly warm, with a dusting of cinnamon and a little splash of Beirão, Portuguese brandy. The tarts can be refreshed in toaster oven the next day, then flavored with brandy or cinnamon, as desired.

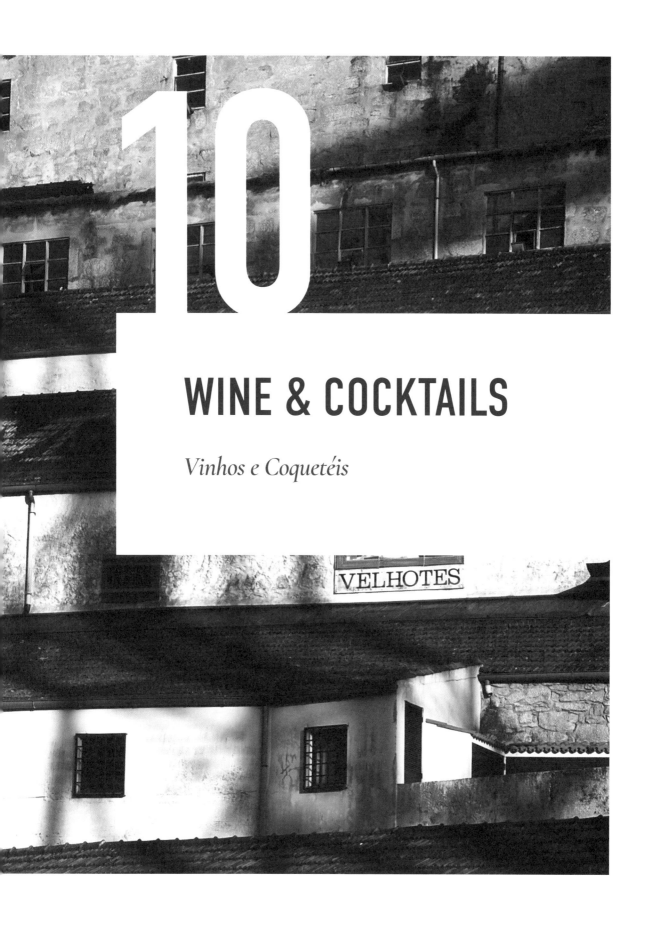

10

WINE & COCKTAILS

Vinhos e Coquetéis

10 WINE & COCKTAILS
VINHOS E COQUETÉIS

When the Portuguese tasted the first drop of wine brought by the Phoenicians, at least 600 years BC, they did not realize where this encounter would lead. Wine eventually became the national drink and was consumed judiciously, but also creatively. Like spices, wine was originally used to preserve meats and mask the flavor of spoiling meat. From that functional beginning, wine has evolved into marinades for meat that enhance flavor and tenderness.

Since the initial popularity of port and Mateus and Lancers wines, the art of wine-making in Portugal has improved tremendously. Before the revolution of 1975, wine cooperatives were controlled by the government. With no incentives, almost all estate bottling disappeared. Although the government sent out inspectors to ensure that vineyards replaced weak vines with strong, high-yielding, disease-resistant stock, it paid the wine producers only for the quantity, not the quality of the grapes produced. Today, estate bottling is back and growing rapidly.

Local homemade wines in Portugal were often sold by the barrel, never reaching the point of bottling. And most of the barrels were purchased by local taverns frequented by farmers and townsmen. They would gather to drink their local wines and discuss local issues, munching on *tremoços* (boiled lupini beans), *petiscos* (small plates) and savory *salgados* (savory snacks).

In these gathering spots, wine was ordered by the *meia bola* or *bola* (half or full glass). It was served in tumblers, not fancy wine glasses, then drunk tavern-fashion, like shots, not sipped. Even in America, my father wasn't the only one who continued to drink his wine in juice tumblers, a charming and unpretentious custom. One of my favorite Italian restaurants served wine in small tumblers as well. But recently, much to my dismay, it caved in to social pressures and replaced the tumblers with wine glasses.

Both in the old days, and now in the United States, Portuguese homemade wines can be stronger or lighter—depending on the maker—than commercial wines. Some wine makers add sugar or a touch of brandy to increase the strength of their wine, particularly if a weak grape is used; others use only grape juice, minimizing contact with the grape skins, in order to make a lighter wine. Of course, not every Portuguese household makes its own wine. Augusto Gabriel, originally from Terceira in the Azores, remembers that during his childhood, from the age of eleven, he would be sent to the local tavern to purchase wine for his family's midday meal. He would take a five-liter jug to be filled. There wasn't such a thing as an age limit then.

Homemade or not, wine is also used by the Portuguese for medicinal purposes. A concoction of warm water, sugar, and wine was a common simple remedy. To help me with my childhood anemia, my father would often take an egg yolk, mix it with a teaspoon or so of sugar, then stir in a small amount of red wine. He would then turn to me and say, "Take this; it will build up your blood."

Agapito Figueira, originally from the island of Madeira, recommends a digestive popular in his homeland: *ponche* is made by macerating sugar with lemon juice and a touch of honey. This is then stirred into a small glass of *cachaça,* a white rum distilled in Madeira from sugar cane.

After 1975, Portugal became more conscientious about growing grapes and wine-making, which was, however, not supported by a consumer demand for quality. Wine continued to be produced for regional local markets such as taverns. In 1986, the European Union opened Portugal to a global market, stimulating a revolution in Portuguese wine-making. Money became available, not only for equipment upgrades and irrigation systems for the vineyards, but for education as well. Enologists needed to learn about better ways to grow the grapes, about the characteristics of grape varieties, and about improved methods of making wine. This type of education made it necessary to travel outside the country.

Those winemakers who first broadened their horizons are now teachers of a new generation of wine makers. The up-and-coming wine makers need to accommodate two types of wine consumers, the new generation and the old generation. "Old" here does not necessarily mean old age. People who drink the Lancers or Mateus wines of the world have always done so and will continue to do so. The new generation of wine drinkers, however, is looking for something different. They want to know the story behind the wine. Today, more than ever, you'll find interesting articles in the world's leading wine magazines about Portuguese wine-making. Having found its own little niche at the dining tables of the world's gourmets, Portuguese table wine no longer sits in the shadow of the world-renowned port.

In Portugal, as in other wine-producing countries, wine is designated by region. When it comes to food, there is a natural tendency to pair wine with dishes of the same region. Since the same soil that flavors the ingredients of a dish flavors the grapes of the same region, the resulting wine complements the food. Portuguese custom throws the red-wine/red-meat white-wine/fish rule right out of the window. Balance should be the goal of pairing Portuguese wines with food. The tannin in red wine, as we know, definitely goes well with red meat, and white wine with fish and its natural oils. But most Portuguese cooking involves fish, while most of our wines are red. How to reconcile the two? The trick is to find a red wine with low tannin content. Low maceration (contact) of the grape juice with the skins produces less tannin, resulting in a more acidic red wine with less tannin—a perfect match for fish. Such a fruity, light-bodied, and acidic wine is the Quinta da Romeira "Tradicão" from the Palmela region. It uses 100% Periquita grapes.

In making a wine selection, you must pay attention to the flavors of the spices and seasoning in the juices or the sauce of the dish as well as the kind of protein it is based on. The acidity of a medium- to full-bodied red wine will certainly stand up to a seafood dish with a spicy, tomato-based sauce without overpowering it. *Caldo Verde* (page 42), a traditional soup, is especially nice with a fine drizzle of Madeira wine over it and a glass of Madeira wine served on the side. This illustrates the idea that when a particular wine is used in a dish—as a marinade or sauce—that same wine should be drunk with that dish.

Serves about 12

SANGRIA ATASCA

Sangria Atasca

Owners of the Atasca Restaurant in Cambridge, Massachusetts, Joe and Maria Cerqueira share their very popular drink. Joe suggests using your favorite full-bodied red wine.

2 cups ice cubes
8 fl oz (1 cup) orange juice
5 fl oz (⅔ cup) either soda water, tonic water, ginger ale, or lemon soda
1½ fl oz (3 tablespoons) Triple Sec
1½ fl oz (3 tablespoons) brandy
½ medium apple, peeled, cored, cut into cubes
½ medium orange, peeled, cut into cubes
1¼ bottles (4 cups) full-bodied red wine

1. In a punch bowl or 2-liter pitcher, combine the ice, orange juice, soda, Triple Sec, and brandy. Stir to blend. Mix in the fruit, top off the ingredients with the wine, and stir. Serve immediately.

Serves 6

MADEIRAN PUNCH

Poncha

My friend Agapito raves about this typical Madeiran drink. In Madeira there is a special tool made of wood that is used to stir up this concoction that is sworn by some to aid in your digestion. A great substitute for the *mexelhote* is a wooden honey spoon, typically found in kitchen shops. It can be served warm like a hot toddy as well. Make sure the white rum is made from sugar cane.

2 fl oz (¼ cup) honey, or to taste
2½ fl oz (⅓ cup) fresh lemon juice, or to taste
12 fl oz (1½ cups) *cachaça* (white rum), *aguardente* (see page 177), or brandy
6 lemon slices

1. In a small pitcher, using a whisk or honey spoon, vigorously mix the honey into the lemon juice until thoroughly dissolved.
2. While continuing to mix, pour in the brandy. Pour over ice into 6 small glasses. Garnish with a slice of lemon.

PORTUGUESE WINES

Grape varieties that were introduced by the Phoenicians long ago are still grown in Portugal today. Portuguese wines today encompass light, effervescent *vinho verdes* and smooth and refined ports and a range in between. The following list is an overview of wines by region, with some suggestions for pairing with food.

Vinho Verde

Vinho verde wines come from a region located in the northwest corner of Portugal. The name "green wine" does not reflect the color of the wine; it is made from immature grapes that have not yet developed a high sugar content. The wine is fresh, uncomplicated, and fruity. It has a low alcohol content (9 to 10%), with varying degrees of effervescence, depending on the grapes used. In some locales, dryer *vinho verdes,* like the Alvarinhos, may have 11 to 12% alcohol. *Vinho verdes* can also be red, although white varieties are more commonly imported to the United States. Lightly chilled, the lively *vinho verde* wine is not only a perfect aperitif and a good partner to shellfish dishes; it also stands very well on its own as a refresher on a hot summer's afternoon. Prominent names of *vinho verdes* are Casal Garcia, Aveleda, Alvarinho, and one of my favorites, Santola.

Douro

The Douro wines, which at one time were consumed mainly by locals, are produced from grapes grown in the Douro River valley in northern Portugal. Grown in poor soil and under stressful conditions, the grapes from the lower slopes produce wines of low acidity and full flavor and body—the wines with which to make port. The precise blending of these grapes with those of higher acidity from the hills above the river also produces some of Portugal's finest red table wines. The medium- to full-bodied Douro wines can be paired perfectly with full-flavored red meats, especially lamb or game and spicy dishes. Some names to check out are: Van Zellen, Carm Douro, and Papo Figos. Another favorite from the Sanguinhal vineyards in Bombarral is the often overlooked and wonderful wine, the 2016 Quinta de S. Francisco, from Obidos. Aged 12 months in oak barrels, it has a beautiful ruby color and aromas of red berries.

Dão

Like the Douro, the Dão region is protected from the effects of the Atlantic Ocean, giving it a more Mediterranean climate. Consistent temperatures are ideal for slow wine fermentation, which gives rise to medium to heavy, full-bodied wines with good balance and a wonderful aroma. Popular selections are Casa de Santar, Meia Encosta, and Caves Aliança Partigular. These wines pair perfectly with hearty dishes.

Bairrada

These wines are made from grapes grown in the clay soil of the Bairrada region. The Baga grape, which is considered difficult to tame, produces very hearty wines. But take care—Bairrada wines can vary from a very light-bodied and harsh wine to a beautiful full-bodied, well-balanced wine like the Luis Pato. This region also produces some of Portugal's best sparkling wines. Drink them with braises and roasts of lamb, Bairrada-style roasted suckling pig, and root vegetable dishes. Some names to choose are Luis Pato and Aliança.

Alentejo

Some of the country's more complex, well-balanced, and full-bodied wines are produced in the Alentejo region of southern Portugal. The predominant grapes grown in these plains and hills are Periquita, Aragonez, and Trincadeira Preta. Font Roupeiro is the dominant grape for the Alentejo's white wine. The estate-bottled wines tend to be fuller bodied and good for cellaring. Suggested wines from this region are Esporão, Quinta do Carmo, Dona Maria's Amanti, and João P. Ramos, a noted top-quality, light-bodied, well-balanced wine.

The upcoming trend in Portuguese wines is the single-grape varietal wines we refer to as *monocasta*. Top-quality wineries are now concentrating on producing small batches of wine made of a single-grape variety. Some varietal red wines go by the names Touriga Naçional, Tinta Roriz, Tricadeira, Aragonêz, and Baga. Alvarinho and Arinto are varietal whites. These are the new generation in Portuguese wines. They are more expensive than the average regional wines, but they are of superb quality. Small amounts are now available in the United States, but the future bears watching. (Some of these grapes are already grown in California and are used for the state's port wine.) Most regions in Portugal produce white wines along with their reds, but there are only a few regions that specialize in white wine: a region in the northwest produces *vinho verde*, which is in a category by itself; Boucelas, which produces some of the best Arinto grape wines; and Terra do Sado, which produces the fabulous dry muscat João Pires. Dry muscat pairs nicely with dishes that are lightly spiced. For special dinners, I like the 2015 Dona Maria "Amantis" Reserva, and the 2017 Quinta do Carmo Dom-Martinho.

HOMEMADE WINE

The art of making Portuguese wine is one of the strands that make up the fabric of Portuguese culture. Continentals and Azorean Portuguese alike transplanted their craft to their new homeland, teaching it to their children in the hopes of a continuing tradition. Like other culinary traditions, wine-making techniques are handed down through the generations. Wooden grape boxes piled high on neighborhood sidewalks during early fall are a dead giveaway that wine is in the making. Some home wine makers use the grapes grown on their backyard vines; others purchase California grapes or combine the two. A few months later, the work gives way to wine-tasting socials, at which delicious dinners are enjoyed accompanied by the age-old debate of who made the best wine this year.

Our friend Manuel Santos Silva came to the United States in 1968 from the town of Luz on the island of Graciosa in the Azores. He brought with him his family's wine-making techniques. His wife, Maria, whom he married in Portugal in 1971, joined him here in 1972, and together they raised a family in which cultural traditions remain strong.

Manuel learned to make wine as a small child, when he would help crush the grapes. Over the years, he has perfected the art of wine-making. Though he does have a vineyard in his backyard in eastern Massachusetts, he chooses to purchase the grapes he needs each fall in the wholesale markets of Boston.

The process begins some three months before he makes the wine, when Manuel cleans his oak barrels, using the old-world method. He inserts clean stones into each barrel and adds cold water. He corks the side hole in each barrel and rolls the barrels around to loosen sediment and residue. (In the Azores it is common to see the barrels being rolled on the road.) After that, he removes the corks, rinses the barrels well, removing the stones. He then turns the barrels on their sides to dry for three days.

The barrels are then given a final cleaning. Manuel folds a teaspoon of Sulphur Sublime in a three-inch square of broadcloth tied to a thin wire. Holding the wire, he places the cloth near the opening, ignites the cloth, and quickly inserts it into the barrel. He corks the hole and lets the sealed barrel sit. The barrels will be ready for use in three months.

In the fall, Manuel goes to Boston to taste different varieties of grapes before making his selection. Recently his preference has been Uva de Collina, a Select Alicante Bouchet, marked California Special. This grape is also used in Portugal. One box of grapes (42 pounds) yields about 3½ gallons of grape juice. Manuel purchases 33 boxes to obtain approximately 112 gallons of wine.

As a child in the Azores, Manuel used his feet to crush grapes. Now he uses a hand-cranked grape crusher instead. Since fermentation begins as soon as the grapes are crushed, the grapes are placed immediately in a large, upright barrel and allowed to ferment for three or four days. The barrel is not filled to the top because space is needed for the skins and pulp that will rise to the surface during fermentation. Near the bottom of the barrel is a corked opening 1 inch in diameter. When the level of juices has increased sufficiently and the pulp and skins have all risen to the surface, the cork is replaced by a 5-inch-long wooden spigot. The juice is poured into a large container and strained before being transferred to the clean barrels Manuel prepared three months ago. Filled to within six inches of the top, the barrels are left uncorked and lying on their sides during fermentation, to permit accumulating gases to escape. Otherwise, the tops would blow off. In the Azores, an apple is placed over the hole, allowing ventilation while preventing contamination, and Manuel continues to use this custom. Extra grape juice is held in glass bottles and used to replenish the volume lost in the barrels during fermentation.

The skins and pulp are removed from the large barrel and placed in a press, where any remaining juices are extracted, strained, and added to the fermenting juice. The compacted pulp is then removed from the press, and may be reserved for distilling *cassis*.

After two or three weeks, when fermentation stops (Manuel knows this because the sound of the fizzing stops!), the apples are removed and the barrels are corked. When the wine is ready, in two or three more months, Manuel will draw first from the smallest barrel, refilling from the next, until the wine is consumed. And the tradition of making homemade wine continues as Manuel teaches his son.

If you are interested in making your own wine at home, there are many suppliers now selling equipment and information with which you can produce wines that not only capture the essence of late summer's sweet harvest but also put you in contact with this age-old tradition.

Porto

It is true that sometimes when you are trying to accomplish one thing, your efforts result in creating something new, something more wonderful than you could have ever imagined. For example, say you were trying to prevent a prepared meat dish from drying out while waiting to serve it to tardy guests. You decide to pour some brandy or other liquid over it to stabilize it. Then, lo and behold, it tastes even better. An event occurred regarding the stabilization of Portuguese wine for transportation to England. When wine producers of the Douro region in Northeast Portugal made their routine preparations for shipments of Portugal's best wines to England, it was customary to add a percentage of brandy to the wines to stabilize them from further fermentation during their journey. The accidental creation of Porto occurred in the year 1820 when a particularly sweet grape was gathered from the year's harvest. Since the grapes were more heavily laden with natural sugar, adding the customary amount of brandy at the customary time prevented all the natural sugars in that year's wine from being fully converted into alcohol. The British, upon tasting the fortified wines of the 1820 harvest, recognized that something special was in their midst. Since not every harvest will yield the same amount of sugar in the grapes, wine producers experimented with quantities of brandy and lengths of fermentations. Over time, the technique evolved until it was perfected.

What, besides fermentation and the addition of brandy, make the perfect Porto wine, you ask? It really is a combination of things. The climate and soil are a major factor, as is the grape. The climate, be it wet, dry, or humid, has an effect on the growing and quality of the grapes and the amount of natural sugar they will contain at harvest time. Believe or not, the soil also affects the flavor of the grape—whether it is acidic or sweet, and what minerals it contains. Did you ever taste one particular variety of vegetable, like peppers, grown in Italy or elsewhere, and then try the same variety grown in your backyard to discover the flavor is different? It is the same for wine, and the reason why imitation is difficult. What makes the Porto wine of the Douro so wonderful is its combination of climate, soil, and the grapes grown in that valley. Fortunately for us, Portos are regulated by the Porto Wine Institute in the city of Porto and the Casa do Douro in Régua. With exacting standards, and a requirement that the bottles carry a seal of authenticity, one can tell these apart from imitators. The ultimate experience for one's palate is to enjoy a meal, with locally grown ingredients, meats, and wine. The culminating flavors are enhanced by the common thread of climate and soil. To round out your meal with a Porto is a perfect finish. Whether it is Vintage, a late Bottled Vintage, Reserva, tawny, ruby, white, or the newest addition—a pink Rosé Porto introduced recently by Croft—you will not be disappointed.

The Porto Wine Institute has stringent rules relating to the harvest, grapes, and verbiage on labels, what constitutes each category, and the quality required for their release. It scrutinizes samples dictating a certain time frame from the point of harvest, the aging in casks to the point of bottling, aging in bottles, and the time of release. After bottling, depending on the Porto, it can spend years aging, as many as 15 or more. Vintage is the most expensive, and its slow maturation produces a lot of sediment making it necessary to be decanted. A late Bottled Vintage, which is not as full bodied as Vintage, is usually less expensive and can be consumed sooner. Then you have one of my husband's favorites, the Colheitas (meaning harvest), also called Reserva Tawny. The name Colheitas indicates a Porto made from the grapes of one harvest as opposed to the grapes of more than one harvest. You can tell a Colheita because the year of harvest is always indicated on the label. According to Pasquale Iacocca, rules apply here as well. Colheitas are usually bottled after at least seven years of aging in a cask. Labels will indicate if the Porto has been aged in oak casks, as well as the year it was bottled. Reserva Tawny Portos of this caliber are available in bottles, which indicate whether they were aged 10 years, 15 years, 20 years, and so on. Ruby Porto is sweeter, and has a deeper, richer red color than the caramel-colored Tawny. Tawny has a smooth semi-dry, nutty flavor with essence of raisins. Regular tawny and ruby are from the west side of the Valley. White Porto, made from white grapes, can be sweet to very dry. The latest member of the Porto family, the pink Rosé Porto, is a light Porto meant to be a refreshing summer drink which, like the semi-dry white Porto (as well as some others), can be served over ice. Reviews so far are very favorable to this newcomer. Whether you purchase a Porto with a label of Croft, Wares, Sandeman, Calem, Ferreira, Anderson, Old Port, or Dow, to name a few, read the label and know what you are buying. Check out books by Pasquale Iocca, for further reading on the subject.

In addition to its wine, wheat, olives, and pork, the Alentejo area is well known for cork, supplying a large demand in the global market. On cork farms like the one owned by my cousin Senhor Jose Oliveira, the harvested bark of the cork trees is piled high, leaving the naked trunks of the trees blushing with a cinnamon color—an unforgettable sight. Cork trees take nine years to produce bark, which is used for wine-bottle corks, insulation, wall and floor tiles, cork liners in shoes, and so on. Usually a cork farm has several groves that are harvested in rotation; a different one each year. The year is marked on the trees of a freshly harvested grove to keep track of when their next harvest will be ready.

INDEX

REFERENCES

Açores, by Francisco Carreira Da Costa. Lisbon: Editorial de Publicações Turistas, R. DeSanta Barbara, 81 5°D, 1967.

Dicionário Portugués Inglés, P. Julio Albino Ferreira. Porto, Portugal: Editorial Domingos Barreira de Manuel Barreira, Rua Oliveira, Monteiro, 1965.

The Complete Book of Herbs, by Lesley Bremness. Studio, 1994.

Great Sausage Recipes and Meat Curing, by Rytek Kutas. Buffalo, NY: The Sausage Maker Company, 1984.

Food and History, by Eduardo Mayone Dias. LusaWeb Comunidades Project, 1997. lusaweb. com/comunides/foods

Food in History, by Reay Tannahill. New York: Crown, 1988.

The Way to Cook, by Julia Child. New York: Albert A. Knopf, 1989.

Wines of Portugal, by Pasquale Iocca. New York: Portuguese Trade Commission.

RESOURCE GUIDE

Portuguese products and housewares
Portugalia Market Place
489 Bedford Street
Fall River, MA 02720
Portugaliamarketplace.com

Tremont Market
70 Tremont Street
Peabody, MA 01960
Tel: 978-531-2764

Pottery, tableware
Provincia
 140 Commercial Street
Provincetown, MA 02657
Tel: 508-487-5610
provinciausa.com

Wines
Grape Moments
PO Box 40607
New Bedford, MA 02744
Tel: 508-997-0100
Fax: 508-997-0155
grapemoments.com

Sanguinhal, LDA
Vinyards
vinhos-sanguinhal.pt

Sausage-making supplies
The Sausage Maker, Inc.
1500 Clinton Street,
Building 123
Buffalo, NY 14206
Tel: 716-824-5814
Fax: 716-824-6465
sausagemaker.com

In the Ironbound section of Newark, NJ, Ferry Street, often referred to as "Little Portugal," possesses the widest variety of products imported from Portugal

Seabra's Market
260 Lafayette Street
Newark, NJ 07105
Tel: 973-587-8606

Ferry Wine and Liquors
158 Ferry Street
Newark, NJ
Tel: 973-589-8251

Lisbon Liquors
114 Ferry Street
Newark, NJ 07105
Tel: 973-344-0139

Oporto Liquors
178 Ferry Street
Newark, NJ 07105
Tel: 973-589-3325

ACKNOWLEDGMENTS

When this book was yet in its infancy, the enthusiasm and support that arose from family, relatives, friends, colleagues, and strangers was overwhelming. This book would not have been possible without the help of those listed here. There are not enough words to express the tremendous appreciation I have for everyone, in Portugal and America, who contributed in some way, big or small, to make this book a reality; some have assisted in nearly every phase of this book.

Words have not yet been invented that could possibly thank my husband, Philip, enough. In his own quiet way, he urged me onward repeatedly with his tremendous patience and boundless good nature—through the researching, proofreading, the many and sometimes repeated testing, the tasting dinners. My thanks especially for picking up the slack when I was totally immersed and, most of all, for believing in me and this book.

Thank you with much love and affection to my daughter, Nancy, for her diligent editing; son-in-law, Michael Savage, always a willing taste tester; my son, Marc, for his enthusiasm and generous help with photography; and his dear friend Sara Zegzdryn for her testing, to all of them for their suggestions, creativity, critiques, and constant support and patience. Heart-filled thank-you to "Titi," my aunt Ana Patuleia Valente, for being there from the beginning and for the wonderful cooking lessons; to my uncle Ilidio Valente for being a valuable source of history, discussions, and tastings; and to my mother, Evelyn, for answering my many questions.

To Aureolinda Bettencourt, Alvarina Boga, "Mother" Julia Fernandes, Olinda Fernandes, Dilia Luz, and Isaura Nogueira—I want to thank you immensely for not only sharing your heirloom recipes and standing with me as we tested them, but for your patience every time I stuck a measuring spoon or cup under your hand, for answering my questions, and for explaining the unspoken Portuguese touches that are sometimes forgotten.

Thanks to my testers and tasters, who not only gave their time and provided me with feedback that helps even the novice home cook, but who also offered their family recipes: Pat Almeida, Lark and Bob Bolduc, John and Barbara Ciman, Dolores and John Figuereido, Mary Gil, Catherine and Bill Hosman, Missy McKinnon, Joe and Marguerite Mendonca, Laraine and Bob Ortins, Mary and Tony Dos Santos. To Mike Benson for his assistance with photography of previous edition, and Hiltrud Schulz for her photography of this edition. Many, many hugs to my friend and computer troubleshooter Mike Bassichis for his timely assistance. Much appreciation to Jack Couto Augusto Gabriel and Joe Saraiva for sharing their passion and knowledge of Portugal's best wines.

So many of you not only offered up your treasured family recipes and the little secret tricks that you do, the helpful hints, and patience while I measured and recorded, but were a great source of information as well. Thank you for sharing it all—Lucinda Almeida, Edelberto Ataide, Edite Biscaia, Deolinda Bettencourt, Elsa Bettencourt, Fatima Bettencourt, Senhorinha Bettencourt, Antonio Cardosa, Leonia Clarimundo; the kitchen crew of Club Luis de Camões of Peabody, Massachusetts; Maria and Rogerio Coimbra, Jose and Ismailda Coelho of Lisbon, Portugal; Alberto F. Cunha of Lisbon Portugal; Evelyn Ortins Cunha, Manuel Cunha, Sonia Cunha, Lili Oliveira Ferreira of Lisbon, Portugal; Maria Fidalgo, Adelaide Figueira, Agapito Figueira, Holy Ghost Society of Peabody, Massachusetts (Irmanda de Açoreana do Espirito Santo); Fatima Lima, Teresa Mendonca, Isaura Nogueira, Rich Nunes, Jennifer Nunes, Connie Oliveira, Antonio and Noelia Ortins, Arthur

Ortins, Denise Ortins, Dorothy Ortins, Joseph and Jeannette Ortins, Maria de Luz Ortins, Rose Pais, Teresa Coutinho Patuleia, Elena Pavick, Mario Pinto, Lucia Rebelo, Antonio Rosa, Alvarinha Silva, Eliodoro Silva, John F. Silva, Manuel and Maria Silva, Manuel Q. Silva, Fernanda and Gaspar Simões, and Juliana Sylvester.

I would like to thank Pat Kelly, who not only was the first to get involved, but whose encouragement, proofreading, and advice were very instrumental in my pursuing this expanded project that went beyond a simple community cookbook. Profound gratitude to Jackie Ankeles, Luis Azevedo, Alfonso Barclamonte; to Linda Bassett for her constant push, suggestions, and tremendous help; Antonio Bragança, Antonio Cardosa, Ken Costa, Mario and Lucia Costa, Eduardo M. Dias, Lisa Ekus, Joan Irons, William LeBlond, Jeanne Lemelin, Giorgio Manzana, Rux Martin, Linda Mendonca, Carlos Pinto, Jorge Ramos and the Portuguese Trade Commission, Beth Riely, Greg Repucci, Mary Rodrigues, John Selski, Ernest Vieira—all who have given invaluable information, advice, product testing, cultural history, contacts, or proofreading—and much more.

Many thanks to Jack Couto and especially Augusto Gabriel, both from Whitehall Imports, for their tremendous help in sharing their knowledge of Portuguese wines and the latest trends in the industry.

Thank you to professional bakers Alex Couto, owner of Central Bakery, Peabody, Massachusetts, retired baker Manuel Galopim, to John Silva owner of Danversport Bakery, Danvers, Massachusetts, for their invaluable help and patience and to Lourival Mello, an enormous thank you for suggestions and technical input.

Last, but not least, I would like to thank my publisher, Michel Moushabeck, and the whole team at Interlink Publishing, especially Harrison Williams for his design, and my editor Leyla Moushabeck, who has been there every step of the way, for her great eye for details, her editorial insight, and enthusiasm.